THE NEW CAMBRIDGE SHAKESPEARE

FOUNDING GENERAL EDITOR
Philip Brockbank

GENERAL EDITOR
Brian Gibbons, *Professor of English Literature, University of Münster*

ASSOCIATE GENERAL EDITORS
A. R. Braunmuller, *Professor of English, University of California at Los Angeles*
Robin Hood, *Senior Lecturer in English, University of York*

MUCH ADO ABOUT NOTHING

Much Ado has always been popular on the stage. This edition pays especial attention to
the history and range of theatrical interpretation. The most famous actors, from the time
of Garrick to the present, have appeared as the sparring lovers Beatrice and Benedick. In
recent times the play's matched plots of two pairs of lovers have been of interest to
feminist critics. A full commentary includes annotation of the many sexual jokes in the
play that have been obscured by the complexity of Elizabethan language.

THE NEW CAMBRIDGE SHAKESPEARE

MUCH ADO ABOUT NOTHING

Edited by

F. H. MARES

Honorary Visiting Research Associate in English,
University of Adelaide

The right of the
University of Cambridge
to print and sell
all manner of books
was granted by
Henry VIII in 1534.
The University has printed
and published continuously
since 1584.

CAMBRIDGE UNIVERSITY PRESS

Cambridge
New York   Port Chester   Melbourne   Sydney

Published by the Press Syndicate of the University of Cambridge
The Pitt Building, Trumpington Street, Cambridge CB2 1RP
40 West 20th Street, New York, NY 10011–4211, USA
10 Stamford Road, Oakleigh, Victoria 3166, Australia

First published 1988
Reprinted 1989, 1991 (twice)

Printed in Great Britain at
the University Press, Cambridge

British Library cataloguing in publication data

Shakespeare, William
Much ado about nothing. – (The New
Cambridge Shakespeare).
I. Title   II. Mares, F. H.
822.3′3   PR2828

Library of Congress cataloguing in publication data

Shakespeare, William, 1564–1616.
Much ado about nothing.
(The New Cambridge Shakespeare)
Bibliography: p.
I. Mares, F. H. (Francis Hugh)   II. Title.
III. Series: Shakespeare, William, 1564–1616. Works.
1984. Cambridge University Press.
PR2828.A2M37   1988   822.3′3   87–10268

ISBN 0 521 22152 8 hardback
ISBN 0 521 29367 7 paperback

WV

THE NEW CAMBRIDGE SHAKESPEARE

The *New Cambridge Shakespeare* succeeds *The New Shakespeare* which began publication in 1921 under the general editorship of Sir Arthur Quiller-Couch and John Dover Wilson, and was completed in the 1960s, with the assistance of G. I. Duthie, Alice Walker, Peter Ure and J. C. Maxwell. *The New Shakespeare* itself followed upon *The Cambridge Shakespeare*, 1863–6, edited by W. G. Clark, J. Glover and W. A. Wright.

The New Shakespeare won high esteem both for its scholarship and for its design, but shifts of critical taste and insight, recent Shakespearean research, and a changing sense of what is important in our understanding of the plays, have made it necessary to re-edit and redesign, not merely to revise, the series.

The *New Cambridge Shakespeare* aims to be of value to a new generation of playgoers and readers who wish to enjoy fuller access to Shakespeare's poetic and dramatic art. While offering ample academic guidance, it reflects current critical interests and is more attentive than some earlier editions have been to the realisation of the plays on the stage, and to their social and cultural settings. The text of each play has been freshly edited, with textual data made available to those users who wish to know why and how one published text differs from another. Although modernised, the edition conserves forms that appear to be expressive and characteristically Shakespearean, and it does not attempt to disguise the fact that the plays were written in a language other than that of our own time.

Illustrations are usually integrated into the critical and historical discussion of the play and include some reconstructions of early performances by C. Walter Hodges. Some editors have also made use of the advice and experience of Maurice Daniels, for many years a member of the Royal Shakespeare Company.

Each volume is addressed to the needs and problems of a particular text, and each therefore differs in style and emphasis from others in the series.

PHILIP BROCKBANK
General Editor

CONTENTS

ILLUSTRATIONS

PREFACE

The best an editor of Shakespeare can hope for is to emulate the wren that flew a little higher from the back of the eagle – only in this case there are a number of eagles. I have made considerable use of my predecessors. Of particular value have been Quiller-Couch and Dover Wilson's New Shakespeare (1923), R. A. Foakes's Penguin edition (1968) and A. R. Humphreys's Arden (1981). A. G. Newcomer's edition (Stanford Studies in English, 1929), which brings together similar uses of language or imagery from other plays of Shakespeare, was often enlightening.

My work was almost complete when I retired from the University of Adelaide at the end of 1985. I am grateful to the University for its support, especially for various periods of leave which allowed me to meet other scholars and visit great libraries in America and Europe. These include the Huntington and Folger Libraries, and the British Library. Other institutions are mentioned in my Note on the Text and in other places. In the spring of 1981 I had a Fellowship at the Institute for Advanced Studies in the Humanities in Edinburgh. There one day I had a clear illustration of Benedick's simile 'like a man at a mark, with a whole army shooting at me' (2.1.193–4). I saw the Royal Company of Archers at practice in the Meadows, and they had a man at the mark, who would run in with a little flag, to show where the arrows fell in relation to the target: Her Majesty's bodyguard in Scotland were preparing for a Royal visit. In 1983 I spent a semester as an exchange professor at the University of Trondheim in Norway, where my generous colleagues asked me to do so little teaching that my research flourished. To all these institutions, and to the librarians who serve in them, I am most grateful. My greatest obligation is to the staff at the Barr-Smith Library of the University of Adelaide.

I have many debts to many colleagues, but would thank specifically Alan Brissenden and Marea Mitchell in Adelaide and Sigmund Ro in Trondheim, who have all read various parts of my work in progress, and commented on it to my advantage. The secretaries of the Adelaide English Department have been most helpful; Joan Alvaro has produced elegant copy on the word-processor from my corrected and recorrected drafts with unfailing patience and skill. My colleague and companion Robin Eaden has given me much help, especially in research and in matters of style – and my gratitude to her is for much more than that.

From the start Philip Brockbank, the General Editor, and later Brian Gibbons have given valuable advice and – along with Cambridge University Press – been patient with my slow progress. Sarah Stanton of the Press has been very helpful in obtaining illustrations, and checking the quality of photographs which, from this side of the world,

I could not examine for myself. The meticulous reading of my typescript by Paul Chipchase has saved me from many errors and solecisms and spared my readers many confusions and ambiguities. The shortcomings which remain, in spite of all this help, I must acknowledge mine.

F.H.M.

Adelaide

ABBREVIATIONS AND CONVENTIONS

Shakespeare's plays, when cited in this edition, are abbreviated in a style modified slightly from that used in the *Harvard Concordance to Shakespeare*. Other editions of Shakespeare are abbreviated under the editor's surname (Newcomer, Knight) unless they are the work of more than one editor. In such cases, an abbreviated series name is used (NS, Riverside). When more than one edition by the same editor is cited, later editions are discriminated with a raised figure (Rowe[2]). All quotations from Shakespeare, except those from *Much Ado About Nothing*, use the text and lineation of *The Riverside Shakespeare*, 1974, under the general editorship of G. Blakemore Evans.

1. Shakespeare's plays

Ado	*Much Ado About Nothing*
Ant.	*Antony and Cleopatra*
AWW	*All's Well That Ends Well*
AYLI	*As You Like It*
Cor.	*Coriolanus*
Cym.	*Cymbeline*
Err.	*The Comedy of Errors*
Ham.	*Hamlet*
1H4	*The First Part of King Henry the Fourth*
2H4	*The Second Part of King Henry the Fourth*
H5	*King Henry the Fifth*
1H6	*The First Part of King Henry the Sixth*
2H6	*The Second Part of King Henry the Sixth*
3H6	*The Third Part of King Henry the Sixth*
H8	*King Henry the Eighth*
JC	*Julius Caesar*
John	*King John*
LLL	*Love's Labour's Lost*
Lear	*King Lear*
Mac.	*Macbeth*
MM	*Measure for Measure*
MND	*Midsummer Night's Dream*
MV	*The Merchant of Venice*
Oth.	*Othello*
Per.	*Pericles*
R2	*King Richard the Second*
R3	*King Richard the Third*
Rom.	*Romeo and Juliet*
Shr.	*The Taming of the Shrew*
STM	*Sir Thomas More*
Temp.	*The Tempest*
TGV	*The Two Gentlemen of Verona*
Tim.	*Timon of Athens*

Tit.	*Titus Andronicus*
TN	*Twelfth Night*
TNK	*The Two Noble Kinsmen*
Tro.	*Troilus and Cressida*
Wiv.	*The Merry Wives of Windsor*
WT	*The Winter's Tale*

2. Other works cited and general references

Abbott	E. A. Abbott, *A Shakespearian Grammar*, 1869 (references are to numbered paragraphs)
Arber	E. Arber (ed.), *A Transcript of the Registers of the Company of Stationers*, 5 vols., 1875–94
Bang	W. Bang (ed.), *Materialien zur Kunde des älteren Englischen Dramas*, 44 vols., Louvain, 1902–14
BL	British Library
Boas	F. S. Boas (ed.), *Much Ado About Nothing*, 1916
Brissenden	A. T. Brissenden, *Shakespeare and the Dance*, 1981
Bullough	Geoffrey Bullough (ed.), *Narrative and Dramatic Sources of Shakespeare*, 8 vols., 1957–75 (for *Much Ado*, vol. II, 1958)
Campbell	T. Campbell (ed.), *The Dramatic Works of Shakespeare*, 1838
Capell	Edward Capell (ed.), *Mr William Shakespeare his Comedies, Histories, and Tragedies*, 10 vols., 1767–8
COED	*Concise Oxford English Dictionary*, 1982 edn
Collier	J. Payne Collier (ed.), *The Works of William Shakespeare*, 8 vols., 1842–4
Collier²	J. Payne Collier (ed.), *The Works of William Shakespeare*, 6 vols., 1858
conj.	conjecture
corr.	corrected forme in Q
Cotgrave	Randall Cotgrave, *A Dictionarie of the French and English Tongues*, 1611
CQ	*Critical Quarterly*
Dyce	Alexander Dyce (ed.), *The Works of William Shakespeare*, 6 vols., 1857
ELR	*English Literary Renaissance*
ES	*English Studies*
F	*Mr William Shakespeares Comedies, Histories, and Tragedies*, 1623 (First Folio)
F2	*Mr William Shakespeares Comedies, Histories, and Tragedies*, 1632 (Second Folio)
F3	*Mr William Shakespeares Comedies, Histories, and Tragedies*, 1664 (Third Folio)
Foakes	R. A. Foakes (ed.), *Much Ado About Nothing*, 1968
FQ	Edmund Spenser, *The Faerie Queene*, ed. J. C. Smith, 2 vols., 1909
Furness	H. H. Furness (ed.), *Much Ado About Nothing*, 1899 (Variorum)
Garrick	'*Much Ado About Nothing*' . . . *as it is acted at the Theatres-Royal in Drury Lane and Covent Garden*, 1777 (Garrick's acting text, published after his retirement in 1776)
Greg, *EP*	W. W. Greg, *The Editorial Problem in Shakespeare*, 1951
Greg, *FF*	W. W. Greg, *The Shakespeare First Folio*, 1955
Halliwell	James O. Halliwell (ed.), *The Complete Works of Shakespeare*, 1850
Hanmer	Thomas Hanmer (ed.), *The Works of Shakespear*, 6 vols., 1743–4
Hinman, *PPFS*	Charlton Hinman, *The Printing and Proof-Reading of the First Folio of Shakespeare*, 2 vols., 1963

Hinman, *Q*	Charlton Hinman (ed.), *Much Ado About Nothing*, Shakespeare Quarto Facsimiles, no. 15, 1971
Honigmann	E. A. J. Honigmann, *The Stability of Shakespeare's Text*, 1965
H&S	C. H. Herford and P. and E. Simpson (eds.), *The Works of Ben Jonson*, 11 vols., 1925–52
Hulme	Hilda Hulme, *Explorations in Shakespeare's Language*, 1977 (first edn, 1962)
Humphreys	A. R. Humphreys (ed.), *Much Ado About Nothing*, 1981 (Arden Shakespeare)
Irving	*'Much Ado About Nothing' . . . As Arranged for the Stage by Henry Irving*, 1882
Johnson	Samuel Johnson (ed.), *The Plays of William Shakespeare*, 8 vols., 1765
Knight	C. Knight (ed.), *The Pictorial Edition of the Works of Shakspere*, 8 vols., 1838–43
Kökeritz	Helge Kökeritz, *Shakespeare's Pronunciation*, 1953
Lewalski	Barbara Lewalski (ed.), *Much Ado About Nothing*, 1969
Long	J. H. Long, *Shakespeare's Use of Music*, 1955
Malone	Edmond Malone (ed.), *The Plays and Poems of William Shakespeare*, 10 vols., 1790
Manifold	J. S. Manifold, *Music in English Drama: From Shakespeare to Purcell*, 1965
Mason	J. M. Mason, *Comments on the Last Edition of Shakespeare's Plays*, 1785
MLN	*Modern Language Notes*
MLQ	*Modern Language Quarterly*
MLR	*Modern Language Review*
MLS	*Modern Language Studies*
Nashe, *Works*	Thomas Nashe, *Works*, ed. R. B. McKerrow, 5 vols., 1905–10, revised by F. P. Wilson, 1958
Newcomer	A. G. Newcomer (ed.), *Much Ado About Nothing*, 1929
N&Q	*Notes and Queries*
NS	Sir Arthur Quiller-Couch and John Dover Wilson (eds.), *Much Ado About Nothing*, 1923 (New Shakespeare)
OED	*Oxford English Dictionary*
Oxberry	W. Oxberry, Comedian (ed.), *The New English Drama, with Prefatory Remarks*, 20 vols., 1818–23
PMLA	*Publications of the Modern Language Association of America*
Pope	Alexander Pope (ed.), *The Works of Shakespear*, 6 vols., 1723–5
Prouty	C. T. Prouty, *The Sources of 'Much Ado About Nothing'*, 1950
Q	*Much Ado About Nothing*, V.S. for Andrew Wise and William Aspley, 1600 (quarto)
REL	*Review of English Literature*
RES	*Review of English Studies*
Ridley	M. R. Ridley (ed.), *Much Ado About Nothing*, 1935 (New Temple Shakespeare)
Ritson	J. Ritson, *Remarks Critical and Illustrative*, 1783
Riverside	G. Blakemore Evans (textual ed.), *The Riverside Shakespeare*, 1974
Rowe	Nicholas Rowe (ed.), *The Works of Mr William Shakespear*, 6 vols., 1709
Rowe²	Nicholas Rowe (ed.), *The Works of Mr William Shakespear*, 2nd edn, 1714
RSC	Royal Shakespeare Company
SB	*Studies in Bibliography*
SD	stage direction
SEL	*Studies in English Literature*
Seng	P. J. Seng, *The Vocal Songs in the Plays of Shakespeare: A Critical History*, 1967
Seymour	E. H. Seymour, *Remarks, Critical, Conjectural and Explanatory*, 1805
SH	speech heading
SJ	*Shakespeare Jahrbuch*

SP	*Studies in Philology*
SQ	*Shakespeare Quarterly*
S. Sur.	*Shakespeare Survey*
Staunton	H. Staunton (ed.), *The Plays of Shakespeare*, 4 vols., 1858–60
Steevens	Samuel Johnson and George Steevens (eds.), *The Plays of William Shakespeare*, 10 vols., 1773
Steevens²	Samuel Johnson and George Steevens (eds.), *The Plays of William Shakespeare*, 15 vols., 4th edn, 1793
subst.	substantively
Theobald	Lewis Theobald (ed.), *The Works of Shakespeare*, 7 vols., 1733
Thirlby	Styan Thirlby contributed notes to Theobald's editions of Shakespeare
Tilley	M. P. Tilley, *A Dictionary of the Proverbs in England in the Sixteenth and Seventeenth Centuries*, 1950 (references are to numbered proverbs)
Trenery	G. Trenery (ed.), *Much Ado About Nothing*, 1924 (Arden Shakespeare)
uncorr.	uncorrected forme in Q
Walker	W. S. Walker, *A Critical Examination of the Text of Shakespeare*, 1860
Warburton	William Warburton (ed.), *The Works of Shakespeare*, 1747
Wells, *Foul Papers*	'Editorial treatment of foul-paper texts: *Much Ado About Nothing* as a test case', *RES* n.s. 31, 121 (1980), 1–16
Wells, *Spelling*	Stanley Wells and Gary Taylor, *Modernizing Shakespeare's Spelling, with Three Studies in the Text of 'Henry V'*, 1979
Wright	W. Aldis Wright (ed.), *The Works of William Shakespeare*, 1894

Biblical references, including the Apocrypha, are taken from the Bishops' Bible, 1572.

INTRODUCTION

Sources

Stories of the calumniation of a chaste woman, as in the plot concerning Hero, are many and ancient. The story of Susanna and the Elders in the Biblical Apocrypha is one of the best-known. The version of this motif to which *Much Ado* is most closely related is found in the twenty-second story of Matteo Bandello's collection of *Novelle* printed in Lucca in 1554; this was not, so far as is known, translated into English until the end of the nineteenth century. Bandello's story in its turn may depend directly or indirectly on the late Greek romance by Chariton, *Chaereas and Callirrhoe*.[1] A translation and expansion by Belleforest was published in French in the third volume of his *Histoires Tragiques* in 1569, but it seems most likely that Shakespeare was working from the Italian rather than the French – unless he had some other source no longer known to us. From Bandello's story of Timbreo and Fenecia come the main plot, the setting in Messina and the names of important subsidiary characters: King Piero of Arragon as the local source of authority and Messer Lionato de' Lionati as the father of the heroine. However there are significant differences. The presence of King Piero in Sicily is a sequel to the 'Sicilian Vespers' – when 'the Sicilians, no longer able to endure French domination, rose one day at the hour of Vespers and . . . murdered all the French in Sicily'.[2] His triumph in Messina follows a sea-victory against King Carlo II of Naples. Don Pedro of Arragon's war is only hazily adumbrated, but seems to have been a revolt by his bastard brother Don John. Sir Timbreo di Cardona (the Claudio figure) is a 'baron of great esteem', not a very young man who has been recognised for his precocious prowess in the recent war. He is well above the lady Fenecia (Hero) in rank, for Messer Lionato is a (comparatively) poor gentleman, though of ancient family. It is only after Timbreo realises that he will not be able to seduce Fenecia that he resolves to marry her, and makes the proposal which is accepted with alacrity by her father. The defamation is engineered by Sir Girondo Olerio Valenziano, a friend of Sir Timbreo, and also in love with Fenecia. He uses this means to break off the intended match, so that he will be able to marry her himself. His agent is a young courtier, 'more pleased with evil than with good' (Bullough, II, 115), who tells Sir Timbreo that Fenecia has had a lover for many months past. He claims that his motive is to protect Sir Timbreo from dishonour, and he sets up a situation where Sir Timbreo sees a servant, dressed and perfumed like a gentleman, climb a ladder and enter a window of a distant and little-used part of Lionato's house. There is no impersonation of Fenecia by a female servant wearing her clothes. Sir Timbreo is enraged and sends a messenger to Lionato, accusing Fenecia of unchastity, and breaking off the engagement. Fenecia swoons, and is apparently dead; when she revives she is sent

---

[1] Furness, p. 344. The connection was first suggested by Konrad Weichberger in *SJ* 34 (1898), 34.
[2] Bullough, II, 112. Later references in brackets in the text.

secretly to the country house of her uncle Girolamo, where she can assume a different identity. Meanwhile her funeral goes ahead with all due ceremony. The story of her unchastity is not believed, but is assumed to be a pretext by Sir Timbreo to get out of a marriage which on mature consideration had seemed too socially demeaning. But Sir Timbreo himself is struck by remorse and realises that he has jumped to conclusions on dubious evidence. Sir Girondo is also grief-stricken and much troubled in his conscience. A week after the funeral he takes Sir Timbreo to visit Fenecia's tomb, and there confesses, offering Sir Timbreo his dagger and inviting him to kill him in revenge. Timbreo forgives him and the two gentlemen confess to Lionato and are forgiven, on condition that Timbreo, when he comes to marry, will take a wife on Lionato's recommendation. Fenecia spends a year in the country and becomes even more beautiful and scarcely recognisable as the same person. Then Lionato tells Timbreo that he has found a wife for him and takes him to meet her. Sir Timbreo marries the beautiful Lucilla (as she is now called) but does not recognise her. At the wedding breakfast he recounts with deep grief the story of Fenecia and the true identity of his new bride is then revealed to him. To bring everything to a satisfactory conclusion Sir Girondo asks, and is granted, the hand of Fenecia's younger sister Belfiore, who is only not the most beautiful girl in the world because Fenecia is. After the double wedding King Piero bestows a splendid dowry on each of Lionato's daughters.

Another story of this type, in which the servant is beguiled into appearing in her mistress's clothes, is found in the fifth book of Ariosto's *Orlando Furioso*. This was translated into 'English heroical verse' by Sir John Harington in 1591. Renaldo, shipwrecked on the coast of Scotland, is told of Genevra, the King of Scotland's daughter, who has been accused of unchastity and

> on this point the lawes are so expresse,
> Except by combat it be proov'd a lie,
> Needs must *Genevra* be condemned to die.[1]

No champion has appeared to defend her, so Renaldo at once sets off for the Scottish court. On the way he comes across two villains trying to murder a young woman; he saves her and as they travel on together she tells him of her unwitting responsibility for Genevra's situation. She was a maid of honour to Genevra, and had fallen in love with Polynesso, Duke of Alban, 'the second person in the land', and become his mistress. Polynesso aspired to marry the princess, and persuaded Dalinda, the maid, to assist him. But Genevra loved the noble Ariodante, and the rejected Polynesso devised a plan to destroy the princess's reputation. He persuaded Dalinda to dress in Genevra's clothes and imitate her hair-style as a preparation for one of their assignations – which often took place in the princess's rooms in the palace. He then told Ariodante that he was Genevra's lover, and offered him ocular proof on condition that he never revealed the secret. Ariodante concealed himself where he would see Polynesso secretly welcomed to Genevra's bedroom, but he did not trust his rival, so stationed his brother Lurcanio where he could see nothing, but could hear and come to his help if he was attacked. Lurcanio, worried by Ariodante's deep distress, did not stay where he was placed, but

[1] *Orlando Furioso*, trans. Sir John Harington (1591), Book V, Canto IV stanza 66.

came much nearer. They saw Polynesso welcomed by Dalinda – whom they both assumed, because of her clothes, to be Genevra. Lurcanio prevented Ariodante from killing himself on the spot, but he disappeared soon after, and a peasant later brought a message that he had leaped into the sea. Lurcanio, who had not recognised Polynesso, blamed Genevra for his brother's death, and accused her of unchastity. No challenger appeared to defend her. Dalinda became frightened and Polynesso proposed that she should go away to a castle of his until after Genevra's case was ended, when he would marry her. Instead he planned her murder, and this was only prevented by Renaldo's arrival.

When Renaldo and Dalinda arrive at the court of Scotland, they discover that an unknown champion has appeared to defend Genevra, and the combat is even then in progress. Renaldo begs the King of Scotland to stop it, and tells Dalinda's story. He then fights and defeats Polynesso, who, at the point of death, confesses his wickedness. The unknown defender turns out to be Ariodante, who had thought better of suicide on hitting the cold water; hearing of Genevra's danger he loved her so much that he came to challenge his own brother to save her, even though he believed in her guilt. All ends well – and Dalinda retires to a nunnery.

Harington attributes a version of the story of Ariodante and Genevra to George Turbervile, but no such poem is known. There is *The Historie of Ariodonto and Jenevra*, by Peter Beverley, which was entered in the Stationers' Register in 1566.[1] It elaborates Ariosto's story in lumbering fourteeners. There is a similar story, but with a tragic outcome, in Book Two of *The Faerie Queene*. In Canto IV Sir Guyon rescues Phedon from Furor and Phedon then tells his story. He grew up with Philemon, and they were faithful friends for many years. Phedon loved the Lady Claribell and their marriage was soon to be celebrated when Philemon told him that she was unfaithful, and that her paramour was a groom of low degree,

> Who used in a darksome inner bowre
> Her oft to meet: which better to approve,
> He promised to bring me at that houre,
> When I should see, that would me nearer move,
> And drive me to withdraw my blind abused love.   (stanza 24)

Philemon had seduced Claribell's maid Pyrene, and persuaded her that to demonstrate how much more beautiful she was than her mistress she should array herself in Claribell's 'most gorgeous gear'. Pyrene did so, Phedon observed the lovers' dalliance in the 'darkesome inner bowre' and assumed that it was Claribell with the groom of low degree. He departed 'chawing vengeance all the way' and when he next saw Claribell he killed her. When she heard his reason for doing so, Pyrene confessed 'how Philemon her wrought to change her weede'. Phedon poisoned Philemon, and then pursued Pyrene with his sword drawn to kill her too. It was in this pursuit that he fell into the hands of Furor and his mother Occasio, from whom Sir Guyon had saved him.

In George Whetstone's *The Rock of Regard* (1576), among other heavily moralised

---

[1] The only known copy is in the Huntington Library. It was reprinted by C. T. Prouty in *The Sources of 'Much Ado About Nothing'*, 1950.

stories and poems is a 'Discourse of Rinaldo and Giletta', which combines parts of the stories of Ariosto and Bandello.

Obviously this tale owes much to Ariosto. The trick is watered down, but the hero tries to commit suicide and then disappears. Nearer to Bandello are the general tone and the novella method, and maybe the fact that misunderstanding is caused mainly by overhearing. The maid's part is less central than in Ariosto, and there is no friendship between Rinaldo and Frizaldo as in both Italian sources.   (Bullough, II, 67)

There are a number of dramatic versions of similar stories, none of them particularly close to *Much Ado*, but indicating the wide popularity of stories of Bandello's type. *Il Fedele* by Luigi Pasqualigo (1579) was imitated by Abraham Fraunce in his Cambridge Latin play *Victoria* and by M. A. [Anthony Munday] in *Fedele and Fortunio* (1585).[1] Della Porta's *Gli Duoi Fratelli Rivali* is quite close to Bandello, though the rival lovers are brothers and the method of deception is different. It remained in manuscript until 1911. Jacob Ayrer's play *Die Schoene Phaenicia* was probably written in Nuremberg about the same time as *Much Ado*; it derives from Belleforest's version of the story and is much closer to its source than Shakespeare's play. There is no direct connection between them, nor does either of them correspond closely with the Dutch play of *Timbre de Cardone* by I. I. Starters (1618) which seems independently derived from Belleforest.[2] On New Year's Day 1575 the Earl of Leicester's Men performed a 'matter of Panecia', no other trace of which survives, and it has been suggested that this may be an error for Fenecia or Phaenicia, and the play based on Bandello's story. More obviously related to Ariosto – perhaps, as Prouty suggests, via Beverley's poem – is *Ariodante and Genevra*, performed at court on 12 February 1583 by the boys of the Merchant Taylors' School under Richard Mulcaster,[3] but this play too is lost.

It is clear that the Claudio–Hero plot of *Much Ado* makes use of episodes and actions which are closely related to Ariosto's poem and Bandello's novel and that these stories were popular, widely known and much imitated. Where Shakespeare departs from the pattern of these sources and analogues, the variations all tend in one direction. There is a reduction in the status of the lovers, and in their power to act, and a lessening of the difference of social status between them. Genevra is the king's daughter, and Ariodante owes his prestige at the Scots court to the king's favour; he is clearly her inferior. In Bandello the situation is reversed, and it is a condescension for Sir Timbreo to propose marriage to Messer Lionato's daughter. The lovers in Ariosto discover their love for each other, and Genevra remains firm in spite of Polynesso's suit and urgings from Dalinda. Fenecia recognises that Timbreo is in love with her and begins 'to watch him and bow discreetly to him' (Bullough, II, 113). Claudio says not a word to Hero, and has the prince to do his courting for him. Hero makes no expression of her feelings until

---

[1] *Victoria* survives in a single manuscript, which was edited by G. C. Moore Smith for Bang's *Materialien* (Louvain), 1906. It is most unlikely that it could have been known to Shakespeare. *Fedele and Fortunio*, ed. Percy Simpson, was printed by the Malone Society in 1906.

[2] Accounts of and extracts from both are available in Furness, pp. 329–39.

[3] A. Feuillerat, *Documents Relating to the Office of the Revels in the Time of Queen Elizabeth* in Bang's *Materialien* (Louvain), 1908; *Panecia* on p. 238, *Ariodante and Genevra* on p. 350. The connection of *Panecia* with *Much Ado* was first suggested by F. S. Boas in his edition in 1916, p. xiii.

Claudio is actually presented to her – and earlier in the same scene she, with all her family, is happily expecting a proposal from Don Pedro. Fenecia's father is not wealthy – the king provides her dowry after the wedding. Claudio is concerned from the start with Hero's expectations: 'Hath Leonato any son, my lord?' (1.1.220). The opposition to the match in both source stories comes from a rival lover of equal status (Girondo) or even greater power (Polynesso). In *Much Ado* it is the spiteful machination of a minor villain; and one of his hangers-on is substituted for the Duke of Albany as the lover of the lady's maid. There is no threat against Margaret's life, and disclosure comes not from the errant champion Renaldo, nor from the confession of the grief-stricken Girondo, but, in spite of the bungling of Dogberry, from the drunken boasting of Borachio. It is worth noting, too, that the effects proposed by Friar Francis for his plan do not occur.

> When he shall hear she died upon his words
> Th'idea of her life shall sweetly creep
> Into his study of imagination,
> And every lovely organ of her life,
> Shall come apparelled in more precious habit,
> More moving-delicate, and full of life,
> Into the eye and prospect of his soul
> Than when she lived indeed: then shall he mourn,
> If ever love had interest in his liver,
> And wish he had not so accusèd her:
> No, though he thought his accusation true.   (4.1.216–26)

Claudio's callous jesting in 5.1 shows not a trace of remorse, or even mild regret, at the supposed death of Hero. Both Girondo and Timbreo are deeply distressed by the news of Fenecia's death, and this remorse leads to confession – first by Girondo to Timbreo, and then by both to Lionato – and forgiveness. Ariodante in Ariosto's story loves Genevra so much that – though he thought the accusation true – he is prepared to challenge his brother to mortal combat to defend her life and honour. Perhaps Friar Francis had been reading too many Italian novellas. On the other hand, by his diagnosis, it appears that love never did have interest in Claudio's liver.

In Shakespeare's play there is a systematic reduction of the attitudes of characters in cognate stories. Romantic infatuation and violent jealousy are to be found in the immature: Claudio's youth is stressed, and while Hero's age is not stated (Fenecia was sixteen) she is clearly small ('Leonato's short daughter', 1.1.158) and as a 'very forward March-chick' (1.3.41) must be assumed young. The Princess Genevra seems a mature person, and the knights in both stories are seasoned soldiers. At the same time as the power and status of Claudio are reduced from the sources, his reaction is made more objectionable. Sir Timbreo sends a private messenger to Lionato with the accusation of unchastity; Lurcanio makes his accusation against Genevra to protect his brother's reputation, and it is in the nature of a challenge to all comers which he will defend with his life. Claudio repudiates Hero in the most public and sensational way, and there is no one – until Benedick undertakes it – to challenge him to maintain her honour: Hero has no relations but two old men and her cousin Beatrice and has even been deprived of the mother and sister who support Fenecia. It seems unlikely, in view of this systematic departure from the tendency of well-known analogues, that Claudio was intended as a particularly admirable or sympathetic character.

It is notorious that critical interest in the play has concentrated on Beatrice and Benedick (apart from wondering whether or not Claudio is a cad),[1] and that these two also provide the parts that make actors and actresses famous. There is no obvious source for their story: it seems – like the Petruchio–Katherina plot of *The Taming of the Shrew* in its departure from the brutality of traditional 'shrew' stories[2] – to be Shakespeare's own invention. It provides a strong contrast to the Claudio–Hero plot in many ways. It is not a traditional (or an archetypal) story. Beatrice and Benedick have been seen as the forerunners of the 'witty couple' of Restoration comedy, with their banter, the assumption by Beatrice of intellectual and sexual equality, and their distrust of the attitudes and also the language of conventional lovers. At the same time they demonstrate in action a genuineness and strength of feeling that shows up the superficiality of the other characters. Hero is rejected by her lover with scarcely a protest – on evidence, however circumstantially convincing, presented by a man he knows to be his enemy. She is rejected by her father on hearsay alone, and he falls at once into the platitudes of anti-feminism. It is her cousin who defends her, and does it on the simplest and most obvious grounds: Beatrice *knows* Hero, and knows, consequently, that the accusation is absurd. Friar Francis defends her because he observes her response to the accusation, and sees that it is one of innocence, not guilt. Benedick shows an immediate concern for Hero, and becomes her champion because, essentially, he trusts Beatrice's judgement. These things again reflect back on the source stories. None of Fenecia's family believes the accusations of Sir Timbreo; Ariodante is prepared to fight to defend the honour of Genevra, even though he believes her guilty.

Although no specific source has been located for the plot of the double gulling of Beatrice and Benedick, hints, parallels and anticipations can be found. The sparring witty lovers are anticipated by Shakespeare himself at a rumbustious level in *The Taming of the Shrew* and more elegantly in *Love's Labour's Lost* – particularly in the pair Berowne and Rosalind. The rapid, elegantly articulated prose and the equally matched lovers have precedents in the comedies of John Lyly. M. A. Scott long ago drew attention to Castiglione's *Il Cortegiano* as a model of courtly conversation, where wit and raillery could be maintained in a good-humoured war of the sexes.[3] Bullough extends this by citing a passage which, without providing the plot, suggests that people might come to be in love with each other by hearing it confidently reported that this was the case.[4]

---

[1] In spite of its stage popularity *Much Ado* has had a good deal less critical discussion than some plays – *Measure for Measure*, for example – which are less frequently performed. This may be changing, since *Much Ado* seems amenable to certain kinds of criticism that have recently become more widely practised: for example, Anthony B. Dawson, 'Much ado about signifying', *SEL* 22.2 (1982), 211–21; or Keir Elam, 'Much ado about doing things with words (and other means): some problems in the pragmatics of theatre and drama', *Australian Journal of French Studies* (Sydney, NSW), 20 (1983), 261–77.

[2] See Ann Thompson's discussion in her edition of *The Taming of the Shrew*, 1984, pp. 27–8.

[3] '*The Book of the Courtier*: a possible source of Beatrice and Benedick', *PMLA* 16 (1901), 475–502.

[4] Bullough, II, 79; the passage is quoted here from the Everyman edition, 1975, of Sir Thomas Hoby's translation (1561), p. 248. In the second line Bullough reads 'they heard say': 'she heard say' seems preferable.

I have also seen a most fervent love spring in the heart of a woman, toward one that seemed at the first not to bear him the least affection in the world, only for that she heard say, that the opinion of many was, that they loved together. And the cause of this (I believe) was that so general a judgement seemed a sufficient witnes, that he was worthy of her love. And it seemed (in a manner) that report brought the ambassad on the lover's behalf much more truer and worthier to be believed, than he himself could have done with letters or words, or any other person for him: therefor sometime this common voice not only hurteth not, but farthereth a mans purpose.

In her edition of *Much Ado* Barbara Lewalski argues strongly for a more pervasive influence from Castiglione in 'the play's evident debt to the Neoplatonic love philosophy, one classic source of which is Bembo's discourse in Book IV of *The Courtier*', and also that the 'thematic centre' of the drama – 'as in Bembo's discourse – is the relation of kinds of loving or longing to ways of knowing' (p. xiv). The parallels here, though, are very much more distant than those for the Claudio–Hero plot, and can have provided no more than hints to be developed, if they were consciously remembered in the process of composition at all. The idea of a benignly intended falsehood interacting in a double plot with the malicious falsehood to lead the witty lovers to a fuller state of awareness is an elegant and effective variation on the well-worn theme of the calumniated and redeemed good woman, and it also provides a drastic criticism of the values implicit in such stories. Shakespeare's real originality is not so much in inventing the Beatrice and Benedick plot as in the way he uses it to comment on the story that he borrows from Bandello and Ariosto.

The date of the play

The quarto of *Much Ado About Nothing* was printed in 1600. The fact that the names Kemp and Cowley appear as speech headings in 4.2 means that the composition must

1   An arbour in an Elizabethan garden, such as might have been the imagined location for Act 2, Scene 3 and Act 3, Scene 1

2   A stage-property arbour from the title page of the 1615 edition of Thomas Kyd's *The Spanish Tragedy*

precede Will Kemp's departure from the Lord Chamberlain's company early in 1599.[1] A date after which the play was written is less easily established, but it is not mentioned in Francis Meres's *Palladis Tamia*, which was entered in the Stationers' Register on 7 September 1598. Towards the end of this book of moral reflections Meres lists the works of the major English writers of his day and compares them with the Greek, Latin and Italian poets. His comment on Shakespeare, 'the most excellent in both kinds for the stage', is well known. The 'kinds' are tragedy and comedy, and of the latter Meres names 'his *Gentlemen of Verona*, his *Errors*, his *Love's Labour's Lost*, his *Love's Labour's Won*, his *Midsummer Night's Dream*, and his *Merchant of Venice*'.[2] That *Much Ado* is not named is in no way conclusive that it was not in existence, but the quality of the play makes it likely that had Meres known it he would have named it. It is most commonly held that the play was written in the latter part of 1598, and this fits in well with other circumstantial evidence and with the style. *A Midsummer Night's Dream* and *The Merchant of Venice* are usually dated in 1595–6, followed by the two *Henry IV* plays and *The Merry Wives of Windsor* in 1597–8. Meres lists 'his *Henry the 4*' among the tragedies. In 1599 come *As You Like It* and *Henry V*; and Touchstone in *As You Like It* is the first part Shakespeare wrote for Robert Armin's more intellectual and gentle style of comedy, after Armin took Kemp's place in the company. *Love's Labour's Won* in Meres's list presents a mystery and

---

[1]   It was on 'the first Monday in clean Lent' of 1599 that Kemp set off on his *Nine Days Wonder*. The record of his morris dance from London to Norwich was published in 1600.

[2]   *Palladis Tamia*, ed. D. C. Allen, 1932, p. 282. Meres uses the form *Love Labours Lost* and *Love Labours Won*.

Balthasar

Leonato

Claudio   Prince

Benedick

"See you where Benedick hath hid himself?"

"I will hide me in the arbour"

3   Alternative stagings for the arbour scene in Act 2, Scene 3, by C. Walter Hodges.
a 'Arbour' simulated simply by use of stage posts
b Arbour as a carried-on property

it has been argued – originally by A. E. Brae in *Collier, Coleridge, and Shakespeare*, 1860 (pp. 131 ff.) – that this title refers to *Much Ado*. The case was never more than speculative: Quiller-Couch wrote in 1923 that Bray's (*sic*) 'ingenious arguments . . . serve sundry good by-purposes while missing to convince us on the main' (NS, p. viii). The discovery in 1953 of a list dating from 1603 of the stock of Christopher Hunt, a London bookseller, made the theory even less tenable, for the list includes *Love's Labour's Won* three years after the publication of *Much Ado About Nothing*.[1]

There have also been revision theories – the most influential being that of Dover Wilson (NS, pp. 102 ff.) – which attempt to account for the problems of the quarto text by postulating an 'old' play on the Claudio–Hero plot on to which the 'new' material of Beatrice and Benedick was (sometimes clumsily) cobbled. In this view the verse parts of the play belong to the earlier strata while the vigorous colloquial prose of Beatrice and Benedick represents the later work. Such 'explanations' can never prove anything.[2]

Stage history

The 1600 quarto assures us that *Much Ado About Nothing* had 'been sundry times publicly acted', but the only performance in Shakespeare's lifetime for which we have documentary evidence took place three years before he died. In 1613 John Heminge received two payments on behalf of the company from Lord Treasurer Stanhope on warrants dated 20 May.[3] These were for twenty plays that had been performed as part of the celebrations for the marriage of James I's daughter Elizabeth to Prince Frederick of Bohemia, the Elector Palatine. The first list contains fourteen plays and includes '*Much adoe abowte nothinge*'. The second list of six plays includes '*Benedicte and Betteris*', and, according to Halliwell-Phillips, Charles I inscribed these names against the title of *Much Ado* in his copy of the 1632 Second Folio.[4] It is usually assumed that this was the same play, though as no other item on either list was given twice, other conjectures have been made. Although no other performance is certainly recorded for more than a century, and *Much Ado* was not republished before the Folio, there is little doubt that it was a popular play, at least until the closing of the theatres. In the verse eulogy provided for the edition of Shakespeare's *Poems* in 1640 Leonard Digges wrote:

> let but Beatrice
> And Benedick be seen, lo in a trice
> The Cockpit, galleries, boxes, all are full.

This, like Charles I's title, confirms the early popularity of the sparring lovers.[5]

---

[1] T. W. Baldwin, *Shakespeare's 'Love's Labour's Won'*, 1957. However, R. F. Fleissner in '*Love's Labour's Won* and the occasion of *Much Ado*', S.Sur. 27 (1974), 105–10, has maintained the identification of *Much Ado* and *Love's Labour's Won*.

[2] Ridley offers a neat *reductio ad absurdum* by producing an 'early' version of Friar Francis's speech at 4.1.148 ff in rhyming couplets.

[3] E. K. Chambers, *William Shakespeare*, 2 vols., 1930, II, 343.

[4] Charles was born in 1600, and would certainly have shared in the festivities of his sister's wedding. He was heir apparent, following the death of his brother Henry in the previous year, though he was not created Prince of Wales until 1616. For Halliwell-Phillips's note see Furness, pp. xxii and 6.

[5] There is clear evidence of the frequency of productions of *Much Ado* after the Restoration. In spite of a late

After the Restoration *Much Ado* was one of nine plays by Shakespeare assigned to Davenant and the Duke of York's company, and not to Killigrew with the King's company.[1] As a result the tradition of the play in the theatre may have been lost, for Davenant chose to hybridise *Much Ado* with *Measure for Measure*, also reserved for his company, under the title of *The Law Against Lovers*, first performed on 15 February 1662. Pepys saw it at Lincoln's Inn Fields on February 18 and thought it 'a good play'. He particularly admired the singing and dancing of a little girl who played Beatrice's baby sister. Beatrice was the ward of Angelo from *Measure for Measure*, and – a significant variation – a great heiress. The Claudio is the one in *Measure for Measure*, and Hero is not there.

When Rich revived *Much Ado* at Lincoln's Inn in 1721, where it was performed on February 9, 10 and 11, with Ryan as Benedick, Quin as Leonato and Mrs Cross as Beatrice, it was advertised as not having been acted for 'thirty years': this perhaps meant only 'for a long time', since so far as surviving records go it had not been acted since the Restoration, though in Rowe's 1709 edition of Shakespeare there is an illustration of the church scene (4.1, see illustration 4) which suggests a post-Restoration stage set. In 1723 some passages from *Much Ado* were incorporated in *Love in a Forest* (mostly *As You Like It*) at Drury Lane. In 1737 another adaptation appeared, James Miller's *The Universal Passion*, which involved substantial parts of Molière's *Princesse d'Elide* as well as passages borrowed from *Twelfth Night* and *Two Gentlemen of Verona*.[2] In November *Much Ado* itself was seen three times at Covent Garden, with Chapman as Benedick and Miss Bincks as Beatrice. There was a one-night benefit at the same theatre two years later on 25 May, with much the same cast in the main roles. In 1746 it ran for three nights at Covent Garden, with Ryan as Benedick – the part he had played in 1721 – and Mrs Pritchard as Beatrice. She had played Delia – an enlarged 'Margaret' – in *The Universal Passion*. Garrick first played Benedick at Drury Lane on 14 November 1748; Mrs Pritchard was his Beatrice. The production was most successful, being seen on ten nights before the end of the year. Benedick became one of Garrick's most admired comic parts and he played it every year until his retirement in 1776, when his final performance was seen on 9 May. Mrs Pritchard was a distinguished Beatrice and played the role until 1757, when the part was taken by her daughter. Miss Pope played Beatrice in 1764 and continued in it for ten years. In the last two years of Garrick's *Much Ado* his Beatrice was Mrs Abington, whose performance was also highly praised.

Both Miss Pope and Mrs Abington continued to play Beatrice, with other Benedicks. Sarah Siddons (who had worked with Garrick's company in 1775) played Beatrice with

---

start it was twentieth in order of popularity among Shakespeare's plays in the first half of the eighteenth century, ahead of *All's Well*, *Twelfth Night* and *The Comedy of Errors*. By the end of the century it had moved up to fifteenth place, overtaking *A Midsummer Night's Dream* and *The Merry Wives of Windsor*, according to the tables in C. B. Hogan's *Shakespeare in the Theatre 1701–1800*, 2 vols. 1952, 1957, I, 461; II, 717. I have no statistical evidence for the nineteenth century, but it was clearly staged very often. J. C. Trewin provides a census of productions at Stratford-upon-Avon between 1879 and 1964 in *Shakespeare on the English Stage, 1900–1964*. *Much Ado* is listed 35 times, like *Twelfth Night*, while *The Merchant of Venice* was produced 40 times, and *As You Like It* 41.

[1] G. C. Odell, *Shakespeare from Betterton to Irving*, 2 vols., 1920 (reprinted 1963), I, 24.

[2] For an outline of the joinery see Hogan, I, 341. Much of the information for early stage history is taken from this source.

4 Claudio repudiates Hero in church, Act 4, Scene 1. From Nicholas Rowe's edition of 1709

success in Bristol in 1779. Her brother John Philip Kemble established himself as Benedick with Elizabeth Farren as Beatrice in 1788. Ten years later Mrs Jordan took over as Beatrice at Drury Lane on 24 May. Miss Farren became Countess of Derby; Dorothy Jordan was mistress to the Duke of Clarence – later King William IV – and bore ten FitzClarence children between the acts (she already had five, by two other fathers). Her Beatrice seems to have been robust and cheerful; she was noted for 'the hearty laugh . . . that made the listener doubt if such a woman could ever be unhappy'.[1] In the same year – on 14 May 1798, at the age of 61 – Mrs Abington played Beatrice for the last time at Covent Garden. Charles Kemble, eighteen years younger than his brother John Philip, also made his début in *Much Ado* in 1798 when he played Claudio at the Haymarket on 21 August; Mrs Jordan was Beatrice. He took Benedick for the first time in 1803, and it became one of his outstanding parts. His daughter, Fanny Kemble, played Beatrice after she joined his company at Covent Garden in 1829. At his retirement in 1836, when he was 61, Charles Kemble chose Helen Faucit, then 19, as his Beatrice, and she records that he passed on to her Fanny Kemble's acting-texts of Shakespeare[2] – Fanny by then was married and living in America. Her Beatrice was refined and generous, and was distinguished both from the large good humour of Dorothy Jordan and the shrewish anger of some other current interpretations. Forty-three years later, in 1879, Helen Faucit (by then Lady Martin) gave her final performance as Beatrice at the opening of the Shakespeare Memorial Theatre in Stratford-upon-Avon. Her Benedick was the Irish-American actor Barry Sullivan.

Three years later Henry Irving and Ellen Terry played Benedick and Beatrice at the Lyceum in a lavish production that ran for 212 performances from 11 October 1882, and then went on an American tour with great success before returning to London in 1884. Irving 'had taken the part of Benedick at one of Helen Faucit's readings at Onslow Square' in July 1882.[3] Beatrice was one of Ellen Terry's most popular parts, and she continued to perform it until the end of her career. She was famous for the sunny good nature of her Beatrice and for her generous loyalty to Hero in her distress; a great lady of charm, wit and entire self-confidence.

Even today no actress [playing Beatrice] has a fair chance with me . . . because Ellen Terry's voice and gestures keep coming between me and her . . . Others have had gaiety and humour, grace and vivacity, tenderness, dignity and deep feeling, but not as Ellen Terry had them.[4]

She had played Hero at the Haymarket in 1863, when she was 15, to Louisa Angell's

---

[1] Furness, p. 387, from George Fletcher, *Studies of Shakespeare*, 1847, p. 282.
[2] Lady Martin, *On Some of Shakespeare's Female Characters*, 1891, in Furness, p. 357. The letter that accompanied the gift is recorded as follows.

11 Park Place, St James's

MY DEAR LITTLE FRIEND, – To you alone do these parts, which were once Fanny Kemble's, of right belong; for from you alone can we now expect the most efficient representation of them. Pray oblige me by giving them a place in your study; and believe me ever your true friend and servant,

C. Kemble

[3] Laurence Irving, *Henry Irving: The Actor and his World*, 1951, p. 401.
[4] Gordon Crosse, *Shakespearean Playgoing 1890–1952*, 1953, p. 15.

5   Ellen Terry as Beatrice in the Lyceum production, 1882. The episode is probably from the end of the play,
5.4.89, when the sonnet 'Containing her affection unto Benedick' is produced

Beatrice.[1] Her first performance as Beatrice had been at Leeds in 1880, with Charles Kelly – Charles Wardell, her second husband – as Benedick. He gave

in many ways a splendid performance, perhaps better for the play than the more subtle and deliberate performance Henry Irving gave at the Lyceum.   (*Memoirs*, p. 115)

Her account of that Lyceum production shows clearly that she had considerable reservations about it, in spite of its enormous success.

When Henry Irving put on 'Much Ado About Nothing' – a play which he may be said to have revived for me, as he never really liked the part of Benedick – I was not the same Beatrice at all. A great actor can do nothing badly, and there was very much to admire in Henry Irving's Benedick. But he gave me little help. Beatrice must be swift, swift, swift! Owing to Henry's rather finicking, deliberate method as Benedick, I could never put the right pace into my part. I was also feeling unhappy about it, because I had been compelled to give way about a traditional 'gag' in the church scene, with which we ended the fourth act. In my own production we had scorned this gag, and let the curtain come down on Benedick's line: 'Go, comfort your cousin; I must say she is dead, and so farewell.' When I was told that we were to descend to the buffoonery of:
    Beatrice: Benedick, kill him – kill him if you can.
    Benedick: As sure as I'm alive, I will.
I protested, and implored Henry not to do it. He said that it was necessary: otherwise the 'curtain' would be received in dead silence.[2]   (*Memoirs*, p. 127)

In her lecture on 'Shakespeare's Triumphant Women' she records another piece of traditional business for *Much Ado* from the early part of the nineteenth century.

When I first rehearsed Beatrice at the Lyceum I was told by Mr Lacy, an actor of the old school who was engaged by Henry Irving to assist him in some of his early Shakespearean productions, of some traditional 'business' which seemed to me so preposterous that I could hardly believe he really meant me to adopt it. But he was quite serious. 'When Benedick rushes forward to lift up Hero after she has fainted, you "shoo" him away. Jealousy, you see. Beatrice is not going to let her man lay a finger on another woman.' I said, 'Oh, nonsense, Mr. Lacy!' 'Well, it's always been done', he retorted, 'and it always gets a laugh.'[3]

She had known Walter Lacy since her first stage appearance at the age of 11 with Charles Kean's company in 1856. When she was playing Mamillius, Puck and the good fairy Goldenstar in the Christmas pantomime, he was playing John of Gaunt to Charles Kean's Richard II; he was then 47.[4] Ellen Terry's comment on Forbes-Robertson's Claudio is – typically – generous.

His Claudio . . . was beautiful. I have seen many young actors play the part since then, but not one of them made it anywhere near as convincing. Forbes-Robertson put a touch of Leontes into it, a

[1] 'Miss Angell was a very modern Beatrice, but I . . . played Hero beautifully.' *Ellen Terry's Memoirs*, ed. Edith Craig and Christopher St John, 1933, p. 41. Page numbers for later references are included in the text.
[2] Odell (II, 296) reports a similar interpolation in the version of *Much Ado* used by Charles Kean for his revival on 20 November 1858, at which time Walter Lacy (see n. 4 below) and Ellen Terry were in Kean's company.
[3] Ellen Terry, *Four Lectures on Shakespeare*, ed. Christopher St John, 1933, pp. 95–6.
[4] Playbill for Charles Kean's company at 'The Princess's Theatre, Oxford Street', Friday, 8 January 1858, now in the Victoria and Albert Museum. NS reports that Walter Lacy played Benedick at the St James's Theatre 'a few years' after 1858 (p. 163) and the *Dictionary of National Biography* lists it among his roles.

6 The church scene, Act 4, Scene 1, in Irving's 1882 production. Benedick (Irving) is right of centre, with Don John further right; Don Pedro is in the centre, with Claudio (played by Johnston Forbes-Robertson, who painted the picture) further left; Hero kneels before Friar Francis and her father, while Beatrice (Ellen Terry) is on the extreme left. The remarkable set is by William Telbin

part which some years later he was to play magnificently, and through the subtle indications of consuming and insanely suspicious jealousy made Claudio's offensive conduct explicable at least.

(*Memoirs*, p. 172)

In 1891 *Much Ado* was revived at the Lyceum, and this time Irving's Benedick suited Ellen Terry better. 'Went most brilliantly', she noted in her diary, 'Henry has vastly improved upon his *old* rendering ... acts larger now' (*Memoirs*, p. 175). In this production her son Edward Gordon Craig played the part of the Messenger.

But the great Lyceum partnership was coming to an end, and she did not play Beatrice with Irving again, though the influence of that partnership probably continues still in the theatre. In 1903 Ellen Terry went into theatrical management with Gordon Craig. It was artistically adventurous, but financially disastrous. Their second production was *Much Ado*, in the hope of recouping the losses made on the first, Ibsen's *The Vikings*.[1] It was to be the only Shakespeare play directed by Gordon Craig in England. Oscar Asche was Benedick and Conway Tearle Claudio. In a provincial tour that followed, these parts were taken by Matheson Lang and Harcourt Williams. Bernard Shaw wrote to Ellen Terry on 3 June 'your Beatrice is a rather creditable performance, considering that I didn't stage manage it', and 'As usual Ted [Gordon Craig] has the best of it. I have never seen the church scene go before – didn't think it *could* go, in fact', but he ends with a warning: 'do no more unless Ted finds the money as well as the scenery'.[2]

Gordon Craig's setting was revolutionary in its day. Telbin's set for Irving for Act 4, Scene 1 had thirty-foot-high built-out pillars and a red plush canopy from which hung golden lamps, and all the gorgeousness of an Italian cathedral. 'Gordon Craig indicated the church simply by the widening light that illuminated the many colours of a huge cross. Otherwise he used only curtains that hung in folds and were painted with pillars.'[3] This bare and impressionistic setting of the play was used throughout its eleven months of provincial touring. It had advantages of transportability, but must have been very strange to audiences used to the architectural splendours of late-nineteenth-century staging. Max Beerbohm's response can be found in his *More Theatres 1898–1903*, 1969, pp. 573–6.

Another revolution was also under way: William Poel's efforts to produce Shakespeare's plays in conditions something like those for which they had been written, and with music of the Elizabethan period, were beginning to have some influence. Between 23 February and 4 March 1904 the Elizabethan Stage Society 'by arrangement with Mr Ben Greet and at the special request of the Rev. Stewart D. Headlam, Chairman of Evening Continuation Schools ... for the London School Board' gave seven performances of *Much Ado* in halls in poor areas of London – Shoreditch, Bow, New Cross, Hammersmith, St Pancras, Battersea and Bermondsey. There was subsequently a public matinée at the Royal Court (where Granville-Barker was beginning his partnership with Vedrenne with a production of *The Comedy of Errors*) on 19 March

[1] 'He persuaded her [Ellen Terry] to do Ibsen's *The Vikings of Heligoland* and play a part quite unsuited to her, and she had to put on a revival of *Much Ado* to replace it. Craig exhausted all the money she had saved to put it on' (John Gielgud, *An Actor and his Time*, 1981, p. 145).

[2] *Ellen Terry and Bernard Shaw: A Correspondence*, ed. Christopher St John, 1949, p. 370.

[3] Trewin, *Shakespeare on the English Stage*, p. 27.

7 Edward Gordon Craig's preliminary sketch for the church scene in his production of 1903

8   Edward Gordon Craig's design for Leonato's garden, used for the arbour scenes and for Benedick's meeting with Beatrice, Act 5, Scene 2

and (with a lecture from Dr Furnivall) at Burlington House on 22 April. William Poel was the producer and the musical direction was by Arnold Dolmetsch. The music included Edward Johnson's 'Pavana Delight' and a 'Cinque Pace or Galliard'; there was a jig by William Byrd, and Dowland's 'Lachrymae' was used for the scene at Hero's tomb. Not all the actors can be identified with the parts they played, but the cast included Nugent Monck, Lewis Casson (Don Pedro) and Poel himself as Friar Francis, the part supposed to have been taken by Shakespeare.[1] Rita Jolivet played Beatrice and Victor Dougal Benedick. An account of the Royal Court performance (*The Pilot*, 9 April 1904,

[1]   T. W. Baldwin, *The Organisation and Personnel of the Shakespearean Company*, 1954, p. 411.

signed W.H.H.) disliked Benedick, who laughed too much, praised Beatrice, and said that Dogberry (unfortunately without identification) was 'the best seen in London these forty years'.[1] *The Times* (23 April) reported the lecture, but found 'the representation does not call for detailed notice'; it 'owed more to . . . antiquarian interest than to the histrionic talents of the players', and was 'painfully slow'.

There was a production of *Much Ado* by Beerbohm Tree at His Majesty's in January 1905, with Winifred Emery as Beatrice. This was in the lavish Victorian style, once more used Telbin's set for the church scene, and lasted four hours – which some thought too long. Shaw praised Tree with his heaviest irony: 'Totally insensible to Shakespear's qualities, he puts his own qualities into the work' and does it 'astonishingly' well. To Winifred Emery, who was evidently reacting against the golden-hearted Beatrice of Ellen Terry, Shaw was kinder: 'she was clever enough to play Lady Disdain instead of playing for sentimental sympathy; and the effect was keenly good and original'. Shaw, of course, was on the side of the revolution, but his recommendation of the production included nostalgia as well as irony.

All the lovely things Shakespear dispensed with are there in bounteous plenty. Fair ladies, Sicilian seascapes, Italian gardens, summer nights and dawns (compressed into five minutes), Renascential splendours, dancing, singing, masquerading, architecture, orchestration carefully culled from Wagner, Bizet, and German, and endless larks in the way of stage business devised by Mr Tree, and carried out with much innocent enjoyment, which is fairly infectious on the other side of the footlights . . . On the whole, my advice is, go and see it: you will never again have the chance of enjoying such an entertainment.[2]

And Shaw was right: almost without exception later productions in the major London theatres are influenced by the work of Poel and Granville-Barker and have a strong connection with Stratford or the Old Vic or – in due course – the National Theatre. The next London production of *Much Ado* was in the 1915–16 season at the Old Vic, the director was Ben Greet, and Sybil Thorndike (married in 1908 to Lewis Casson) played Beatrice. This production went to Stratford for the festival in 1916. *Much Ado* was seen at the Old Vic in the seasons beginning 1918, 1921 and 1924. In 1925–6 Edith Evans – who had first acted Shakespeare as an amateur with Poel in 1912, and later toured with Ellen Terry – played Beatrice to Baliol Holloway's Benedick. In the 1927–8 season Sybil Thorndike returned as Beatrice with Lewis Casson as Benedick. In 1930–1 Harcourt Williams directed Gielgud and Dorothy Green. The last two productions of *Much Ado* at the Old Vic, in 1934 and 1956, were not among the most distinguished.

At Stratford-upon-Avon *Much Ado* was also frequently produced. It had opened the Memorial Theatre in 1879, and Barry Sullivan's company presented it again in the next two years. After a ten-year break Benson's company did it; and again in 1894. Ben Greet directed his company in *Much Ado* in 1895, but Benson maintained the festival until 1914, presenting *Much Ado* almost every year. Apart from the visit of the Old Vic

---

[1] This could perhaps refer to Robert Keeley, who had worked with Charles Kean and whose Dogberry was highly praised by Dickens. He died in 1869. Westland Marston reports of Macready's Benedick of 1843 that he 'roused the house to such shouts of mirth, one might have thought Keeley, not Macready, was on the stage' (*Our Ancient Actors*, 1888, quoted by Gāmini Salgādo, *Eyewitnesses of Shakespeare*, 1975, p. 154).

[2] *The Saturday Review*, 11 February 1905, quoted in *Shaw on Shakespeare*, ed. Edwin Wilson, 1961, pp. 140–9.

9   John Gielgud as Benedick in the arbour, Act 2, Scene 3, in his production at the Shakespeare Memorial
Theatre, 1950. Leonato (Andrew Cruickshank), Don Pedro (Leon Quartermaine) and Claudio (Eric Lander)
are seated on the left

company in 1916, with Sybil Thorndike, there was not another *Much Ado* until W.
Bridges-Adams produced it for the first time in 1920. (In 1910, fresh from Oxford, he
had been assistant stage-manager for Poel in a production of *Two Gentlemen of Verona*.)
Of his sixteen years' work at Stratford J. C. Trewin wrote that

> his productions would be among the most distinguished of the century: they have been under-rated
> because too few London critics went regularly to the Memorial Theatre.[1]

Bridges-Adams included *Much Ado* in the Stratford repertory roughly every other year
until 1934. In February 1926, he produced it at the New Theatre with Henry Ainley and
Madge Titherage as Benedick and Beatrice. He also designed the simple multiple set for
that successful production. It was the last in a London theatre until Donald Wolfit took
his company to the Kingsway in 1940. Among his leading players at Stratford Bridges-
Adams included George Hayes and Baliol Holloway as Benedick, Dorothy Black and
Fabia Drake as Beatrice and Roy Byford as a much admired Dogberry.

   Under the direction of Iden Payne *Much Ado* was seen at Stratford in 1936 with
Barbara Couper as Beatrice and James Dale as Benedick: Donald Wolfit was also in the
cast. In 1939 Alec Clunes and Vivienne Bennett played these roles, and in 1941 George
Hayes returned to play Benedick with Margaretta Scott.

[1]   Trewin, *Shakespeare on the English Stage*, p. 88.

In the period immediately after the war *Much Ado* was seen several times in the West End: in 1946 Fabia Drake directed, with Renée Asherson and Robert Donat, and Harcourt Williams as Leonato, but it was not very successful. The next year Hugh Hunt's Bristol Old Vic production came to the Embassy with much fun and games, including Dogberry (William Devlin) as an air raid warden on a bicycle. In 1949 there were two London productions, but the outstanding production of that year, and one which like Irving's set a standard for years to come, was John Gielgud's at Stratford. It was a happy production which did not allow the Claudio–Hero plot to develop its potential for distress too far. In it the various traditions of playing Shakespeare seemed to come harmoniously together. It was conventionally dressed in early Renaissance costume and had a colourful though formal Italian palace and garden set by Mariano Andreu,[1] but the set was ingeniously and rapidly adaptable and allowed the free movement from scene to scene that Poel had demonstrated on his bare stage fifty years before. Anthony Quayle and Diana Wynyard were the original Benedick and Beatrice, and played in the Australian tour of 1949–50. In later revivals (1950, 1952 and 1955, with a European tour before another London season) Gielgud played Benedick himself. Subsequently Peggy Ashcroft took over the part of Beatrice. Lewis Casson returned to the play as an admirable Leonato, and when the production went to America in 1959 Margaret Leighton was Beatrice. Gielgud's comments on these Beatrices, and on his own changing view of the role of Benedick, are interesting.

Peggy Ashcroft's Beatrice was most original. Diana Wynyard played it much more on the lines I imagine Ellen Terry did – the great lady sweeping about in beautiful clothes. When Peggy started rehearsing she rather jibbed at that and said 'I'm not going to wear those dresses, they're too grand for me.' She evolved her own approach to the character, just as good as Diana's but totally different – almost with a touch of Beatrice Lillie. She wore much simpler dresses and created a cheeky character who means well but seems to drop bricks all the while (perhaps she got it from me). Everybody thinks Beatrice will never marry because she is too free with her tongue and is rather impertinent to people without intending any rudeness.
  As far as my own performance was concerned over the years, I kept trying to make Benedick into more of a soldier. At first Mariano [Andreu, the designer] encouraged me to be a dandy, wearing comic hats . . . The hats used to get laughs the moment I came on in them. I decided this had not much to do with Shakespeare's play, so I gradually discarded them, and wore leather doublets and thigh boots and became less of a courtier. I tried to inject a good deal more bluffness and strength into the part. Benedick ought to be an uncouth soldier, a tough misanthrope, who wears a beard and probably smells to high heaven. When this went against the grain I tried to console myself with the idea that Irving must have been more of the courtier too, but of course I never saw his performance.[2]

Of the 1959 revival for an American tour Gielgud said 'by that time I thought my production had become rather old-fashioned'. The set was poorly reproduced, looked like 'a Soho *trattoria*' and lacked the 'lovely classical Italian quality' it had had in England.
  The determination not to be 'old-fashioned' seems to have influenced a number of subsequent productions. The period and location of the play have been shifted for

[1] In *Stage Directions*, 1963, p. 39, Gielgud writes that he specified 'scenery and dresses of the Boccaccio period'.
[2] Gielgud, *An Actor and his Time*, pp. 135–6.

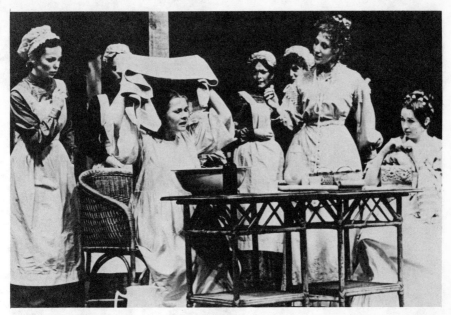

10 'A maid and stuffed! There's goodly catching of cold.' Judi Dench as Beatrice in John Barton's 'Indian'
production for the Royal Shakespeare Company in 1976 (3.4.48). Hero (Cheri Lunghi) is seated on the right
and Margaret (Eliza Ward) stands next to her

reasons not always clearly explained. Douglas Seale's 1958 Stratford production,
costumed in the mid nineteenth century, was played with ease and elegance by Michael
Redgrave and Googie Withers. In 1961 Michael Langham tried an earlier period of the
same century with Christopher Plummer and Geraldine McEwen; the latter was 'pert
and pretty', while Benedick 'quietly and promptly refused to kill Claudio as one might
decline to remove an overcoat'.[1] The most famous of these departures was Zeffirelli's
production for the National Theatre in 1965, set in a Messina of the late nineteenth
century, with strong implications of the Mafia, and a lot of inventive farcical business
which the director is reported to have claimed was intended to enliven a 'very dull play'.[2]
Robert Stephens and Maggie Smith were admired as Benedick and Beatrice, but the star
performance was Albert Finney's macaroni cigar-smoking Don Pedro. In the 1966
revival of this production that visited Stratford-upon-Avon Derek Jacobi took over this
role: he had played Don John in 1965. Trevor Nunn's production at Stratford in 1968
(which came to the Aldwych in London in the following year) was back in period
costume, with Janet Suzman and Alan Howard as Beatrice and Benedick, but it appears
that the 'merry war' never got 'properly under way'.[3] Unusually, the honours in this
production seemed to go to Helen Mirren's Hero. The next Royal Shakespeare
Company production, by Ronald Eyre in 1971, used mid-Victorian costumes and tried

[1] *Theatre World*, May 1961, p. 27.
[2] Quoted by Humphreys, p. 43, from *The Guardian*, 29 October 1977.
[3] Irving Wardle in *The Times*, 15 October 1968.

11 Sinead Cusack and Derek Jacobi as Beatrice and Benedick in the final scene of Terry Hands's Royal Shakespeare Company production, 1982. Jeffrey Dench as Antonio is in the background; the set is by Ralph Koltai

the interesting – but not, it seems, very successful – experiment of casting Derek Godfrey and Elizabeth Spriggs as a Benedick and Beatrice approaching middle age. The 1976 production by John Barton with Judi Dench and Donald Sinden was more widely acclaimed. This was set in British India in the later nineteenth century. An incidental advantage from this setting was an Indian Dogberry played by John Woodvine; his (proleptic) malaproprisms came over well in Bombay Welsh.

In 1982 Terry Hands produced the play at Stratford, and it was seen at the Barbican the following year. The set, by Ralph Koltai, was a lovely abstraction of mirrors and garden images, and the costumes suggested the mid seventeenth century rather than the sixteenth, perhaps in recognition of the affinity that has been seen between Beatrice and Benedick and the 'witty couple' of Restoration comedy. Sinead Cusack played a charming but rather unemphatic Beatrice to a very funny and intelligent Benedick from Derek Jacobi.[1]

The return in this 1982 production to a fairly traditional period and location may indicate that a fashion has passed – but the fashion itself is not without significance. It coincides with a period of greater theatrical respect for the text and (perhaps) for the views of scholars and critics not directly associated with the theatre on what the concerns of the text are. It also coincides with an increase in feminist awareness. As a result of the first the unpleasant aspects of the Claudio–Hero plot are less easily avoided, and as a result of the second the response to Hero's situation thus brought clearly to our attention is likely to be more sympathetic and more vehement. Barbara Everett's admirable article on *Much Ado About Nothing* in *Critical Quarterly*, 3.4 (1961), indicated the direction of change: it stressed the difference between men's and women's experience of the world and suggested that this is the first of Shakespeare's plays in which the clash of the two worlds had been treated seriously. The shifts in period and location in productions from the late 1950s on were perhaps attempts to find an ambience for *Much Ado* less inaccessible for a modern audience than the Elizabethan, or Gielgud's 'Boccaccio period', but one in which the brutal treatment of Hero would still be comprehensible, and the behaviour of Claudio and Don Pedro not too inexcusable. Clearly a world is required where the double standard in sexual morality obtains. That points, in an English context, to the nineteenth century, and, for the military swagger, the earlier part of it. In Zeffirelli's Sicily the situation is even clearer. The male military fraternity of John Barton's British Raj was one of privileged leisure, where the attitudes of the boarding school, and its toleration of humiliating practical jokes, persisted. Women in that world had a particularly sheltered and restricted place.

I have not attempted to give a record of productions of *Much Ado About Nothing* outside Britain, though of course there have been many in Australia, Canada, the United States[2] and elsewhere in the English-speaking world, not to mention translations into other languages. It seemed better to attempt to follow a single tradition, and one

---

[1] The performance I saw – a matinée at the Barbican – may have been influenced by a responsive audience of secondary school children.

[2] One New York production seems to have been unique: the *New York Herald*, 3 February 1903, reports an 'Elizabethan' production of scenes from *Much Ado* at 'Mrs Osborne's playhouse'. The list of players includes 'Imogen [*sic*] Hero's mother', played by 'Mrs Grant', but the report does not comment on this unusual performance.

undoubtedly influential all over the world, where the continuities are strong over a long historical period. The frequent longevity of actors, and their evident ability to grow old gracefully in the parts of Beatrice and Benedick, strengthen these continuities. Nor have I done more than mention in passing a few of the many productions outside London and Stratford-upon-Avon, though provincial and touring companies up to the earlier twentieth century, and local repertory companies after 1945, did a great deal.

A tradition of production, like the tradition of acting, can be traced from the time of Garrick down to the present day. The text of *Much Ado* 'as it is acted at the Theatres-Royal in Drury Lane and Covent Garden' (1777) has a frontispiece of 'Mr Garrick in the character of Benedick' in the arbour scene (illustration 12) and presumably relates to his productions, though published in the year after his retirement. The indications of business and the cuts and alterations from the quarto text are remarkably similar to those made by Irving more than a century later and gags and business can be traced through intervening theatrical editions. The prompt-books of the Stratford Memorial Theatre indicate the continuation of some of these traditions into the second half of this century, though of course other influences become evident. There are more interpolations and gags in the Garrick text – though it is clear from Ellen Terry's *Memoirs* (see above, p. 15) that not all the gags Irving used were incorporated in his text as printed (1882). Both cut Act 1, Scene 2 substantially, and shifted its position so that it served, without a break, as the opening of Act 2, Scene 1. Irving provided an entry for Borachio as an eavesdropper at 1.1.235. I have no evidence that Garrick did so, but this business was used in Bridges-Adams's productions at Stratford in the 1930s, and in one production at least (probably 1934) he brought on Antonio to overhear the last lines of the scene – with the consequent disappearance of the 'good sharp fellow' of 1.2. Borachio's entry in 1.1 was still used in one of Iden Payne's Stratford productions. Garrick cut very substantially 3.4 – the scene as Hero dresses on her wedding morning – reducing it by over 30 lines. Irving cut the scene altogether, but he was following an already established tradition, for the scene is deleted in Oxberry's edition (1818–23), and it was not played by Charles Kean.[1] Irving also cut 3.5, the scene with Leonato, Dogberry and Verges before the wedding, and this too was regularly done. Shaw complains of this cut in his review of Tree's 1905 production, and remarks of Winifred Emery's Beatrice that 'happier than Verges, she had the *carduus benedictus* scene restored, to the great benefit of the play' (*Shaw on Shakespeare*, p. 149). Garrick also cut the scene at Leonato's family vault, 5.3; Irving did not, but he opened it with the song and transposed the epitaph to follow this. The same thing was done in Michael Langham's Stratford production of 1961.

When cuts are made within scenes and in long speeches a surprising consistency is found. Perhaps it is likely that directors will find the same passages dispensable, and this is not evidence of a continuing tradition: nevertheless, it is not without effect on the understanding of the play. For example, both Garrick and Irving made substantial cuts in that part of 5.1 where Benedick finds Don Pedro and Claudio and delivers his challenge. Both cut the prince's jesting speech (145–54) recounting Beatrice's praise of Benedick's wit. The same cut is marked in the 1939 and 1945 Stratford productions. This removal

---

[1] 'His [Oxberry's] most notable cut is the entire useless scene of Beatrice's awakening of Hero on her wedding morning' is how Odell (II, 125) rather strangely records it. For Kean's cut see Odell, II, 297.

12 'Hah! the prince and Monsieur Love, I will hide me in the arbour' (2.3.27–8). David Garrick as Benedick, from the edition of 1777

of unfeeling flippancy in a painful situation must result in a more serious prince, who retains his dignity a little better, who can more easily be seen as the representative of authority.

In the twentieth century the influence of learned editors in the solution of textual cruxes begins to be apparent. In 2.1.74–84 there is a problem about who is Margaret's partner in the dance (see below, p. 150). Garrick used Balthasar throughout, as in this edition. Irving solved the problem by cutting the whole exchange. In Bridges-Adams's early productions the lines go to Balthasar, but in 1933 Margaret danced with Borachio and he got the speeches, although the text used, the Temple Classics, gives Balthasar in its speech headings. It was in the New Shakespeare, which first appeared in 1923, that Dover Wilson had argued for this emendation, and it seems to have become the regular procedure at Stratford. It was used in Gielgud's production (1949 and revivals), Douglas Seale's (1958) and Michael Langham's (1961). I have not seen later prompt-books, but the 1982 production followed Q and had a change of partners for Margaret. The 1961 prompt-book indicated several passages of business for which there is no textual warrant. Beatrice is associated with the housekeeper, implying that her status is that of 'poor relation'. Before 3.2 Benedick is seen with the barber (as he had been in Gielgud's production) and into the middle of 3.3, before the entry of Conrade and Borachio, is interpolated a dumb show which presents Borachio at Hero's window, with a 'heavily cloaked' female – apparently it was the actress of Hero in this production. The two are observed by Claudio, Don Pedro and Don John, who 'throws wallet up to Borachio' before he exits. To this point are transferred words adapted from the end of 3.2.

CLAUDIO Tomorrow in the congregation, where I should wed, there will I shame her.
DON PEDRO And as I wooed for thee to obtain her, I will join with thee to disgrace her.

Other alterations follow from this. Since Borachio has no time to get drunk, he is sober in his confession to Conrade, most of his 'fashion' speech is cut, and as a consequence that 'vile thief' Deformed is never heard of. The text used for this production was the New Shakespeare, and it seems possible that the producer had read Quiller-Couch's introduction.[1]

The omission of the window-scene weakens our sympathy with Claudio in the chapel-scene. We cannot put ourselves in his place, deprived as we have been of the visual evidence that convinced him. (NS, p. xiii)

This summary has indicated several phases in the history of *Much Ado* on the stage after the Commonwealth period. Initially it seems to have been neglected, and used as a quarry for strange compounds like *The Law Against Lovers* or *The Universal Passion*, but once re-established it was regularly played without many liberties (beyond the expected cuts and gags) being taken with it. Always the main interest has been in Beatrice and Benedick, not Hero and Claudio, with the humours of Dogberry in second place. Garrick's Benedick was a witty gentleman, and his Beatrices met him on that level, as magnanimous and spirited ladies of fashion. At the end of the eighteenth and in the early nineteenth century it seems that in some cases Beatrice became more vindictive, and Benedick's humour broader. Macready in the part raised laughter appropriate perhaps for Dogberry (see p. 20 above, n. 1), while the gags and business to which Ellen Terry objected had a long history. With Charles Kean (and of course the development of stage lighting) the scenery begins to become important, and historical reconstructions are the mode. This reached its apogee with Irving, though perhaps it lingered still in Gielgud's 'Boccaccio period' costumes. Ellen Terry, following Helen Faucit, redeemed Beatrice, and while Irving's Benedick may have been 'finicking', he was certainly again the perfect courtier and gentleman. Scenery and business dominated the productions of George Alexander and Beerbohm Tree – though Winifred Emery seems to have attempted a Beatrice with rather more asperity than had been common. Another revolution in stage presentation began with the new century, assisted, in their different ways, by William Poel, Gordon Craig and Harley Granville-Barker. These new methods, which found their fullest application in work at the Old Vic and the Shakespeare Memorial Theatre at Stratford, allowed a speeding-up of the action, and the consequent reinstatement of some of the extensive cuts that had become the rule in the Victorian theatre, because of the time needed for the elaborate spectacles and the shifting of scenes. As it became

---

[1] This information about productions comes from the prompt-books preserved in the Shakespeare Institute Library, Stratford-upon-Avon. I am also grateful for access to Dr Pamela Mason's Birmingham MA thesis, '*Much Ado* at Stratford 1949–1976'.

more possible to perform them, directors became more concerned for the integrity of Shakespeare's texts. Meanwhile the acting tradition continued strong and unbroken, so that, for example, Harcourt Williams, who played Claudio for Ellen Terry in 1904, directed Gielgud in 1930–1, and played Leonato in 1946. Lewis Casson, who played Don Pedro in Poel's 1904 production, played Benedick opposite Sybil Thorndike in 1927–8, and joined the company as Leonato for a revival of Gielgud's production in 1950. Derek Jacobi played first Don John (1965) and then Don Pedro (1966) in Zeffirelli's production, and played Benedick in 1982. Gielgud's production seems to have set a standard of elegance and happiness that lasted for a while. More recent productions have seen the play as a less happy one, and have tried to find a milieu where the calumniation of Hero can be accepted as possible at the same time as social attitudes make it increasingly difficult for it to be condoned or glossed over in a production.

Much Ado About Nothing has an operatic as well as a theatrical history. *Beatrice and Benedick*, an *opéra-comique* in two acts, adapted from Shakespeare, both words and music by Hector Berlioz, was first performed on 9 August 1862 at Baden-Baden. It was Berlioz's last major work, and has remained popular; the overture, at least, being very frequently heard. The title reflects what the adaptation has done. The plot of the calumniation of Hero has disappeared: we have only the happy reunion of the young lovers after the war, counterpointed with the double gulling of Beatrice and Benedick; the dénouement depending on the production of the love sonnet that each has written to the other. Less well known is the opera by Charles Villiers Stanford, *Much Ado About Nothing*, which had its première at the Royal Opera House, Covent Garden, on 30 May 1901. The reviews were on the whole favourable and indicate an enthusiastic reception. The idea that there might be English as well as German and Italian opera seems also to have been welcomed. But in spite of this *Much Ado* does not seem to have stayed in the repertory. It has four acts: the first is the ball in Leonato's house, where the plots, both good and bad, are laid. The second act is in Leonato's garden, and has several episodes: a serenade of Hero by Claudio; the gulling of Benedick – in which Hero takes part; a scene where Benedick woos Beatrice; a love-duet for Hero and Claudio followed by Don John's defamation; Borachio's window scene is enacted, and Claudio vows vengeance. Act three is the church scene: act four opens with Dogberry and Verges, and the arrest of Borachio; Beatrice grieves at Hero's tomb; the plot is revealed, Hero resurrected, and the happy ending, heading for a double marriage, is produced. The libretto by Julian Sturgis was mainly a re-ordering with necessary revision of passages from the play.[1]

The criticism of the play

The history of *Much Ado* in the theatre shows that the play is susceptible of a range of different interpretations. Walter Lacy's justification for the business in the church scene (4.1) when Hero swoons, that 'it always gets a laugh' (p. 15 above), suggests a much more farcical treatment of the play than would be possible today. Ellen Terry found it 'preposterous', but perhaps such business was less at odds with the loud laugh and hoydenish humour of Dorothy Jordan, or those Beatrices whose performances led Thomas Campbell, in his edition of 1838, to call her an 'odious woman' (Furness, p. 289). Even within his own production Gielgud contrasts Diana Wynyard's Beatrice as 'a great lady, sweeping about in beautiful clothes' with Peggy Ashcroft's 'cheeky character who means well, but seems to drop bricks all the while' and records the swings of his own interpretation of Benedick from the 'dandy' to the 'uncouth soldier' and back again towards the 'courtier' (p. 22 above). The chroniclers of the theatre, like editors who see the text systematically deconstructed in the collation, are less likely to be disturbed than traditional literary critics by philosophers who insist on the ineluctable fluidity of texts and the impossibility of arriving at fixed or even especially privileged readings. For them this is a matter of plain common experience, though it may not have been elegantly theorised. This is the case whether the argument depends on the post-structuralist understanding of the unending play of signifiers, on C. S. Peirce's arguments for the existence of 'real generals'[1] or the Marxist insistence that any work comes from one particular set of social–historical conditions and is interpreted in another. The theatre historian need not be astonished that responses to *Othello* should vary with racial stereotypes and these with imperial politics.[2]

My own prejudices and preconceptions inevitably appear – sometimes, no doubt, disguised as scholarly inductions from unimpeachable evidence – both in the stage history and in other parts of this discussion. I do not dispute the infinite variety of possible readings, but in my view that infinite variety is constrained within certain bounds. It is possible to conceive of readings of *Much Ado* which would be, simply, wrong, and wrong for clearly statable reasons. To take a small instance: J. S. Manifold claimed that 'Benedick's little song [in 5.2] is extempore; he makes up his own tune as he goes along.'[3] As an idea for production in the twentieth century this may be attractive, but as a statement of Shakespeare's intention it must be rejected: he knew that Elderton's song was very popular and that his audience would recognise it. The fact that in some cases there might be violent debate about whether a particular reading were inside or outside the boundaries of acceptability does not affect the issue: though we may argue about where green merges into blue on the spectrum, that does not mean that green and blue are the same colour.

As an editor, at least, I would wish to privilege certain readings, and in particular that of the author. The problem is that such a reading is inaccessible – even if it could be supposed that Shakespeare had only one single view of a play that probably remained popular in the repertory of his company (even while the membership of that company changed) for the last sixteen or seventeen years of his life. All the evidence from other writers (as well as common sense) suggests the contrary, and so does the argument that the copy for the 1600 quarto was Shakespeare's 'foul papers', where he seems to be changing his mind about the play even while he is writing it. Even so, an author's reading – at least his *first* reading – of his own text has clear chronological priority. Such a reading

---

[1] *Charles S. Peirce: The Essential Writings*, ed. E. C. Moore, 1972, p. 35.
[2] See Catherine Belsey's discussion of *Othello* in the symposium 'The "text in itself"', *Southern Review* (Adelaide, South Australia), 17.2 (1984), 138–41.
[3] *The Music in English Drama*, p. 181.

can never be obtained, but it may be possible to limit the area within which it would fall. In the light of Shakespeare's treatment of his sources and his presentation of comparable stories in other works it seems unlikely that he intended a highly sympathetic Claudio or an 'odious' Beatrice. At the same time there is no suggestion that a change in the social status of women is desirable. In *Much Ado* there is sympathetic insight into the way women suffer in a world where men control all the property and make all the rules, but no advocacy of change – except perhaps that men should try to behave better, and even sometimes allow women to make their own choices. Marriage is the only career for a woman, so that almost any husband is better than none – which does not alter the fact that some husbands are vastly preferable to others. It is an interesting gap in the story that we know nothing about Beatrice's fortune. She is Leonato's ward, well-bred, virtuous, sharp-tongued – but has she any money? Davenant made Beatrice a 'great fortune' in *The Law Against Lovers*, but some productions of *Much Ado* (such as Michael Langham's for the Royal Shakespeare Company in 1961) imply that she is a poor relation. At least it cannot be unequivocally asserted (in spite of his own statement at 2.3.24) that Benedick is a fortune hunter. On the other hand, this is clearly a concern of Claudio's.

Little of this is controversial, but the boundaries of the area within which an authorial reading would fall are defined partly by historical fact – as with my example of Benedick's song. *Much Ado* was written at the very end of the sixteenth century, and some of the things that we can think about it – that it would 'work' set in late-nineteenth-century British India, say – were literally unthinkable then. We may bring to bear in our reading of the play social or scientific attitudes that belong to the latter part of the twentieth century, without always recognising that we are doing so. These may be perfectly legitimate as a means of interpreting the play in our own time as a representation of human behaviour, so long as we recognise that it works on the assumption that human behaviour is constant, to some extent, under changing social forms. We cannot, though, project such interpretations back into the past: the theoretical structures by which the twentieth century accounts for human behaviour are not those the sixteenth century used. Shakespeare could not have apprehended Marilyn French's 'mythic' reading of *Much Ado*.[1] This is not to claim that her reading is wrong for our time: only that it could not have been accessible for his.

Other limits to interpretation may be internal: that is, they may depend on the relation of parts within the work itself, or between the particular work and the rest of Shakespeare's *œuvre*, or between it and other works around its own time. Arguments in this area – my own discussion of the sources and analogues would be an instance – are much more open to question than those which are simply external and relate to matters of fact. But we have some advantages, for we know much more about Shakespeare's work than he did himself in 1599: at that time he had not written most of it. We can see that certain themes preoccupied him, so that he treated them over again in a variety of ways, and we may assume without too much risk that these re-treatments relate to a deepening and clarification of his attitudes towards his themes.

A virtuous woman is falsely accused and 'dies' in the persons of Desdemona in *Othello*,

---

[1] *Shakespeare's Division of Experience*, 1981, pp. 132–3.

Imogen in *Cymbeline* and Hermione in *The Winter's Tale*; in *All's Well That Ends Well* Helena is rejected by her husband Bertram because of her low birth, and also reported dead. In this and in other ways *Much Ado* has affinities with plays that come after it – particularly, in terms of the Claudio–Hero plot, the problem plays and the romances – more than with the major comedies of the 'green world' that are closer to it in time.[1] The threat or intimation of unhappy outcome is always present in Shakespeare's comedy. It may provide the frame within which the action takes place, as in the death sentence on Egeon at the opening of *The Comedy of Errors*. It may arise within the play itself, as in *Two Gentlemen of Verona* with the perfidy of Proteus. This is the case in *Much Ado*, but because the action is more realistically presented[2] and the characters are more fully developed than in the earlier play it is much more disturbing. Though the complication starts with the machination of a melancholy villain, this could not achieve much if it did not have the weakness of Claudio to operate on. The remorseless pursuit of Helena's virtuous love seems only to provide further occasions for Bertram to show how much he is unworthy of it; Posthumus is prepared to have Imogen murdered on the basis of circumstantial evidence only a little more convincing than that which provoked Claudio; and Leontes requires nothing but his own curious imagination to persuade him of Hermione's infidelity. The sequence of these treatments of extreme possessive jealousy in men suggests that Shakespeare found it increasingly reprehensible, and more deserving of severe punishment. At the same time he seems to have maintained the view that womanly virtue was most manifest in tolerance and forgiveness.[3] Hero is 'dead' for twenty-four hours, and Claudio need only make a formal ostentation of grief; Othello destroyed himself and Desdemona, and Leontes mourned for sixteen years before Hermione was finally returned to him. (Obviously I am paying no attention to the symbolic significance of some of these characters.) Claudio, like these later jealous lovers, is a seriously flawed character, and it is only the happy accidents of a comic plot that save him. These happy accidents are acceptable because the world of *Much Ado* is a world of normal decency. Too high a claim must not be made for it: it is a world where everybody minds everybody else's business, eavesdrops and interferes; Borachio in his cups is only a little uneasy about what he may have done to Hero, and Leonato believes the worst of his daughter with surprising haste. On the other hand Messina does not present an underworld like that of Vienna in *Measure for Measure*, and Beatrice's indignant common sense in defence of Hero does not come up against the immovable obstinacy of a Jacobean divine-right

---

[1] As Barbara Lewalski points out in her edition (p. xiii), borrowing Northrop Frye's phrase. Compare also R. S. White: 'When Beatrice chillingly challenges Benedick to "Kill Claudio!" she is also challenging the playwright to recognise his options in ending the play, inviting him to be consistent to the moral vision of the play which has presented Claudio as reprehensible and untrusting . . . These treacherous hints lead into the . . . "problem comedies"' (*Shakespeare and the Romance Ending*, 1981, p. 45); and Marilyn French: 'The characters are emblematic of moral positions: *Much Ado* is close to the romances' (*Shakespeare's Division of Experience*, p. 136).

[2] Compare Barbara Everett: 'This easy, humorous, and conversational manner, that refers to a past and a future governed by customary event and behaviour, and that carries a sense of habitual reality in a familiar social group, gives the play the quality that it would certainly be unwise to call "realism"; it is an atmosphere easier to feel than to define' ('*Much Ado About Nothing*', p. 323).

[3] There is an interesting discussion by Anne Parten, 'Masculine adultery and female rejoinders', *Mosaic* (Winnipeg, Canada), 17.1 (1984), 9–19.

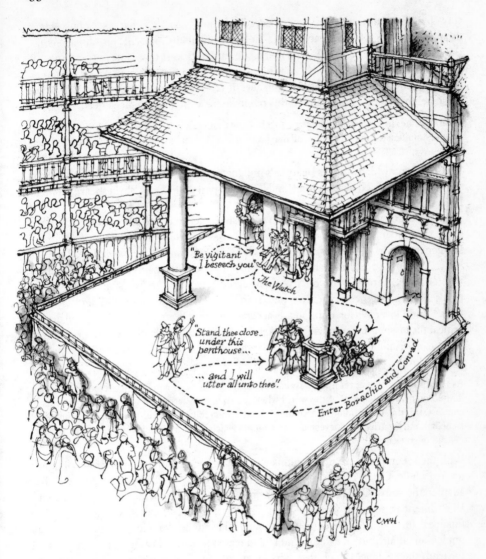

13   The 'penthouse' under which Conrad and Borachio shelter from the rain in Act 3, Scene 3, here supposed as similar to the (known) stage-roof at the Swan playhouse. Under other circumstances, such as the indoor Blackfriars playhouse, a feature of the rear-stage wall, like the space under the balcony shown here, would have been used. Drawing by C. Walter Hodges

king like Leontes, as Paulina's does in *The Winter's Tale*. Hero's unchastity is as imaginary as Desdemona's, as Imogen's, as Hermione's, and all these could be called *Much Ado About Nothing*, with 'nothing' as the 'pudendal joke'[1] – no thing has been in the nothing in any case, except the permitted thing – but in those plays the 'ado' grows to

[1]   See *The Dramatic Use of Bawdy in Shakespeare*, 1976, pp. 15–19, where Adrian Coleman argues the difficulty of proving or disproving the presence of this pun in the title of the play.

very serious issues indeed. When Borachio confesses, the charges against Hero disappear. Though Claudio apologises, he must still justify himself: 'yet sinned I not, / But in mistaking' (5.1.241–2) – and it must be hard to deliver those lines as anything but a querulous whimper, if only because of the sequence of the vowels. It would be a weak excuse in the best circumstances, but here it is exactly wrong. It was not Claudio's 'mistake' that killed Hero – and at this point, so far as he knows, she is dead.

What, bear her in hand, until they come to take hands, and then with public accusation, uncovered slander, unmitigated rancour? Oh God that I were a man! I would eat his heart in the market place.

(4.1.292–5)

The behaviour which arouses Beatrice's indignation was not a necessary consequence of the 'mistake' induced by Don John, and it was not part of the story Shakespeare found in his sources.

The character of Claudio has been extensively debated and his conduct has been variously condemned, condoned or explained away. Of considerable importance in the last generation in justifying Claudio was C. T. Prouty's study *The Sources of 'Much Ado About Nothing'* (1950): more recent criticism with a feminist point of view has reversed this tendency. Prouty starts off from a disagreement with the 'revision' theory of the play's origins, whether explicitly stated as in the New Shakespeare edition of Quiller-Couch and Dover Wilson or implicitly accepted without examination as in a good deal of critical discussion. He argues for Shakespeare's unified conception of the two plots in significant relation to each other, and for the play as a 'realistic' criticism of romantic ideas of love.

As Hero and Claudio represent one aspect of realism, so Benedick and Beatrice represent another. The former follow the way of the world where marriages are arranged by patrons or parents in contrast with the idyllic unions which literary convention followed exclusively. On the other hand Benedick and Beatrice are interested in an emotion which is real and a relationship based on reality instead of convention.

(Prouty, p. 63)

With the second of these propositions we must agree, as with the view of the play as a unified whole. Prouty argues from an examination of the ways in which Shakespeare has adapted the story from his sources, and from a study of Elizabethan marriage customs. But while it is possible to accept that 'Claudio is a careful suitor with an interest in finances' (p. 43), it is harder to agree that 'the public denunciation of Hero is an unpleasant affair [but] . . . Pedro and Claudio are more than justified, since they accept for truth the evidence which they have seen' (p. 46). Few of the later critics who take Claudio for a conventional young man 'really interested in . . . a good and suitable marriage' (p. 43) have been able to accept the whole argument, but rather use his conventionality and youth as an extenuation of his behaviour:

the play offers Claudio's nature in three successive lights: first, in the church crisis, as shocked into almost hysterical anger by conduct which, if true, would be the worst of treacheries towards trusting love; second, in its aftermath, as thrown off balance into adolescent arrogance; and third, on Borachio's confession, as thunderstruck by realization of his error.   (Humphreys, p. 74)

This is still partial to Claudio, though less flagrantly so than Prouty. Prouty accepts without question the business man's view of marriage and completes his whole argument without once mentioning the vehemence of Beatrice's outburst in defence of her cousin, or attempting to explain why Benedick should dissociate himself from the prince and his friend to stay with Hero and her family and finally challenge Claudio to a duel to defend Hero's honour.[1] If he accepts Claudio's explanation as sufficient – 'for the love of Beatrice' (5.1.175) – it seems a very romantic action for the 'realist' comic hero he elsewhere proposes. There is no doubt that arranged marriages in good society were general at the end of the sixteenth century: it does not follow that Shakespeare adhered uncritically to such conventions. What the play presents is a public and premeditated calumny that can only be explained as coming from the male assumptions of property rights in the woman's body, and the injured *amour propre*, of both Claudio and Don Pedro.

> I stand dishonoured that have gone about
> To link my dear friend to a common stale.   (4.1.58–9)

We are shown this act but we are only given a report of the evidence that provoked it. This is 'a fault' and 'weakens our sympathy with Claudio in the chapel-scene', remarked Quiller-Couch (NS, p. xiii), and based his patriarchal apologetics on the theory of a revision of an old play. Prouty, though, insists that Shakespeare was a 'dramatic artist' (p. 2) and knew what he was doing. What Shakespeare did was to put a vehement denunciation of 'princes and counties' (4.1.301) into the mouth of the most sympathetic character in the play. Even Thomas Campbell found Beatrice's defence of Hero 'a relieving and glad voice in the wilderness, which almost reconciles me to [her] otherwise disagreeable character' (Furness, p. 350).

It is true that Claudio and Don Pedro make a formal act of penance for their 'mistake', there is a reconciliation, and marriages impend at the conclusion, but the jokes are still about cuckoldry and male infidelity and fly as fast as ever. The conclusion is not as difficult to accept as the last-minute repentance of Bertram in *All's Well*, but it certainly lacks (*pace* those who see the dance as a powerful symbol of restored social cohesion) the affirmative unity of *As You Like It* or *Twelfth Night*. Our unease might be greater if Hero were a more positive character: Hermione is a great lady of strength and dignity, Desdemona and Imogen both wilfully choose husbands contrary to parental – more strictly paternal – will. Hero does not 'make another curtsy, and say, father, as it please me'. Apart from one little spurt of ill temper – 'My cousin's a fool, and thou art another, I'll wear none but this' (3.4.9) – which may hint at Bianca in *The Shrew*, she is all docility and propriety. But *Much Ado* is like the problem plays in that – though perhaps less intensely – it provokes embarrassment in readers or spectators, who find in themselves complex or even contradictory responses to the dramatic situation. The extreme example of this is the scene in *Cymbeline* (4.2) where Imogen wakes from her drugged sleep to find the headless body of Cloten beside her, and takes it for Posthumus. Our empathy with her horror and deep distress must accommodate the dark comic irony that

---

[1] As Barbara Everett pointed out, by staying with Hero and her family after Claudio's denunciation, Benedick 'has broken the rules of the game, and entered upon a desertion far more serious than Claudio's [falling in love] ever appeared: he is crossing the boundaries of a world of masculine domination' ('*Much Ado About Nothing*', p. 324).

(like Claudio) she takes the clothes for the person, and assumes that the body of the 'puttock' she refused is that of her husband, the 'eagle' she had chosen. The church scene in *Much Ado* is painful, but our sympathies after the departure of Claudio are clearly directed to Hero, in spite of the violence of Leonato's language. More difficult to cope with is 5.1, where the scene starts with the pathos of the father lamenting the disgrace of his daughter, and rejecting the attempts of his brother to offer consolation. The text is inexplicit as to whether Antonio knows at this stage that Hero is not dead. The vehemence with which he asserts her death when the prince and Claudio enter may persuade us that he thinks it true (if he has not been on stage in the church scene) but Leonato also asserts it, and he knows it to be false. In the moment of giving Claudio the lie, Leonato is lying himself. Our knowledge of this – and that Hero is safe – assists the difficult shift from pathos at the opening of the scene to something like farce in Antonio's senile anger. The embarrassment persists when a tense and serious Benedick, coming to deliver his challenge, is met with the usual flippant jesting, which must now appear as the depth of bad taste and insensitivity in Claudio and Don Pedro. I have remarked already how persistently this scene has been cut by directors from Garrick onwards in ways that reduce the offensiveness at least of Don Pedro. The final solution to the problem of the uneasiness caused by the main plot of *Much Ado* was found by Hector Berlioz in his opera: excise it altogether.

It is clear that for some people this concentration on the sub-plot at the expense of the main plot started very early: by 1613, if the reference to *Benedicte and Betteris* in the Lord Treasurer's warrant may be so interpreted. Davenant did not include the Claudio–Hero plot in *The Law Against Lovers* in 1662. Certainly the sub-plot has always been well received, and there is a general chorus of praise for these cheerful, witty, generous-hearted lovers, and approval of the plot that by a false report persuades them to a true valuation of each other's virtues. Campbell prognosticates an unhappy marriage, and Shaw points out – correctly – that neither the gentleman's nor the lady's jokes would have been acceptable in a middle-class Victorian drawing-room (*Shaw on Shakespeare*, p. 135), but generally, in the theatre at any rate, these two characters manifest a good-humoured vitality that lets them shine, however feeble or smutty some of their jokes may be in the library. More importantly, their reaction to the denunciation of Hero is exactly what the audience requires: they are the champions of injured innocence. It is their joint involvement in a serious issue – and in particular Benedick's demonstration with his challenge to Claudio that he is in earnest – much more than the play-acting of the two arbour scenes that brings them together on a basis of mutual trust and fuller understanding.

The Constables and the Watch make up the action: 'what your wisdoms could not discover, these shallow fools have brought to light' (5.1.205–6). In fact, it is the good sense of the 'learned writer' Francis Seacoal that brings things to light, and Borachio's own confession. Left to himself Dogberry would never have managed it. The function of the Watch in the action is both to provide reassurance that all will be well and at the same time to withhold the vital information that will make all well until after the crisis of the church scene. In that scene Claudio, Don Pedro and, indeed, Leonato reveal themselves as upholders of the chattel view of women, more concerned for their own 'honour' than for the well-being of the female person whom they claim to have loved, while Benedick dissociates himself from the man's world and rises to the challenge to 'Kill Claudio.' It is through these actions that that extension of the possibility of good that H. B. Charlton found as the essential of Shakespearean comedy[1] is made possible – at least for Beatrice and Benedick. This delay of information manipulates our sympathies: we want to kick Dogberry or prompt him in the scene with Leonato before the wedding, and his self-congratulation at the prospect of acting as the magistrate is infuriating. At the same time we know that the details of Don John's plot must eventually be revealed, and so the humiliation of Hero is less painful than it would otherwise be.

Dogberry's particular problem with language, which, to a degree, infects all the Watch, parodies the linguistic practices of the other characters. He, with sublime nonchalance, says usually the opposite of what he means, or, where he does achieve his own meaning – 'O that I had been writ down an ass' – it is one that can be subverted by the hearers. The whole play, as has often been pointed out, depends very much on the mistaking of words. Conversations are overheard and misunderstood, or if correctly reported are misapplied. Situations are set up where deliberate falsehoods are taken for truths; these may be benignly intended, as in the arbour scenes, or maliciously, as when Don John and Borachio after the dance tell Claudio that Don Pedro is in love with Hero himself and intends to marry her 'tonight'. The masked Claudio at the same time is presenting himself as Benedick, although in fact the villains have recognised him. Along with the lies which are intended to be believed there are those which are not: the metaphors and hyperboles that decorate the conversation, and the slanders and insults based on mis-taking words that account for much of the wit. The Messenger sets the tone of elegant word-play; Claudio has done 'in the figure of a lamb the feats of a lion', and he is matched by Leonato: 'A kind overflow of kindness'. Beatrice introduces a sharper note.

MESSENGER I see, lady, the gentleman is not in your books.
BEATRICE No, and he were, I would burn my study.

The nearer these shafts come to the truth, the more effective they are: Benedick is hurt by the suggestion that he is 'the prince's jester'. The gulling scenes work on this principle: the plotters assert that Beatrice loves Benedick vainly, combining a calculated praise of her undeniable good qualities with an only slightly exaggerated indication of his weaknesses, as he listens in hiding to their conversation. Hero and Ursula play the same trick on Beatrice.

Dogberry has a taste for well-worn proverbial phrases: much of his conversation with Leonato in 3.5 is made up of such tags. In this too he apes his social superiors:

What need the bridge much broader than the flood?
The fairest grant is the necessity.
Look what will serve is fit.   (1.1.242–4)

A little earlier Benedick had taken the prince and Claudio to task for their use of 'old ends' to ornament the body of their discourse (214). His metaphor from tailoring carries

---

[1] H. B. Charlton, *Shakespearian Comedy*, 1938; pp. 277–8 provides the classic summary of his argument.

the well-known idea of language as the dress of thought, and it recurs elsewhere: 'there's one meaning well suited' (5.1.199). This is appropriate in a play where so frequently people put forward views which they do not hold, and where even the Friar – the representative, presumably, of wisdom and virtue – proposes subterfuge and lies as the means to reinstate injured innocence.

> Let her awhile be secretly kept in,
> And publish it, that she is dead indeed:
> Maintain a mourning ostentation,
> And on your family's old monument
> Hang mournful epitaphs, and do all rites,
> That appertain unto a burial. (4.1.196–201)

This Polonius-like 'assay of bias' does not 'by indirections find directions out', but has no effect on Claudio's behaviour at all. In two major scenes of the play, the mask (2.1) and the final scene (5.4), leading characters are disguised at important points of the action. The crisis turns on the (reported, not presented) disguise of Margaret in Hero's clothes. The discussion of clothes and the use of images related to dress are very frequent in the play. 'What a pretty thing man is, when he goes in his doublet and hose, and leaves off his wit' (5.1.179). Clothes are also an important visual element in the play. We should assume a shift from the martial to the lover-like in Claudio and later Benedick; there are the disguises of the mask, the finery and vestments of the wedding, mourning clothes for the scene at Hero's monument, and a final change to 'other weeds' for the last scene. Borachio engages in a drunken discussion of 'fashion', and the word recurs in many

other places, more frequently than in any other play of Shakespeare's. In short – and again the point has been often made – *Much Ado* is a play very much concerned with appearances: with *ostentation* in its etymological sense of what is held out to be seen. We could put this into modern terms, perhaps, as 'role playing', or 'games people play'. Very early on, when Claudio asks his opinion of Hero, Benedick distinguishes between his 'simple true judgement' and what he might speak after his custom as 'a professed tyrant to their sex' (1.1.123–4). As we all do – all must – the characters in this play play roles in relation to each other, and these roles vary depending on the company and the circumstances. There is no necessary disingenuousness involved: Leonato assumes an appropriate formality to welcome his noble guest, Don Pedro; Balthasar's self-deprecating modesty before his song is still appropriate, if perhaps taken a little too far. On the other hand, Don John presents himself as 'a plain-dealing villain' in some of the most elegantly modulated prose of the play (1.3.20–7). When he first suggests to the prince and Claudio that 'the lady is disloyal' his syntax is much more abrupt and sometimes cryptic (3.2.70–96). He has 'fashion[ed] a carriage to rob love' from someone (1.3.22). In the two arbour scenes Don Pedro, Claudio and Leonato, and later Hero and Ursula, play themselves, but in a text they have invented which does not correspond to the situation. Benedick and Beatrice believe the invented script, and play themselves – in soliloquy – without masks, but with an awareness of the roles they commonly assume in the society around them. The scene in the church ('This looks not like a nuptial') pushes some into conventional responses – the shocked and abused lover, the outraged father – but others are moved out of their roles: the 'professed tyrant to their sex' comes seriously to the defence of a distressed woman – 'How doth the lady?' (4.1.105) – and 'my Lady Tongue' is reduced to tears and silence for a while. At the close of that scene – a little cautiously at first – Beatrice and Benedick talk to each other without masks, and the admission of love is made. It is for both a dangerous admission. Both have made public professions of immunity, and they have just had before them an example of the destructiveness of some kinds of love. When the confession is made Benedick moves back towards a conventional role: the courtly servant–lover: 'Come, bid me do anything for thee.' He nearly destroys the trust that has developed, for Beatrice is not playing when she nails him with that famous injunction, 'Kill Claudio.' She means it: she is obliging him to accept the implications of the role he has offered – indeed the two roles that are implicit in his offer. As the romantic lover he must perform the task set for him by his mistress, however hard it may be. As a gentleman of honour who has made the offer of his love to a lady with the intention of marriage, the honour of her family becomes his responsibility, and by this route also he is obliged to challenge Claudio. It is probable that Beatrice foresees this situation. There is a 'very even way' to right the wrong to Hero, but no 'friend' to do it, and 'It is a man's office, but not yours' (4.1.256, 258). Somewhere near the boundaries of acceptable interpretation is a Beatrice who deliberately manipulates Benedick into a position he cannot escape from; more central is one who sees more clearly than he where the situation is going, and is almost sorry for him. But her anger at the treatment of her cousin is still the dominant consideration. Benedick's response is taken from yet another of his repertory of possible roles: the 'sworn brother', the comrade-in-arms; and feeling the pull of this male freemasonry, he demurs: 'Ha, not for the wide world.' He must be persuaded again by Beatrice's anger – and his fear of losing her – that she is right to fix the blame on Claudio. They return to undisguised sincerity: 'Think you in your soul the Count Claudio hath wronged Hero?' (310). But even after this Benedick cannot refrain from trying on another hat: 'by this hand, Claudio shall render me a dear account'. The brave defender of the family honour of his mistress strides off – thus perhaps providing a cue for that gag which Irving, in spite of Ellen Terry's objections, insisted on: 'Benedick, kill him – kill him if you can' (p. 15 above). We have in this episode, it may seem, the obverse of the beginning of the scene. Claudio's response to the allegation of unchastity in Hero is excessive and objectionable, but perhaps Beatrice also goes too far in demanding the death penalty, as the gag insists. Her problem is that for her there is no alternative: her cousin has been publicly shamed, and her honour can only be restored by the equally public shaming of the man who disgraced her. Beatrice's anger is the anger of impotence,[1] but it is also embarrassing if stressed too much. We do not want a Beatrice who unequivocally wishes Claudio dead. Dogberry again comes to the rescue: as Benedick marches off to deliver his challenge, the trial of Borachio begins. It is soon made clear that there is one sensible man in Messina, as the Sexton takes charge of the

---

[1] Marilyn French associates Don John with what she calls the 'outlaw feminine': 'His revolt is the revenge of the impotent. Rebellion that emerges from the outlaw feminine aspect is often terrifying because it comes out of a sense of powerlessness and seems to want nothing . . . It is an inarticulate, incoherent challenge to the very notion of legitimacy and establishment, a fury inexplicable even to those who feel it' (*Shakespeare's Division of Experience*, pp. 132–3).

a

b

14   Possible ways of staging (*a*) the scene at Leonato's tomb, Act 5, Scene 3, and (*b*) the entrance of the masked ladies, Act 5, Scene 4, by C. Walter Hodges

proceedings, and then sets off to inform Leonato. The duel will not need to take place, and we can look forward to a happy ending, though it will still be delayed for a while. Benedick will appear as the challenger, and then trying out the role of the lover. Claudio and Don Pedro will go through the motions of formal grief at Leonato's family monument, but by the final scene most of the persons of the play will be back in the established social roles they had at the beginning. Some of them, at least, have been through a serious testing, and will play their roles with fuller insight in the future. How far the benefits of this much ado about nothing will spread will continue to be a matter of debate among critics and of interpretation in the theatre.

A note on the text

It has been accepted for a long time that the only authoritative text for *Much Ado About Nothing* is the quarto of 1600:

[ornament] / Much adoe about / Nothing. / *As it hath been sundrie times publikely* / acted by the right honourable, the Lord / Chamberlaine his servants. / *Written by William Shakespeare.* / [ornament] / LONDON / Printed by V.S. for Andrew Wise, and / William Aspley. / 1600.

There seems little doubt that the Folio text of *Much Ado* was set up from a copy of Q, and does not have independent authority, in spite of some interesting variants of theatrical provenance such as the substitution of 'Iacke Wilson' for 'Musicke' in the stage direction at 2.3.28. This and other changes are not inconsistent with Hardin Craig's proposal that the copy for F was a transcript of the foul papers from which Q was set, and which became the playhouse copy (*A New Look at Shakespeare's Quartos*, 1961, pp. 105 ff.). In any case, the higher authority would still remain with Q.

V.S. (Valentine Sims) had printed quartos of *Richard II* and *Richard III* for Andrew Wise in 1597, but when Wise retired in 1603 and transferred his copyrights to Matthew Law he did not include *Much Ado*, so it seems probable that the main agent in this publication was William Aspley. Aspley's right in *Much Ado* and *2 Henry IV* (also printed by V.S. for Wise and Aspley in 1600 and not reprinted before the Folio) is probably recognised in his inclusion in the Folio colophon: 'at the charge of W. Jaggard, Ed. Blount, I. Smithweeke, and W. Aspley' (Hinman, *PPFS*, I, 24–7). *Much Ado* and *2 Henry IV* are entered to Wise and Aspley on 23 August 1600 in what appears a perfectly normal way in the body of the Stationers' Register (Arber, III, 170). However, there is another mention of the play on one of the two front fly-leaves of this volume of the Register. All the other entries on these two leaves are dated 1603, except for this and the one immediately preceding it. Arber transcribes these two as follows (Arber, III, 37).

my lord chamberlens menns plaies Entered

27 may 1600	*viz*
to Master Robertes	*A moral of 'clothe breches and velvet hose'*
27 may	*Allarum to london/*
To hym	

[The next entry has nothing to do with the preceding. The ink of it is now of a different colour.]

4 Augusti [1600]

As you like yt/   a booke

HENRY the FFIFT/   a booke

Every man in his humour/   a booke   }   to be staied

The Commedie of 'much A doo about nothing

   a booke/

Arber justified his insertion of the date '1600' on the grounds of the entry of *Much Ado* to Wise and Aspley in that year on 23 August, and other entries of *Every Man in His Humour* to Burby and Barre, and *Henry V* to Thomas Pavier on 14 August 1600. On the basis of this circumstantial evidence it has been generally assumed that 1600 was the year of the 'staying', and sometimes that James Roberts was involved, in spite of Arber's own careful distinction of the entries. But there is no harm in the speculation that 'Conceivably James Roberts, printer and publisher, who, from July 22, 1598, onwards figures in the Stationers' Register as taking an active interest in plays belonging to the Chamberlain's men, may, after a preliminary attempt which failed, have succeeded eventually in spiking Aspley's guns' (NS, p. 92). It can be no more than speculation, though there was no further printing of *Much Ado* before the publication of the Folio, in spite of the probable popularity of the play.

W. Craig Ferguson has demonstrated (*SB* 13 (1960), 19–30) that the quartos of *Much Ado* and *2 Henry IV* were set throughout by a single person, Sims's 'Compositor A', who had certain clearly distinguishable idiosyncrasies. He rarely used full stops after unabbreviated speech headings, he centred stage directions with an initial capital and set exits to the right, his Latin was usually correct, and he did not use contrasting founts for the names of persons and places within the text. Compositor A almost certainly set some texts in Sims's shop from printed copy (including *The First Part of the Contention* in 1600 and the second quarto of *Richard II*). 'A detailed comparison of these two versions shows that, though the variants between the two are seldom of great importance, the second edition very often fails to reproduce exactly what stands in the first . . . it is characteristic of this man's work that it usually makes sense; and so is not obviously corrupt, even when it does not follow its original' (Hinman, *Q*, pp. xvi–xvii). With these reservations, it seems that the 1600 quarto of *Much Ado* is a not unreliable representation of its copy.

Another question of printing-house procedure remains to be discussed. Some pages of Q are more crowded than others; a standard page of 37 lines of type is sometimes stretched by line spaces above stage directions, sometimes compressed by overruns above or below the line, or by stage directions placed after a speech on the same line. Five pages have 38 lines, and one, G1^r, 39, including the compression of what is usually printed as four lines of verse into two lines of prose, with an overrun on the same line as the signature and catchword. Partly on the basis of evidence of this kind, partly because of assumptions about the relation of plot and sub-plot, and partly because of the inconsistencies which persist in the Q text, Dover Wilson erected his theory of an 'old play' of Shakespeare's, revised and modified, presenting difficult copy to the compositor. This theory is not now widely accepted, but the textual evidence which it was devised to explain still needs to be accounted for. John Hazel Smith (*SB* 16 (1963), 9–26) argued that the crowding and thinning of the text arose from problems involved in casting-off copy for the quarto to be set in formes, rather than page-by-page seriatim. Casting-off – estimating in advance which lines will take up any particular page – is more difficult in a largely prose play like *Much Ado* than with verse. Its advantage is that more than one compositor can work on the text, but that did not happen here. The evidence is anomalous, in any case, for apart from italic *B*s (for which there was an abnormally high demand in the speech headings) 'none of the other . . . types, of which a good many are highly distinctive, are ever found in successive sheets (except, for special reasons, in sheets G–H and H–I at the end)' (Hinman, *Q* p. xiv).[1] This strongly suggests seriatim setting of the text, where inner and outer forme must be made up together, and the last to be machined stands ready while the first goes through the press. It seems possible that the italic capital *B*s that were in such demand for speech headings were simply removed from the forme that had been printed and returned to the compositor before the rest was distributed.

Since it is not clear that Q was set in formes (and seems most likely to have been set seriatim), and since we know that it was set by a single competent, if not always minutely accurate, compositor, the anomalies surviving in the text must be treated as evidence for the nature of the copy from which Sims's Compositor A worked. Greg's statement (*EP*, p. 122), 'Everything points to the copy having been foul papers that lacked final revision', can hardly be disputed. The evidence for this is considered in the Textual Analysis (pp. 148 ff. below), and the particular problems of the crowding of the final lines of G1^r at 4.1.148–51 are commented on in the note to that place.

In attempting to provide a modernised, easily accessible text of *Much Ado* the assumption that the printer's copy for Q was Shakespeare's own manuscript, and that it had not undergone final revision, presents the editor with two obligations. If the quarto provides a careful and generally competent compositor's interpretation of that manuscript, then a conservative treatment is called for. On the other hand the only authoritative text 'includes anomalies that could not possibly have survived in performance [but which] . . . represent correctly what the author wrote',[2] and these must, as far as possible, be resolved. The modernisation of spelling presents few problems: there are not many places where loss of puns or distortion of meaning is involved. There is a scattering of capital letters for nouns that could be considered personifications – Nature, Love, Scorn – but their occurrence is so irregular that I have thought it best to use lower case for all but obvious instances. The punctuation has been treated conservatively. In Q it is very light and consists mainly of commas and colons: full stops are rare except at the ends of speeches: clause-ends within long speeches are usually indicated by colons. Semicolons are not found in Q: I have used a few to replace commas where these may be confusing, but the weight of a colon does not seem justified. My emendation of the crux

---

[1] The 'special reasons' were probably the interruption of the printing of *Much Ado* in order to print the cancellans sheet E3–E[6] for insertion into the Q(b) issue of *2 Henry IV*. This was first suggested by J. G. McManaway, 'The Cancel in the Quarto of 2 Henry IV', *Studies in Honour of A. H. R. Fairchild* (Columbia, Missouri) 1946, pp. 67–80.

[2] Wells, *Foul Papers*, p. 1.

at 5.1.16 is an example. There is a fairly frequent use of brackets for parenthesis. The punctuation seems intended to point the lines for delivery rather than to make clear the grammatical relations.[1]

The Folio compositor usually followed Q, though he did make a few corrections and regularisations, and pointed the text a little more heavily. The quarto punctuation, though light and different from modern systems, is – errors and omissions excepted – consistent and easily comprehensible. I have therefore, as far as possible, preserved it, and where correction seemed necessary have taken it from the Folio whenever possible. If F follows Q in apparent error I have attempted to apply the system found in the quarto, as I understand it. It is my hope that this may represent the system in Shakespeare's manuscript. I have introduced a few full stops, especially where stage directions have been interpolated into speeches, as at 1.1.113. I have also introduced one sign that is not found in the copy-text – the dash. It is used where one character cuts off the speech of another, as where Benedick interjects 'Beat –' into Beatrice's tirade against Claudio (4.1.300). I have also used it with speeches where there is an abrupt change of topic or an anacoluthon: for example 2.3.26–7, 'an excellent musician – and her hair shall be of what colour it please God', or in the disjunction of Borachio's drunken narrative: 'my villainy, which did confirm any slander that Don John had made – away went Claudio enraged ...' (3.3.129–30). Where Q appears to vary randomly in a usage which the New Cambridge Shakespeare treats consistently – an instance is the use of commas before vocatives: 'What, my dear Lady Disdain!' (1.1.88), where Q has 'What my dear Lady Disdain!' – I have, after a little hesitation, followed the convention. Commas precede vocatives in Q only in about one case in three. Similarly, in stage directions, a comma before 'and' and the final name in a list of entries or exits has always been deleted, though it is quite commonly present in Q. On the other hand, where the variations in Q from standard usage seem not to be random, but to have possible theatrical or rhetorical justification, I have preserved them. The most frequent instance here is the use of commas – or not – to mark off interjections or asseverations. 'Marry', 'troth', 'nay' and such like are not usually separated by commas from what follows them in Q. In most cases where commas are found, I think, an argument can be made that a marked pause is intended. So, for example, in Benedick's soliloquy deciding to be in love with Beatrice, at 2.3.197, 'No, the world must be peopled!', the pause after 'No' points the comic effect. However, the normal run-on delivery of such constructions is speeded up still further by Margaret at 3.4.7 and 14, where the contraction of 'by my troth, it is' to 'by my troth's' makes the modern grammatical punctuation impossible.

There are no scene headings to prescribe place in quarto or Folio: this of course is the general rule in the period. The scene locations to which we are accustomed begin with Rowe's generalised 'Scene *Messina*' for the whole play, and accumulate detail as edition follows edition. Any necessary information about setting is always rapidly given in the dialogue. Act 2, Scene 1 opens with Leonato's query 'Was not Count John here at supper?' Clearly the scene is Leonato's house and his guests are leaving the dining room

---

[1] Compare 'Rhetoric ... instructs him ... to observe his commas, colons, and full points, his parentheses, his breathing places and distinctions' (Thomas Heywood, *An Apology for Actors* (1612), in G. E. Bentley (ed.), *The Seventeenth Century Stage*, 1968, p. 12).

where they have just supped: what else do we need to know? Accordingly, any editorial scene locations will be found in the Commentary, not in the text.

Many small alterations of punctuation have not been noted, but in the collation will be found all other departures from copy-text, all substantive variations between Q and F, and some other variations – of spelling or forms of contraction, for example – which may have some intrinsic interest. It is to be assumed in all cases that F agrees in substance with Q unless I have indicated otherwise. In the collation the authority for this edition's reading follows immediately upon the first square bracket if it differs in substance from Q. Other readings follow in chronological order. An asterisk in the lemma of a note in the Commentary is used to call attention to a word or phrase that has been emended in the text. Act divisions are from F; Q is printed continuously. Scene divisions are those of Capell, which have been generally accepted: these are not noted in the collation. James Spedding proposed an alternative division as follows: Act 1 (1.1 only); Act 2 (1.2–2.2); Act 3 (2.3–3.3); Act 4 (3.4–4.2); Act 5 unchanged. These act divisions can be justified as corresponding to natural phases in the development of the action, but they were (as Spedding insisted) for the 'imaginary theatre', not for one that employed 'scene-shifters'. The article, from *The Gentleman's Magazine* (June 1850), is given in Furness, pp. 363–7.

In the preparation of this edition the text provided in the Oxford Shakespeare Quarto Facsimiles, no. 15, 1971, prepared by Charlton Hinman from the Trinity College, Cambridge, copy, has been collated with the copies of the 1600 quarto in the Huntington Library, the Clark Library and the Folger Library in the United States; in the United Kingdom I have consulted the Malone copy in the Bodleian, the two British Library copies, the Dyce copy, the Edinburgh copy, as well as the Trinity copy from which the facsimile was taken. The copy now in the Bodmer Collection in Geneva, the first Rosenbach copy, no. 793, in the Bartlett and Pollard *Census* of Shakespeare's quartos (1939), does not present any variants not recorded by Hinman.[1] A reproduction was not available to him when he prepared his edition. For Folio readings I have used the Norton facsimile of the First Folio, again edited by Hinman. This text has been collated with the two copies of the Folio which are preserved in the southern hemisphere, the Tangye copy in the New South Wales Public Library, and the Grey copy in the Auckland Public Library, New Zealand.

Postscript, March 1987

When preparations for the printing of this edition were already begun I had the good fortune to be involved, as an adviser on the text, in a production of *Much Ado* by the State Theatre Company of South Australia.[2] It was a successful and honest interpretation of the play for a late-twentieth-century audience. I sat in on some rehearsals and I learned

---

[1] Professor Richard Proudfoot, of King's College, London, who has examined the Bodmer copy, kindly provided this information.

[2] The Artistic Director of the State Theatre Company is John Gaden; *Much Ado*, directed by John Gaden and Gale Edwards, design by Ken Wilby and Mark Thompson, was seen at the Playhouse, Adelaide Festival Centre, from February 28 to March 28 1987.

things from the actors that I didn't know I didn't know. A small example: in her early chaffing with the Messenger Beatrice refers to 'my uncle's fool' (1.1.30) who challenged Benedick at the birdbolt. Celia De Burgh, who played Beatrice, decided that she was 'my uncle's fool', and she produced a gesture that made this reflexive identification clear. As rehearsals went on this gesture was reduced until it was vestigial, like the palatal stop with a de-voiced vowel – 'k^u' – that is almost inaudible, but still understood as 'thank you'. I do not recall that any editor has made this indentification of 'my uncle's fool'; it had not occurred to me, but now I have it, I like it. It fits with Beatrice naming Benedick as 'the prince's jester' (2.1.103) and could be a reference to the earlier association between them that is mentioned at 2.1.211–13.

Actors (unlike editors) cannot have it both ways: if there are alternative interpretations of a passage (and of course there always are) they must choose one. William Zappa played a consciously uncouth, almost raffish, Benedick. He played his soliloquies (2.3.6. ff., 2.3.181 ff. and 5.2.17 ff.) not just *to* but *with* the audience, well down stage, and in league with them like a stand-up comic. It worked well, but some austerer lovers of the Bard were a little offended, maybe because it was so funny. The 'merry war' in this production was maintained to the end. After the revelation of Hero in 5.4 the other three ladies remained masked and cloaked, and divided between them the three speeches of Beatrice at 73, 74 and 77, creating a comic exasperation in the now publicly committed Benedick that persisted until the production of the purloined sonnets. There is no textual warrant for this, but it struck me as an invention quite in keeping with the tenor of the play. The comic inventiveness of Zappa's playing enhanced by contrast the strength he found at the end of the church scene and in his challenge to Claudio.

Claudio emerged from this production with more credit than he does from my introduction. He was played by a darkly handsome young Italian-Australian, Luciano Martucci. He was naïve and calculating, diffident and over-confident, a born member of the ruling class who could not conceive of himself doing anything remotely dislikeable. In his confrontation with Antonio he avoided the old man's lunges with hilarious agility but no malice: it was good fun, even though he could not understand what the fuss was about as he had done nothing unbecoming to a gentleman. Antonio (played by Don Reid) was a farcical dodderer without ever losing his dignity as a deeply distressed old man.

The set was very simple: a colonnade, raised three steps, around the back and sides of a bare thrust stage. There were drapes that could be drawn across the arches of the colonnade, and a further set of arches, making a clerestory effect, was flown in above the first, along with a large picture of the Virgin, for the church scene. The play was set in nineteenth-century Sicily, and faded paintings above the arches suggested the murals of an earlier period. It was almost an Elizabethan stage, and allowed the continuous action from scene to scene that is implicit in Shakespeare's dramaturgy. There was no arbour (and this would have pleased C. Walter Hodges, who only provided one in his drawings for this edition under mild protest): the overhearers lurked behind pillars, or crept down stage only to dash back for cover a minute later. The designer's great moment came with 5.3 at Hero's tomb. To a crescendo of ecclesiastical choral music a great baroque tomb ascended through the trap, while two pillars and a sunburst surrounding a holy picture came down from the flies. On top of the tomb a Bernini-like female figure aspired heavenward in bronze; below, a glass panel in the catafalque revealed a body, resembling Hero, wrapped in cerements. I am not sympathetic to Mulryne's argument[1] that this scene can provide an 'impressively meaningful experience' presenting Claudio's remorse. Rather it has seemed to me to show that remorse in an appropriately jejune manner. The high – almost camp – theatricality of the Adelaide presentation conveyed this well. It was a 'mourning ostentation' (4.1.198), a show of grief indeed, and in this appropriate to Leonato's response (more concerned for family honour than his daughter's well-being), as well as making an effective setting for Claudio and Don Pedro's act of contrition.

Future productions that I may see will, I am sure, provide further insights, but I gained particularly from this one because I saw the details of the action emerge from the early readings and rehearsals; I saw the actors deciding what they had to *do* as these or those words were said. This basic issue in the theatre is often given too little attention by readers – and editors – of playtexts.

[1] J. R. Mulryne, *Shakespeare: 'Much Ado About Nothing'*, 1965, p. 11.

Much Ado About Nothing

LIST OF CHARACTERS

LEONATO, *Governor of Messina*
MESSENGER, *servant of Don Pedro*
BEATRICE, *niece of Leonato*
HERO, *daughter of Leonato*
DON PEDRO, *Prince of Arragon*
BENEDICK, *gentleman of Padua, in the court of Don Pedro*
DON JOHN, *bastard brother of Don Pedro, recently reconciled to him after a war*
CLAUDIO, *a count of Florence, in the court of Don Pedro*
ANTONIO, *old man, Leonato's brother*
CONRADE, *associate of Don John*
BORACHIO, *associate of Don John*
BALTHASAR, *musician in the service of Don Pedro*
MARGARET, *gentlewoman in Leonato's household*
URSULA, *gentlewoman in Leonato's household*
BOY, *servant to Benedick*
DOGBERRY, *Constable of Messina*
VERGES, *Headborough, Dogberry's partner in office*
GEORGE SEACOAL, *senior watchman*
WATCHMAN 1
WATCHMAN 2
FRIAR FRANCIS
SEXTON
SOLDIERS, COURTIERS, MUSICIANS, SINGERS, WATCHMEN *and other* ATTENDANTS

Notes

The characters are here listed in the order of first speaking, not entry, with mutes at the end. There is no cast-list in Q or F; one was first provided by Rowe in 1709. The play requires a substantial cast, and it is difficult to reduce this by doubling. There are twelve speaking parts, four boys and eight men, required in 2.1, as well as 'maskers with a drum' and musicians. It is unlikely that Dogberry would have been doubled with any other significant parts, and while Friar Francis does not appear until 4.1 he is present there and in 5.4 with most of the other major characters. He could be doubled with Borachio perhaps. While Q indicates (not very specifically) entries for Antonio and for Verges in the latter part of 5.1, neither is necessarily given a speech, so it would be possible to double the two old men's parts if either (or both) remained off stage at that point. The line given to Verges in this edition (5.1.225) is headed *Con.2* in Q. The brief appearance of Benedick's Boy (2.1) could be picked up by one of the girl's parts, most appropriately, perhaps, by Hero, as the youngest and smallest. But in any case nine or ten men and four boys are needed, along with musicians and such extras as could be found for Don Pedro's entourage at his first entry, for the maskers of 2.1, for the Watch and 'all the gallants of the town' (3.4.72) who come to the church.
LEONATO Lionato di Lionati in Bandello.
MESSENGER A messenger also appears at the end of the play, to announce the capture of Don John. He is not necessarily the same character or the same actor. The messenger who comes to fetch Leonato to the wedding (3.5.42) must be one of his own servants.

BEATRICE Her name means 'the one who blesses'.

HERO Fenecia in Bandello. Marlowe's *Hero and Leander* with Chapman's completion was published in 1598, and there are several references to it in *Much Ado*.

DON PEDRO King Piero in Bandello.

BENEDICK *Benedictus* (Latin) means 'blessed'.

ANTONIO It is not clear that 'Old Man' and 'Brother' in 1.2 and 2.1 and 'Signor Antonio' of the mask in 2.1 were originally conceived as the same person. The association was first made by Rowe (1709); see p. 148 below.

BORACHIO *Borracho* (Spanish) means 'drunk'.

BALTHASAR He is given an entry with Don Pedro in 1.1, but does not speak until 2.1. In F the name Jack Wilson is given in a stage direction; see supplementary note to 2.3.28, p. 146 below.

DOGBERRY His name signifies the dogwood or female cornel, a common hedgerow bush, with red twigs and black-purple berries. Speech headings surviving in 4.2 in Q demonstrate that the part was written for Will Kemp; see p. 7 above.

VERGES Perhaps related to 'verjuice', the acid juice of unripe fruit, formerly widely used in cooking. He is apparently old and small, and he and Dogberry would make 'a Laurel and Hardy pair' (Foakes, p. 21). The speech headings 'Cowley' and 'Couley', which survive in Q in 4.2, show that Richard Cowley was the original Verges; see p. 7 above.

WATCHMAN One of a group (the Watch) who, before the development of regular police, 'watched' (i.e. stayed awake) at night to protect their fellow citizens against theft, fire or other dangers. In plays they are usually presented as incompetent, venal and comic.

FRIAR FRANCIS The wise holy man, who manipulates the evidence for the general good, a stock figure which Shakespeare does not elsewhere present so kindly. Friar Lawrence (*Rom.*) is notably unsuccessful and (in Act 5) pusillanimous. The treatment of the duke disguised as a friar in *MM* calls the whole convention in question.

SEXTON 'Officer charged with care of church and churchyard, often also bell-ringer and grave-digger' (*COED* sv). He is referred to as Francis Seacoal at 3.5.45, but not otherwise connected with George Seacoal, the leader of the Watch. The duplication of the name should probably be seen as part of the evidence for the lack of revision of the copy for Q; see Textual Analysis, p. 148 below.

MUCH ADO ABOUT NOTHING

1.1 *Enter* LEONATO, *Governor of Messina,* HERO *his daughter and* BEATRICE *his niece,*
with a MESSENGER

LEONATO I learn in this letter, that Don Pedro of Arragon comes this
    night to Messina.

MESSENGER He is very near by this, he was not three leagues off when I
    left him.

LEONATO How many gentlemen have you lost in this action?   5

MESSENGER But few of any sort, and none of name.

LEONATO A victory is twice itself, when the achiever brings home full
    numbers. I find here, that Don Pedro hath bestowed much honour on
    a young Florentine called Claudio.

MESSENGER Much deserved on his part, and equally remembered by   10
    Don Pedro. He hath borne himself beyond the promise of his age,
    doing in the figure of a lamb the feats of a lion. He hath indeed better
    bettered expectation than you must expect of me to tell you how.

LEONATO He hath an uncle here in Messina will be very much glad of it.

MESSENGER I have already delivered him letters, and there appears   15
    much joy in him, even so much that joy could not show itself modest
    enough without a badge of bitterness.

LEONATO Did he break out into tears?

MESSENGER In great measure.

LEONATO A kind overflow of kindness: there are no faces truer than   20
    those that are so washed. How much better is it to weep at joy, than to
    joy at weeping!

Act 1, Scene 1   1.1] *Actus primus, Scena prima.* F; *not in* Q   0 SD *Messina*] *Theobald; Messina, Innogen his wife* Q
1, 8, 11 Don Pedro] *Rowe;* don Peter Q

Act 1, Scene 1

0 *SD An entry for Leonato's wife is indicated
here and again at 2.1, but she is given no speeches:
see Textual Analysis, p. 148 below. The scene would
have been on the main stage of the Elizabethan
theatre, using one of the side doors from the tiring-
house, which could then locate Leonato's area for
subsequent entries and exits; see 71 SD and n. below.
Capell provided the location 'before Leonato's
house'.

3 **three leagues** About nine miles or fourteen
kilometres.

6 **sort** rank.

6 **name** reputation.

10 **remembered** recompensed.

10–13 The Messenger's taste for alliteration,
elegant parallels of syntax and tropes sets the tone of
Don Pedro's court.

BEATRICE I pray you, is Signor Mountanto returned from the wars or no?

MESSENGER I know none of that name, lady, there was none such in the
army of any sort.   25

LEONATO What is he that you ask for, niece?

HERO My cousin means Signor Benedick of Padua.

MESSENGER O he's returned, and as pleasant as ever he was.

BEATRICE He set up his bills here in Messina, and challenged Cupid at
the flight: and my uncle's fool, reading the challenge, subscribed for   30
Cupid, and challenged him at the birdbolt. I pray you, how many hath
he killed and eaten in these wars? But how many hath he killed? – for
indeed I promised to eat all of his killing.

LEONATO Faith, niece, you tax Signor Benedick too much, but he'll be
meet with you, I doubt it not.   35

MESSENGER He hath done good service, lady, in these wars.

BEATRICE You had musty victual, and he hath holp to eat it: he is a very
valiant trencherman, he hath an excellent stomach.

MESSENGER And a good soldier too, lady.

BEATRICE And a good soldier to a lady, but what is he to a lord?   40

MESSENGER A lord to a lord, a man to a man, stuffed with all honourable
virtues.

30 flight:] F; flight, Q   31 birdbolt.] *Pope;* Burbolt. F; Burbolt, Q   32 killed? –] killed? Q   37 victual] F; vitaille Q
37 eat] Q; ease F   37 he is] Q; he's F

23 **Mountanto** Beatrice's name for Benedick suggests that he is 'stuck-up' or a social climber, and
mocks his pretensions as a swordsman, since 'Mountanto' is a fencing term: compare Jonson, *Every Man
in His Humour*: 'The special rules of swordsmanship
as your *Punto*, your *Reverso* ... your *Montanto*'
(4.7.77–9, H & S). Cotgrave glosses *montant* as 'an
upright blow or thrust', which perhaps means a blow
with the sword from below upwards. She probably
intends a sexual innuendo also since a stallion
'mounts' a mare. In *Queen Anna's New World of Words*
Florio has: '*Monta* – a mounting or ascent . . . Also a
stallion's covering of mares.' Timon invites
Alcibiades' whores: 'Hold up, you sluts, / Your
aprons mountant' (*Tim.* 4.3.135–6).

29 **bills** advertisements, public notices.
29–30 **at the flight** at long-distance shooting. A
'flight' was a special light arrow for this purpose.
There may also be a pun on 'flight' as a term in
falconry, and on 'flyte', a contest in verbal abuse.
30 **subscribed for** took the part of.
31 **birdbolt** A blunt wooden-headed arrow for
stunning small birds, an appropriate weapon for children or fools, since it could do little injury to larger
targets. As the party challenged (standing in for

Cupid) the fool would have the choice of weapons:
'mine adversary choosing the proof by arms, the
choice of them cometh unto me . . . for it is no reason
nor honesty, that I both call him to arms, and also
take the choice of them' (*Vincentio Saviolo, His Practise* (1595), sig. x2ʳ). Beatrice suggests that a fool's
weapon is appropriate to Benedick, and that he is not
dangerous with Cupid's weapons.

32 **killed and eaten** Another suggestion of brag-
ging: the phrase is proverbial. Cotgrave has under
mangeur de charrettes ferrées 'one that will kill all he
meets, and eat all he kills'. Compare *H5* 3.7.91–2:
'*Ram.* [The Dolphin] longs to eat the English. *Con.* I
think he will eat all he kills.'
34–5 **be meet** get even.
37 *musty victual stale provisions. The Q spelling may represent Shakespeare's choice.
38 **stomach** appetite; but it could also mean
'courage'.
40 **soldier . . . lady** lady-killer.
41 **A lord . . . man** The Messenger claims that
Benedick is a true gentleman, courageous but also
courteous, and showing a proper sense of social
hierarchy.

BEATRICE It is so indeed, he is no less than a stuffed man, but for the
stuffing – well, we are all mortal.

LEONATO You must not, sir, mistake my niece: there is a kind of merry   45
war betwixt Signor Benedick and her: they never meet but there's a
skirmish of wit between them.

BEATRICE Alas, he gets nothing by that. In our last conflict, four of his
five wits went halting off, and now is the whole man governed with
one: so that if he have wit enough to keep himself warm, let him bear it   50
for a difference between himself and his horse, for it is all the wealth
that he hath left to be known a reasonable creature. Who is his
companion now? He hath every month a new sworn brother.

MESSENGER Is't possible?

BEATRICE Very easily possible: he wears his faith but as the fashion of his   55
hat, it ever changes with the next block.

MESSENGER I see, lady, the gentleman is not in your books.

BEATRICE No, and he were, I would burn my study. But I pray you, who is
his companion? Is there no young squarer now, that will make a
voyage with him to the devil?   60

MESSENGER He is most in the company of the right noble Claudio.

BEATRICE O Lord, he will hang upon him like a disease: he is sooner
caught than the pestilence, and the taker runs presently mad. God

44 stuffing –] *Theobald;* stuffing Q   45 not, sir,] Q; not (sir) F   48 that.] F; that, Q   52 creature.] F; creature, Q
58 study.] F; study, Q

43 **stuffed** The word had a military sense, meaning, of a fortified place, 'supplied with arms', and so
was applied metaphorically to persons, as in *Rom.*
3.5.181; 'Stuff'd, as they say, with honourable parts'.
Beatrice takes it in a derogatory sense, 'padded out',
and perhaps continuing the 'stomach' word-play.

48–9 **four . . . off** The five wits were distinguished
from the five senses, as in Sonnet 141: 'But my five
wits nor my five senses can / Dissuade one foolish
heart from serving thee.' The distinction, however,
was not always clear, and 'wits' could be used to
mean 'senses'. The five wits derive eventually from
Aristotle's faculties of the soul in *De Anima*. They are
common sense, imagination, fantasy, judgement and
memory. If Beatrice means 'senses' by 'wits', then
touch will be the sense that governs Benedick, as the
one essential to life and the one most open to the
battery of temptation – as in the assault on Alma's
Castle in *FQ*, II, 11. Her military image perhaps
recollects the psychomachia of the morality play. If
she means 'wits' strictly, then the survivor must be
'common sense'.

50 **wit . . . warm** A proverbial phrase (Tilley K10).
Compare *Shr.* 2.1.265: '*Pet.* Am I not wise? *Kath.*
Yes, keep you warm.'

51 **difference** A mark in heraldry distinguishing a
junior branch of a family.

52 **reasonable creature** Reason is the quality that
distinguishes man from beast. Compare *Tro.*
3.3.306–7: 'Let me bear another [letter] to his horse,
for that's the more capable creature.'

53 **sworn brother** *Fratres iurati* (*iniurati, coniurati*)
had some basis in fact and history as well as chivalric
fiction. Biblical prototypes are David and Jonathan;
classical, Damon and Pythias. As such an oath was
lifelong, the paradox of Beatrice's 'every month' provokes the Messenger's shocked 'Is't possible?'

56 **next block** newest fashion. The block was the
mould on which felt hats were made. Compare 'The
block for his head alters faster than the feltmaker can
fit him' (Dekker, *Seven Deadly Sins of London* (1606),
p. 32).

57 **in . . . books** The phrase is still common, now
usually qualified with 'good' or 'bad'.

58 **study** library.

59 **squarer** quarrelsome person.

62–5 The punctuation of Q is ambiguous. 'if . . .
Benedict' could be attached to what follows just as
well as to what precedes it.

63 **pestilence** plague.

63 **presently** immediately.

help the noble Claudio, if he hath caught the Benedict. It will cost
him a thousand pound ere a be cured.   65

MESSENGER I will hold friends with you, lady.

BEATRICE Do, good friend.

LEONATO You will never run mad, niece.

BEATRICE No, not till a hot January.

MESSENGER Don Pedro is approached.   70

Enter DON PEDRO, CLAUDIO, BENEDICK, BALTHASAR *and* JOHN *the
bastard*

DON PEDRO Good Signor Leonato, are you come to meet your trouble?
The fashion of the world is to avoid cost, and you encounter it.

LEONATO Never came trouble to my house in the likeness of your grace:
for trouble being gone, comfort should remain: but when you depart
from me, sorrow abides, and happiness takes his leave.   75

DON PEDRO You embrace your charge too willingly. I think this is your
daughter?

LEONATO Her mother hath many times told me so.

BENEDICK Were you in doubt, sir, that you asked her?

LEONATO Signor Benedick, no, for then were you a child.   80

DON PEDRO You have it full, Benedick: we may guess by this, what you
are, being a man. Truly, the lady fathers herself: be happy, lady, for
you are like an honourable father.

BENEDICK If Signor Leonato be her father, she would not have his head
on her shoulders for all Messina, as like him as she is.   85

BEATRICE I wonder that you will still be talking, Signor Benedick,
nobody marks you.

64 Benedict.] Benedict, Q   65 a be] Q; he be F   68 You will never] Q; You'l ne're F   71 are you] Q; you are F
79 doubt, sir,] doubt sir Q; doubt F

64 Benedict The only instance of this spelling in
Q. Beatrice makes Benedick's name that of a disease,
likely to lead to insanity: 'Benedict' priests were
exorcists, and so associated with madness. Leonato
makes the point that Beatrice is not likely to 'catch
the Benedict' at 68.

65 thousand pound The singular with numbers
is still common in spoken English. As well as making
a gibe at the traditional avarice of the medical pro-
fession, Beatrice is suggesting that Benedick will
lead Claudio into extravagance, or borrow money
and not repay it.

70 SD Don Pedro, returning from a successful
campaign and reconciled to his brother, should make
an informal but triumphal entry, with as large a com-

pany as possible. Balthasar is included in the Q SD,
though he does not speak. They would use the door
on the opposite side of the stage from Leonato's
entry.

70 SD.2 *the bastard* This relationship is not made
explicit until 4.1.171. Spectators would not know it
unless provided with a detailed cast-list, or unless
John were distinguished in some conventional way.

81 full completely. Leonato's reply is tit-for-tat.

82 fathers herself has a strong resemblance to
her father.

84–5 head ... shoulders The proverbial
reference to 'an old head on young shoulders'
perhaps derives from the icon of Prudence.

BENEDICK What, my dear Lady Disdain! Are you yet living?

BEATRICE Is it possible Disdain should die, while she hath such meet
food to feed it, as Signor Benedick? Courtesy itself must convert to   90
Disdain, if you come in her presence.

BENEDICK Then is Courtesy a turn-coat: but it is certain I am loved of all
ladies, only you excepted: and I would I could find in my heart that I
had not a hard heart, for truly I love none.

BEATRICE A dear happiness to women, they would else have been   95
troubled with a pernicious suitor. I thank God and my cold blood, I
am of your humour for that: I had rather hear my dog bark at a crow
than a man swear he loves me.

BENEDICK God keep your ladyship still in that mind, so some gentleman
or other shall scape a predestinate scratched face.   100

BEATRICE Scratching could not make it worse, and 'twere such a face as
yours were.

BENEDICK Well, you are a rare parrot-teacher.

BEATRICE A bird of my tongue is better than a beast of yours.

BENEDICK I would my horse had the speed of your tongue, and so good a   105
continuer: but keep your way a God's name. I have done.

BEATRICE You always end with a jade's trick: I know you of old.

DON PEDRO That is the sum of all: Leonato, Signor Claudio and Signor
Benedick, my dear friend Leonato, hath invited you all. I tell him we
shall stay here at the least a month, and he heartily prays some   110
occasion may detain us longer: I dare swear he is no hypocrite, but
prays from his heart.

LEONATO If you swear, my lord, you shall not be forsworn. [*To Don John*]
Let me bid you welcome, my lord, being reconciled to the prince your
brother: I owe you all duty.   115

DON JOHN I thank you, I am not of many words, but I thank you.

LEONATO Please it your grace lead on?

DON PEDRO Your hand, Leonato, we will go together.

Exeunt all except Benedick and Claudio

---

104 yours] Q; your F   108 all: Leonato,] Q; all, Leonato. *Collier²*   113 forsworn.] forsworne, Q   118 SD *Exeunt all
except*] *Exeunt. Manent* Q

89–90 meet . . . **it** suitable food for her (i.e. Disdain's) disdain.

95 dear happiness great good fortune.

100 scape escape.

103 parrot-teacher Parrots can be taught to
repeat a few familiar phrases.

104 beast of yours Perhaps she means that Benedick's is the double tongue of the serpent: she
accuses him of duplicity of some kind at 2.1.211.

105–6 so . . . **continuer** so much staying-power.

107 jade A broken-down and vicious horse.

108 *This speech is commonly repunctuated to
make the first 'Leonato' a vocative concluding the
first sentence. The Q reading, where it is the subject
of the second sentence (with the second 'Leonato'
phrase in apposition), makes perfect sense, and has
been retained in substance.

111 occasion event, happening.

CLAUDIO Benedick, didst thou note the daughter of Signor Leonato?

BENEDICK I noted her not, but I looked on her.   120

CLAUDIO Is she not a modest young lady?

BENEDICK Do you question me as an honest man should do, for my simple true judgement? Or would you have me speak after my custom, as being a professed tyrant to their sex?

CLAUDIO No, I pray thee speak in sober judgement.   125

BENEDICK Why i'faith, methinks she's too low for a high praise, too brown for a fair praise, and too little for a great praise. Only this commendation I can afford her, that were she other than she is, she were unhandsome, and being no other, but as she is – I do not like her.   130

CLAUDIO Thou thinkest I am in sport. I pray thee, tell me truly how thou lik'st her?

BENEDICK Would you buy her, that you enquire after her?

CLAUDIO Can the world buy such a jewel?

BENEDICK Yea, and a case to put it into. But speak you this with a sad 135
brow? Or do you play the flouting Jack, to tell us Cupid is a good hare-finder, and Vulcan a rare carpenter? Come, in what key shall a man take you, to go in the song?

CLAUDIO In mine eye, she is the sweetest lady that ever I looked on.

BENEDICK I can see yet without spectacles, and I see no such matter.   140
There's her cousin, and she were not possessed with a fury, exceeds her as much in beauty as the first of May doth the last of December. But I hope you have no intent to turn husband, have you?

CLAUDIO I would scarce trust myself, though I had sworn the contrary, if Hero would be my wife.   145

BENEDICK Is't come to this? In faith, hath not the world one man, but he

120 **I ... not** I didn't pay particular attention to her.

126–7 From this we may infer that the boy who played Hero was small and dark-haired. Compare 158 below.

135 **sad** serious.

136 **flouting Jack** provocative and contradictory person.

136–7 **Cupid ... carpenter** These are contraries or 'flouts'. Newcomer quotes from the bad quarto of *Hamlet*: 'the warme Clowne cannot make a iest / Vnlesse by chance, as the blinde man catcheth a hare' (Furness (ed.), *Hamlet*, 1877, II, lines 1216–17). As well as being blindfold, Cupid is associated with Venus, not Diana the chaste huntress. Vulcan is smith, not carpenter: a carpenter might produce birdbolts, not steel-tipped arrows for Cupid.

137–8 **in what ... song** What key must I sing in to harmonise with your voice?

141 **cousin** Beatrice, who must be the child of a deceased sibling of Leonato and Antonio. We learn at 2.3.143 that Leonato is her guardian, but there is no information in the play about whether she has any fortune of her own.

141 **and** if.

141 **with** by.

141 **fury** A spirit of torment and punishment in Greek mythology.

146–7 'Isn't there a man in the world who will avoid the risk of being a cuckold?' The cap would conceal the cuckold's horns.

will wear his cap with suspicion? Shall I never see a bachelor of three
score again? Go to, i'faith, and thou wilt needs thrust thy neck into a
yoke, wear the print of it, and sigh away Sundays. Look, Don Pedro is
returned to seek you.   150

Enter DON PEDRO

DON PEDRO What secret hath held you here, that you followed not to
    Leonato's?
BENEDICK I would your grace would constrain me to tell.
DON PEDRO I charge thee on thy allegiance.
BENEDICK You hear, Count Claudio, I can be secret as a dumb man – I   155
    would have you think so. But on my allegiance (mark you this, on my
    allegiance) he is in love. With who? Now that is your grace's part:
    mark how short his answer is. With Hero, Leonato's short daughter.
CLAUDIO If this were so, so were it uttered.
BENEDICK Like the old tale, my lord: 'It is not so, nor 'twas not so, but   160
    indeed, God forbid it should be so.'
CLAUDIO If my passion change not shortly, God forbid it should be
    otherwise.
DON PEDRO Amen, if you love her, for the lady is very well worthy.
CLAUDIO You speak this to fetch me in, my lord.   165
DON PEDRO By my troth, I speak my thought.
CLAUDIO And in faith, my lord, I spoke mine.
BENEDICK And by my two faiths and troths, my lord, I spoke mine.
CLAUDIO That I love her, I feel.
DON PEDRO That she is worthy, I know.   170
BENEDICK That I neither feel how she should be loved, nor know how

---

150 SD PEDRO] *Hanmer; Pedro, Iohn the bastard* Q   155 man –] man, Q   156–7 so. But ... allegiance (mark ...
allegiance)] so (but ... allegiance, mark ... allegiance) Q   157 love.] love, Q   168 spoke] Q; speake F

148–9 **Go to ... Sundays** Draught animals were
yoked in pairs, and the yoke is a common image of
matrimony; compare *AYLI* 3.3.79–82. Sunday was a
day of rest and relaxation from work: the married
man would have less liberty for his bachelor
amusements.
  150 ***SD*** It is necessary to remove Don John from
the Q stage direction if Borachio's news at 1.3.40 ff.
is to be news to him.
  154 **allegiance** The oath of allegiance to a lord
was most binding. Compare *Lear* 1.1.166–7: 'Hear
me, recreant, / On thine allegiance, hear me!' Here
Benedick jocularly asks to be obliged to disclose
Claudio's secret.

158 **short** See 126–7 and n. above, and compare
the references to Hermia's short stature in *MND*
3.2.289 ff.
  159 **If ... uttered** If this were the case, he would
tell everybody.
  160–1 **It is ... be so** This formula, in which a fact
is repeatedly denied but finally revealed as true, was
first located in the fairy tale of *Mr Fox* by Halliwell
(Furness).
  165 **fetch me in** make a fool of me.
  168 **two ... troths** Benedick's allegiance to Don
Pedro, and his faithful friendship to Claudio. Benedick jocularly swears by his own duplicity.

she should be worthy, is the opinion that fire cannot melt out of me: I
will die in it at the stake.⟍

DON PEDRO Thou wast ever an obstinate heretic in the despite of beauty.

CLAUDIO And never could maintain his part, but in the force of his   175
will.

BENEDICK That a woman conceived me, I thank her: that she brought
me up, I likewise give her most humble thanks: but that I will have a
recheat winded in my forehead, or hang my bugle in an invisible
baldrick, all women shall pardon me. Because I will not do them the   180
wrong to mistrust any, I will do myself the right to trust none: and the
fine is (for the which I may go the finer) I will live a bachelor.

DON PEDRO I shall see thee, ere I die, look pale with love.

BENEDICK With anger, with sickness, or with hunger, my lord, not
with love: prove that ever I lose more blood with love than I will get   185
again with drinking, pick out mine eyes with a ballad-maker's pen,
and hang me up at the door of a brothel house for the sign of blind
Cupid.

DON PEDRO Well, if ever thou dost fall from this faith, thou wilt prove a
notable argument.   190

BENEDICK If I do, hang me in a bottle like a cat, and shoot at me, and he
that hits me, let him be clapped on the shoulder, and called Adam.

DON PEDRO Well, as time shall try: 'In time the savage bull doth bear the
yoke.'

---

173 stake Burning at the stake was the notorious
punishment for heretics (174).

175 part position, argument.

176 will A further play on the idea of heresy, the
essence of which lay not in holding, but in wilfully
persisting in, proscribed beliefs. There is also a sexual allusion in 'part' (penis) and 'will' (sexuality).

179 recheat A hunting call played on the horn.

179–80 bugle . . . baldrick A further variation on
the old joke about the cuckold's horns. A bugle is a
horn; an invisible baldrick – a fancy shoulder-belt, to
hang a sword or bugle on – would be one to make the
horn invisible. The cuckold's horns are never actually seen.

182 fine conclusion. Hamlet makes a similar pun
(5.1.106–8): 'Is this the fine of his fines . . . to have
his fine pate full of fine dirt?'

185 lose . . . love The lover's sighing consumed
his blood; consequently, lovers looked pale. Compare *MND* 3.2.97: 'With sighs of love, that costs the
fresh blood dear'.

186 drinking This leads to a sanguine complexion. Red wine, with its high iron content, was
prescribed for anaemia until quite recently.

186 pick . . . pen Lovers were often
ballad-makers.

187–8 blind Cupid Cupid is blind to show the
irrationality of love. Brothels, like inns and other
shops at this time, carried signs to indicate the nature
of the business carried on.

190 argument subject of discussion. The connotation, as with 'notable', is usually uncomplimentary.

191 bottle A wicker bottle or basket. Various folk-
customs of this barbarous kind are noted in Furness.

192 Adam Probably from Adam Bell, an outlaw,
archer and ballad hero.

193 try Bring to trial, test. Compare *WT* 4.1.1: 'I,
that please some, try all.'

193–4 In time . . . yoke A quotation, slightly
astray, from Thomas Kyd's *The Spanish Tragedy*
(1587), 2.1.3. Kyd perhaps borrowed it from the
forty-seventh poem in Thomas Watson's
Hecatompathia (1582). Watson refers his line to *Son-
netto 103* of Seraphina, and this in turn may derive
from Ovid, *Ars Amatoria* I, 471 (Furness). It leads to
further play on the cuckold's-horns theme.

BENEDICK The savage bull may, but if ever the sensible Benedick bear it,   195
pluck off the bull's horns, and set them in my forehead, and let me be
vilely painted, and in such great letters as they write, 'Here is good
horse to hire', let them signify under my sign, 'Here you may see
Benedick the married man.'

CLAUDIO If this should ever happen, thou wouldst be horn-mad.   200

DON PEDRO Nay, if Cupid have not spent all his quiver in Venice, thou
wilt quake for this shortly.

BENEDICK I look for an earthquake too then.

DON PEDRO Well, you will temporise with the hours. In the mean time,
good Signor Benedick, repair to Leonato's, commend me to him, and   205
tell him I will not fail him at supper, for indeed he hath made great
preparation.

BENEDICK I have almost matter enough in me for such an embassage,
and so I commit you –

CLAUDIO To the tuition of God: from my house if I had it –   210

DON PEDRO The sixth of July: your loving friend Benedick.

BENEDICK Nay, mock not, mock not: the body of your discourse is
sometime guarded with fragments, and the guards are but slightly
basted on, neither: ere you flout old ends any further, examine your
conscience: and so I leave you.   *Exit*   215

CLAUDIO My liege, your highness now may do me good.

DON PEDRO My love is thine to teach, teach it but how,
And thou shalt see how apt it is to learn
Any hard lesson that may do thee good.

---

197 vilely] *Rowe²;* vildly Q   **209** you –] you. Q   **210** it –] ìt. Q

195 sensible The modern meaning – 'showing
pragmatic intelligence' – was coming into use at this
time, but perhaps Benedick's intention is nearer the
modern French *sensible*, capable of fine feelings and
delicate sensations – unlike the savage bull.

197 *vilely The spelling 'vile' and 'vild' were both
current at this time, and for some while later. The
shade of difference felt between them is hard to
define, but the substitution of one for the other is
'sheer perversion' according to Greg, *EP*, p. li.

200 horn-mad stark mad; but with the expected
pun. Compare *Err.* 2.1.58–9: 'I mean not cuckold-
mad / But sure he is stark mad.'

201 Venice Notorious at this time for its libertin-
ism. Compare *Oth.* 3.3.202–3: 'In Venice they do let
God see the pranks / They dare not show their
husbands.'

203 earthquake A very unlikely event.

204 temporise ... hours put off the evil hour.
Or, perhaps, as Furness suggested, 'become

tempered, change your attitude, with the passage of
time'.

210 tuition safe-keeping. The whole, as continued by Claudio and the prince, is a common formula for the conclusion of a letter.

211 sixth of July 'Old Midsummer day, an
appropriate date for such midsummer madness'; this
is attributed to Aldis Wright by NS, but I have not
found it in any edition by him. P. H. Ditchfield (*Old
English Customs*, 1896, p. 207) gives 5 July.

212–14 The extended metaphor of this passage is
from tailoring. Benedick says the prince and Claudio
abuse these bits and pieces of language as freely as
he does. The 'body' of a garment is its essential
construction; 'guards' are decorations, laces, trim-
mings; 'basting' is loose temporary sewing, to hold
things in place while they are fine-sewn. 'Old ends'
are the tailor's scraps (which might be used for
'guards') as well as literary tags.

CLAUDIO Hath Leonato any son, my lord?   220
DON PEDRO No child but Hero, she's his only heir:
    Dost thou affect her, Claudio?
CLAUDIO   O my lord,
    When you went onward on this ended action,
    I looked upon her with a soldier's eye,
    That liked, but had a rougher task in hand,   225
    Than to drive liking to the name of love;
    But now I am returned, and that war-thoughts
    Have left their places vacant, in their rooms
    Come thronging soft and delicate desires,
    All prompting me how fair young Hero is,   230
    Saying I liked her ere I went to wars.
DON PEDRO Thou wilt be like a lover presently,
    And tire the hearer with a book of words:
    If thou dost love fair Hero, cherish it,
    And I will break with her, and with her father,   235
    And thou shalt have her. Wast not to this end,
    That thou began'st to twist so fine a story?
CLAUDIO How sweetly you do minister to love,
    That know love's grief by his complexion!
    But lest my liking might too sudden seem,   240
    I would have salved it with a longer treatise.
DON PEDRO What need the bridge much broader than the flood?
    The fairest grant is the necessity.
    Look what will serve is fit: 'tis once, thou lovest,
    And I will fit thee with the remedy.   245
    I know we shall have revelling tonight,

---

228 vacant,] vacant: Q   **235–6** and with . . . have her] Q; *not in* F   **241** salved] salude Q; salu'd F   **246** tonight] to night Q

220–1 son . . . heir From the start Claudio is a prudential lover; he checks on Hero's prospects. See p. 34 above.

222 affect (1) feel affection for, (2) aim at.

223 onward . . . action on your way to the war now ended.

227 that The displacement of 'that' from the first to the second clause makes the line a little difficult: 'But now that I am returned . . .'

233 book of words long discourse.

235 break with discuss the matter with.

239 know . . . complexion understand the way a lover suffers by the way he looks. The 'complexion'

(four syllables) was originally the 'mixture of humours', but became transferred to the outward manifestation as shown in facial colour. Lovers were pale: see 185 n. above.

241 *salved (1) smoothed with ointment to make it more acceptable; (2) salued (i.e. saluted, greeted). The second meaning is faintly possible.

243 The fairest . . . necessity 'The best boon is that which answers the necessities of the case' (Staunton, in Furness).

244 fit appropriate.

244 once once for all.

245 fit provide.

I will assume thy part in some disguise,
And tell fair Hero I am Claudio,
And in her bosom I'll unclasp my heart,
And take her hearing prisoner with the force   250
And strong encounter of my amorous tale:
Then after, to her father will I break,
And the conclusion is, she shall be thine:
In practice let us put it presently.

Exeunt

[1.2] *Enter* LEONATO *and an old man* [ANTONIO,] *brother to Leonato*

LEONATO How now, brother, where is my cousin your son? Hath he
provided this music?
ANTONIO He is very busy about it: but, brother, I can tell you strange
news that you yet dreamed not of.
LEONATO Are they good?   5
ANTONIO As the events stamps them, but they have a good cover: they
show well outward. The prince and Count Claudio walking in a
thick-pleached alley in mine orchard, were thus much overheard by a

Act 1, Scene 2   3, 6, 14 SH ANTONIO] *Old* Q   3–4 strange news] Q; news F

248 tell . . . Claudio This is the first of the many
impersonations proposed in the play. For Pedro to
do the wooing with an 'amorous tale' as well as acting
as broker and go-between seems (to us) odd. And he
says 'my heart', 'my amorous tale', which can be seen
as the origin of the misunderstanding by the 'good
sharp fellow' (1.2.14) who overhears. The whole
proposal shows little concern for Hero's possible
feelings.
  249 in her bosom in confidence.

Act 1, Scene 2
  0 SD They probably enter by separate doors, since
Leonato's 'How now' suggests a greeting as they
meet. There is a bustle of several extras across the
stage indicated at 19. 'A room in Leonato's house'
was Capell's location.
  1 cousin your son 'Cousin' was loosely used at
this time of members of the extended family; so here
it means 'nephew' as at 2.1.58 it means 'niece'; at 19
the plural could almost include family servants.
There is a contradiction if Rowe's identification of
'old man', 'brother' and 'Antonio' is accepted, since
at 5.1.257 Hero is asserted to be 'heir to both of us'.
  6–7 As . . . outward It depends on how they turn
out, but they look good.

6 events stamps Though this appears to be a
plural noun with a singular verb, 'events' is in fact
seen as collective (= outcome). See Abbott 338 for a
discussion of similar anomalies.
  8 thick-pleached . . . orchard 'Orchard' could
still mean 'pleasure garden' in Shakespearean England – though such a garden would probably contain
fruit trees. A 'thick-pleached alley' could be a walk
between carefully trimmed and intertwined trees, or
an arbour composed of intertwined or naturally
climbing plants. A description of the Duke of Buck-
ingham's estate at Thornbury when confiscated to
the Crown after his execution in 1521 includes the
following: 'Beside the same privy garden is a large
and a goodly orchard full of young graftes, well laden
with fruit, many roses, and other pleasures; and in
the same orchard are many goodly allies to walk in
openly: and round about the same orchard is covered
on a good height, other goodly allies with roosting
places covered thoroughly with white thorn and
hazel' (*Archaeologia* 25 (1834), 312). See also William
Lawson, *A New Orchard and Garden* (1618), chapter
17. Compare 2.3.4 and 28, and 3.1.7–9, and see
illustration 1, p. 7 above.

man of mine: the prince discovered to Claudio that he loved my niece
your daughter, and meant to acknowledge it this night in a dance, and   10
if he found her accordant, he meant to take the present time by the
top, and instantly break with you of it.

LEONATO Hath the fellow any wit that told you this?

ANTONIO A good sharp fellow, I will send for him, and question him
yourself.   15

LEONATO No, no, we will hold it as a dream till it appear itself: but I will
acquaint my daughter withal, that she may be the better prepared for
an answer, if peradventure this be true: go you, and tell her of it.

[Several persons cross the stage]

Cousins, you know what you have to do. O I cry you mercy, friend, go
you with me and I will use your skill: good cousin, have a care this   20
busy time.

Exeunt

[1.3] *Enter* DON JOHN *the bastard and* CONRADE *his companion*

CONRADE What the good year, my lord, why are you thus out of measure
sad?

DON JOHN There is no measure in the occasion that breeds, therefore the
sadness is without limit.

CONRADE You should hear reason.   5

19 SD] *Theobald; not in* Q   Act 1, Scene 3   0 SD DON JOHN] *sir Iohn* Q   3 SH DON JOHN] *John* Q *(and throughout scene)*

11 **accordant** in accord, willing.

12 **top** forelock. The allusion is to the icon of *Occasio*, a female figure who was bald behind but had a long forelock hanging down in front; see the illustration from Geoffrey Whitney's *A Choice of Emblems* (1586), in Russell Fraser (ed.), *All's Well That Ends Well*, 1985, p. 26. This forelock symbolised the auspicious moment that must not be allowed to pass (Tilley T311). Compare Spenser's description of Occasion:

> Her lockes, that loathly were and hoarie gray
> Grew all afore, and loosely hong vnrold,
> But all behind was bald, and worne away,
> That none thereof could ever taken hold . . .
>
> (*FQ* II, 4, iv)

This comes from the beginning of the story of Phedon, one of the analogues of *Much Ado*; see p. 3 above.

16 **appear itself** (1) makes itself appear, (2) till the event itself appear. (1) is reflexive, (2) elliptic.

18 *SD Theobald's stage direction is needed, since the disjunctions of Leonato's speech suggest at least two people, and possibly more.

Act 1, Scene 3

0 SD NS suggests that the servants of 1.2 were used to set the stage with properties required for 2.1, in the mask. 1.3 is then played 'above' and the direction 'A door opens in the gallery' is provided. Assuming that some large properties were required this would be an economical use of time and space on the Elizabethan stage. The scene is unlocalised, and editors have suggested variously a room in Leonato's house (Capell) or 'the street' (Hanmer).

1 **What . . . year** A mild expletive of obscure origin.

1 **measure** moderation. In 3 Don John takes 'measure' in the sense of limit, boundary.

DON JOHN And when I have heard it, what blessing brings it?

CONRADE If not a present remedy, at least a patient sufferance.

DON JOHN I wonder that thou (being as thou sayest thou art, born under
Saturn) goest about to apply a moral medicine to a mortifying
mischief. I cannot hide what I am: I must be sad when I have cause,   10
and smile at no man's jests: eat when I have stomach, and wait for no
man's leisure: sleep when I am drowsy, and tend on no man's
business: laugh when I am merry, and claw no man in his humour.

CONRADE Yea, but you must not make the full show of this till you may do
it without controlment. You have of late stood out against your   15
brother, and he hath ta'en you newly into his grace, where it is
impossible you should take true root, but by the fair weather that you
make yourself: it is needful that you frame the season for your own
harvest.

DON JOHN I had rather be a canker in a hedge, than a rose in his grace,   20
and it better fits my blood to be disdained of all, than to fashion a
carriage to rob love from any. In this (though I cannot be said to be a
flattering honest man) it must not be denied but I am a plain-dealing
villain. I am trusted with a muzzle, and enfranchised with a clog,
therefore I have decreed not to sing in my cage. If I had my mouth, I   25
would bite: if I had my liberty, I would do my liking. In the mean time,
let me be that I am, and seek not to alter me.

CONRADE Can you make no use of your discontent?

DON JOHN I make all use of it, for I use it only. Who comes here?

---

6 brings] Q; bringeth F   7 at least] Q; yet F   17 true root] Q; root F   29 make] Q; will make F

9 **Saturn** The saturnine were 'sad, sour, lumpish,
melancholy' (Cotgrave); Conrade, born under
Saturn, should have a temperament like Don John's
own.

9–10 **moral ... mischief** medicine of moral precepts to an incurable disease. Don John is melancholy by temperament, as, he claims, Conrade
should be by the dominance of Saturn in his horoscope. Good advice can have no effect.

10–13 'An envious and unsocial mind, too proud
to give pleasure, and too sullen to receive it, always
endeavours to hide its malignity from the world and
from itself, under the plainness of simple honesty, or
the dignity of haughty independence' (Johnson).

12 **tend** attend, wait.

13 **claw** flatter, 'scratch the back of'; but it contains a hint of cruelty as well.

15 **stood out** rebelled. Compare *R2* 1.4.38: 'Now
for the rebels which stand out in Ireland'. This is the
clearest indication of the cause of the war and Don
John's disgrace: it is not very clear.

17 **root** This vegetable image of friendship is
found elsewhere in Shakespeare: compare *Mac.*
1.4.28–33.

17–19 **fair weather ... harvest** Conrade insists
that if John is to benefit from his reconciliation with
Don Pedro, he must make sure that good relations
are maintained between them.

20 **canker** wild rose. It is also a general term for
diseases of malformation, excessive growth or ulcers
in animals and plants (cognate with modern 'cancer')
and this connotation attaches to Don John.

20 **grace** Newcomer suggests a pun on 'grass'.

21–2 **fashion a carriage** devise a way of behaving.

24 **muzzle ... clog** Restraints for animals. A clog
is a heavy block of wood to which an animal is tied to
prevent straying.

26 **liking** what I like.

29 **only** alone.

Enter BORACHIO

What news, Borachio?   30

BORACHIO I came yonder from a great supper, the prince your brother is
royally entertained by Leonato, and I can give you intelligence of an
intended marriage.

DON JOHN Will it serve for any model to build mischief on? What is he for
a fool that betroths himself to unquietness?   35

BORACHIO Marry, it is your brother's right hand.

DON JOHN Who, the most exquisite Claudio?

BORACHIO Even he.

DON JOHN A proper squire! And who, and who, which way looks he?

BORACHIO Marry, on Hero, the daughter and heir of Leonato.   40

DON JOHN A very forward March-chick. How came you to this?

BORACHIO Being entertained for a perfumer, as I was smoking a musty
room, comes me the prince and Claudio, hand in hand, in sad
conference: I whipped me behind the arras, and there heard it agreed
upon, that the prince should woo Hero for himself, and having   45
obtained her, give her to Count Claudio.

DON JOHN Come, come, let us thither, this may prove food to my
displeasure, that young start-up hath all the glory of my overthrow: if I
can cross him any way, I bless myself every way. You are both sure,
and will assist me?   50

CONRADE To the death, my lord.

DON JOHN Let us to the great supper, their cheer is the greater that I am
subdued. Would the cook were a my mind: shall we go prove what's to
be done?

BORACHIO We'll wait upon your lordship.   55

Exeunt

39 squire!] squier, Q   40 on Hero,] F; one Hero Q   44 whipped me] Q; whipt F   53 a] Q; of F

32 **intelligence** information of a valuable or secret
kind. The meaning is preserved in such phrases as
'military intelligence'.

34 **model** builder's or architect's plan.

34–5 **What . . . fool** What kind of a fool is he?

39 **proper squire** smart little fellow. The tone is
contemptuous, but hard to render in modern
English.

40 *****on** The Q reading 'one' is possible, but
unlikely since it suggests that Hero is unknown to
John and Borachio.

41 **March-chick** precocious child. A March chick
is early hatched.

42 **entertained** employed.

42–3 **perfumer . . . room** Elizabethan domestic

hygiene was rudimentary, so that strong and
unpleasant odours had to be disguised by burning
sweet-smelling substances such as juniper.

43 **me** The ethical dative: The speaker, me (i.e.
Borachio), is perceiver of the action reported.

43–4 **sad conference** serious conversation.

48 **start-up** upstart. But 'start-ups' were also high
shoes – 'lifts' in modern stage terms – and so may
refer, like 'young' and 'squire', to Claudio's youth
and small stature; compare 1.1.11–12.

49 **sure** trusty, to be relied upon.

53 **cook . . . mind** i.e. that the cook would agree
to poison them.

53 **prove** find out. Or perhaps, for the whole
phrase, 'see what we can do'.

2.[1] *Enter* LEONATO, *his brother* [ANTONIO], HERO *his daughter and*
BEATRICE *his niece*

LEONATO Was not Count John here at supper?

ANTONIO I saw him not.

BEATRICE How tartly that gentleman looks, I never can see him but I am
heart-burned an hour after.

HERO He is of a very melancholy disposition.   5

BEATRICE He were an excellent man that were made just in the mid-way
between him and Benedick: the one is too like an image and says
nothing, and the other too like my lady's eldest son, evermore tattling.

LEONATO Then half Signor Benedick's tongue in Count John's mouth,
and half Count John's melancholy in Signor Benedick's face –   10

BEATRICE With a good leg and a good foot, uncle, and money enough in
his purse, such a man would win any woman in the world if a could get
her good will.

LEONATO By my troth, niece, thou wilt never get thee a husband, if thou
be so shrewd of thy tongue.   15

ANTONIO In faith, she's too curst.

BEATRICE Too curst is more than curst, I shall lessen God's sending that
way: for it is said, God sends a curst cow short horns, but to a cow too
curst, he sends none.

LEONATO So, by being too curst, God will send you no horns.   20

Act 2, Scene 1 2.1] *Actus Secundus.* F; *not in* Q   0 SD] *Enter Leonato, his brother, his wife, Hero his daughter, and Beatrice
his neece, and a kinsman.* Q   2, 16, 38 SH ANTONIO] *brother* Q   12 if a] Q; *if he* F

Act 2, Scene 1

0 *SD There are problems about the entries here
and later (60) in this scene: compare 1.1.0 n. and see
Textual Analysis, p. 148 below. It is a large-scale
full-stage scene, and requires musicians, presumably
in the gallery, out of the way of the dancers in the
mask. The hall or great chamber of Leonato's house
is the usual editorial location, though Furness suggested the garden.

3 **tartly** sourly.

7 **image** statue.

8 **eldest son** i.e. a spoilt child.

8 **tattling** chattering.

9–13 Leonato teases Beatrice by proposing a
hybrid Benedick/John monster; she hastily adds further conditions for an acceptable husband. He must
be well-built, wealthy, and able to get her good will.
'Leg' implies both physique and elegance; a 'good
leg' could be a graceful bow. At the same time there

is an extended sexual pun: 'leg' leads to foot, but
'foot' can mean 'penis', and occurs in the Bible as a
euphemism for the sexual organs (e.g. 'The Lord
shall shave with a razor the head and the hair of the
feet: and it shall also consume the beard' (Isa. 7.20)).
There is also the association of 'foot' with French
foutre; compare *H5* 3.4.50–9. A well-filled purse is
also the scrotum – 'purse' is still colloquial in this
sense. Finally 'will' can mean sexual passion or the
sexual organs as in Sonnets 135 and 136. It is all this
that provokes Leonato's comment on Beatrice's
'shrewd tongue' (15); for 'shrewd' in this sense compare *Wiv.* 2.2.223.

16 **curst** ill-natured.

18–19 A proverb (Tilley G217): God limits the
power of the vicious to do harm. There is also the
sexual innuendo on 'horn' – a short horn/penis con-
noting an unsatisfactory husband.

BEATRICE Just, if he send me no husband, for the which blessing I am at
him upon my knees every morning and evening: Lord, I could not
endure a husband with a beard on his face, I had rather lie in the
woollen!

LEONATO You may light on a husband that hath no beard.   25

BEATRICE What should I do with him – dress him in my apparel and
make him my waiting gentlewoman? He that hath a beard is more
than a youth: and he that hath no beard is less than a man: and he that
is more than a youth, is not for me, and he that is less than a man, I am
not for him: therefore I will even take sixpence in earnest of the   30
bearward, and lead his apes into hell.

LEONATO Well then, go you into hell.

BEATRICE No, but to the gate, and there will the devil meet me like an old
cuckold with horns on his head, and say, get you to heaven, Beatrice,
get you to heaven, here's no place for you maids. So deliver I up my   35
apes, and away to Saint Peter: for the heavens, he shows me where the
bachelors sit, and there live we, as merry as the day is long.

ANTONIO Well, niece, I trust you will be ruled by your father.

BEATRICE Yes faith, it is my cousin's duty to make curtsy, and say, father,
as it please you: but yet for all that, cousin, let him be a handsome   40
fellow, or else make another curtsy, and say, father, as it please me.

LEONATO Well, niece, I hope to see you one day fitted with a husband.

BEATRICE Not till God make men of some other metal than earth: would
it not grieve a woman to be overmastered with a piece of valiant dust?
to make an account of her life to a clod of wayward marl? No, uncle,   45

25 on] Q; upon F   31 bearward] *Knight;* Berrord Q   39 curtsy,] F; cursie Q   39 father] Q; *not in* F   41 curtsy] cursie
Q, F

21 **husband** This adds the cuckold's horns to the
extended joke.

23–4 **in the woollen** between blankets, without
sheets (Capell thought it meant 'in my shroud').
Scratchy blankets would be preferable to a man's
beard. In the following lines Beatrice rejects beardless men as well. It appears that early in the play
Benedick is heavily bearded (compare 3.2.33–6
below), while Claudio is as yet too young to have
grown a beard.

28 **less than a man** immature or impotent.

30 **sixpence in earnest** A token payment, given
and taken to confirm a contract or bargain.

31 **bearward** keeper of the bears. The tragic actor
Edward Alleyn with his father-in-law Philip
Henslowe bought the office of 'Master of the Royal
game of bears, bulls and mastiff dogs' in 1604.
Though primarily concerned with the 'sport' of bear-
baiting, the bearward would also keep other animals.

31 **apes into hell** The proverbial fate of old maids

(Tilley M37). There are many instances of the
phrase, but no satisfactory explanation of its origin.

36 **for the heavens** 'when I get to heaven', or
perhaps just a mild intensive expletive, 'good
heavens!'

37 **bachelors** The word 'bachelor' could, at this
time, mean the unmarried of either sex, but the
usage is rare and Beatrice probably means that she
will be with the single men in heaven – another
'shrewd' jest.

42 **fitted** Leonato carries on Beatrice's game of
sexual puns.

43 **metal** material; but also punning on 'mettle' –
spirit, energy. Of the four elements – Earth, Water,
Air, Fire – Earth was the dullest and heaviest.

43–5 **earth ... dust ... marl** Beatrice is referring to the creation of Adam out of the dust of the
earth (Gen. 2.7), and perhaps suggesting the
superior nature of Eve's creation out of Adam's rib.
Marl is a soil of clay and lime.

I'll none: Adam's sons are my brethren, and truly I hold it a sin to
match in my kindred.

LEONATO Daughter, remember what I told you: if the prince do solicit
you in that kind, you know your answer.

BEATRICE The fault will be in the music, cousin, if you be not wooed in   50
good time: if the prince be too important, tell him there is measure in
everything, and so dance out the answer. For hear me, Hero, wooing,
wedding, and repenting, is as a Scotch jig, a measure and a
cinquepace: the first suit is hot and hasty like a Scotch jig (and full as
fantastical), the wedding mannerly modest (as a measure) full of state   55
and ancientry, and then comes Repentance, and with his bad legs falls
into the cinquepace faster and faster, till he sink into his grave.

LEONATO Cousin, you apprehend passing shrewdly.

BEATRICE I have a good eye, uncle, I can see a church by daylight.

LEONATO The revellers are entering, brother, make good room.   60

                                                              [*Exit Antonio*]

Enter DON PEDRO, CLAUDIO, BENEDICK *and* BALTHASAR, *Maskers with
a drum;* [*re-enter* ANTONIO, *masked, followed by*] DON JOHN [*and*
BORACHIO *and others including* MARGARET *and* URSULA. *The dance begins*]

DON PEDRO Lady, will you walk a bout with your friend?

HERO So you walk softly, and look sweetly, and say nothing, I am yours for
the walk, and especially when I walk away.

60 SD.1 *Exit Antonio*] NS *subst.* 60 SD.2–3] *Enter prince, Pedro, Claudio, and Benedicke, and Balthaser or dumb Iohn.* Q;
F *adds/Maskers with a drum.* 60 SD.2 *re-enter* ANTONIO *masked*] NS *subst.* 60 SD.3 MARGARET *and* URSULA] *conj.*
Wells, 'Foul Papers' 61 SH DON PEDRO] *Pedro* Q (*and throughout scene*) 61 a bout] NS; *about* Q

47 kindred A Table of Kindred and Affinity at
the end of the Book of Common Prayer lists the
'forbidden degrees' of affinity, those relations a man
or woman may not marry.

48–9 solicit ... kind approach you about that
matter (i.e. propose marriage). At this stage the
assumption of Leonato and all his family is that Don
Pedro will woo for himself.

50–2 Beatrice has heard the report of Antonio's
'good sharp fellow' (1.2.14) that Don Pedro is going
to propose during the dance. 'Music', 'good time',
'measure' and 'dance' play on this.

51 important importunate.

51 measure (1) moderation, (2) tempo in music,
(3) a specific stately dance.

53–4 Beatrice's gloss adequately differentiates
these three dances.

55–6 state and ancientry formality and tradition.

57 cinquepace ... grave The pronunciation
'sink apace' is used for a pun: the dying may be said
to be 'sinking fast'. It is perhaps the approach of
death that gives Repentance (56) bad legs. The
cinquepace was a capering dance of five steps followed by a leap.

58 Cousin Compare 1.2.1 n.

58 passing shrewdly very sharply.

59 see ... daylight perceive the obvious. Compare *AYLI* 2.7.52: 'The why is plain as way to parish
church.' Beatrice can also see a wedding approaching.

60 make ... room Antonio is to be one of the
maskers, so Leonato warns him to leave the stage
and join them. Alternatively, it may be a request for
Antonio to organise the clearing of the space for
dancing.

60 *SD For the problems here and with speech
headings at 71–81 see Textual Analysis, p. 150 below.

61 *a bout The NS reading, meaning a turn, the
duration of the dance, is attractive. Compare *Rom.*
1.5.17, where the Q1 reading 'have about' (emended
in later editions to 'walk about') suggests 'a bout' was
the sense intended. The difference in intonation
between 'walk about' and 'walk a bout' could hardly
be perceived by a theatre audience, in any case.

63 walk away Words spoken, probably, as the pair
move apart in the formal movements of the pavan:
see Brissenden, pp. 49–50.

DON PEDRO With me in your company.

HERO I may say so when I please.   65

DON PEDRO And when please you to say so?

HERO When I like your favour, for God defend the lute should be like the
case.

DON PEDRO My visor is Philemon's roof, within the house is Jove.

HERO Why then your visor should be thatched.

DON PEDRO   Speak low if you speak love.   70

[They move on in the dance]

[BALTHASAR] Well, I would you did like me.

MARGARET So would not I for your own sake, for I have many ill
qualities.

[BALTHASAR] Which is one?

MARGARET I say my prayers aloud.   75

[BALTHASAR] I love you the better, the hearers may cry amen.

MARGARET God match me with a good dancer.

BALTHASAR Amen.

MARGARET And God keep him out of my sight when the dance is done:
answer, clerk.   80

BALTHASAR No more words, the clerk is answered.

[They move on in the dance]

URSULA I know you well enough, you are Signor Antonio.

ANTONIO At a word, I am not.

URSULA I know you by the waggling of your head.

ANTONIO To tell you true, I counterfeit him.   85

URSULA You could never do him so ill-well, unless you were the very

---

69 Jove] Q; Love F   71, 74, 76 SH BALTHASAR] *Theobald; Bene.* Q; *Borachio/NS*   78, 81 SH BALTHASAR] Q *subst.;*
Borachio/NS   82 Antonio] Anthonio Q   83, 85, 88 SH ANTONIO] *Anth.* Q

67 defend forbid.

67–8 lute . . . case face like the mask. Don Pedro
wears a rustic or grotesque mask.

69–70 These lines make up a fourteen-syllable
rhyming couplet. This was the measure used in
Arthur Golding's translation of Ovid (1567). The
story of Baucis and Philemon who entertained Jove
and Mercury in their humble cottage is found in
Metamorphoses, Book 8, and was widely known.

one cottage afterward
Receivèd them, and that was but a pelting one indeed,
The roof thereof was thatchèd all with straw and
fennish reed.   Fol. 113ᵛ, sig. O7ᵛ
Newcomer suggests that Hero is joking at the
expense of a balding Don Pedro. Hilda Hulme

argues that 'thatch' could also mean 'pubic hair' and
that even if this is 'not for Hero to say, it may be for
some of the audience to hear' (p. 150). Shakespeare
uses 'thatch' for false hair in *Tim.* 4.3.145–6: 'And
thatch your poor thin roofs / With burthens of the
dead'.

75–8 Praying aloud was a practice of enthusiastic
reformers in religion and, like the interjection of
hearty 'amens', probably comic to Shakespeare's
audience.

80 clerk The parish clerk led the responses in
church.

83 At a word In short.

84 waggling . . . head trembling caused by age.

86 do . . . ill-well imitate his failings so skilfully.

man: here's his dry hand up and down, you are he, you are he.

ANTONIO At a word, I am not.

URSULA Come, come, do you think I do not know you by your excellent
wit? Can virtue hide itself? Go to, mum, you are he, graces will   90
appear, and there's an end.

[They move on in the dance]

BEATRICE Will you not tell me who told you so?

BENEDICK No, you shall pardon me.

BEATRICE Nor will you not tell me who you are?

BENEDICK Not now.   95

BEATRICE That I was disdainful, and that I had my good wit out of *The
Hundred Merry Tales*: well, this was Signor Benedick that said so.

BENEDICK What's he?

BEATRICE I am sure you know him well enough.

BENEDICK Not I, believe me.   100

BEATRICE Did he never make you laugh?

BENEDICK I pray you, what is he?

BEATRICE Why he is the prince's jester, a very dull fool, only his gift is, in
devising impossible slanders: none but libertines delight in him, and
the commendation is not in his wit, but in his villainy, for he both   105
pleases men and angers them, and then they laugh at him, and beat
him: I am sure he is in the fleet, I would he had boarded me.

BENEDICK When I know the gentleman, I'll tell him what you say.

BEATRICE Do, do, he'll but break a comparison or two on me, which
peradventure (not marked, or not laughed at) strikes him into   110

96–7 *The Hundred Merry Tales*] *Hanmer;* the hundred merry tales Q   106 pleases] Q; pleaseth F

87 **dry hand** Another sign of age, as a young hand
was supposed moist. Compare *2H4* 1.2.180, and
Oth. 3.4.36–7: 'This hand is moist . . . / It yet hath
felt no age.'

87 **up and down** in every respect, exactly.

90 **mum** be silent, don't protest any more.

96–7 **The Hundred Merry Tales** A famous and
proverbially unsophisticated jest book, first printed
by John Rastell in 1526, but popular long after.

103 **jester** A menial office though a privileged
one. Benedick is clearly hurt by this for he reverts to
it at 155.

103 **only his gift** his only gift. For such transposi-
tions see Abbott 420, 421.

104 **impossible** unbelievable.

104 **libertines** loose livers and speakers.

105 **his villainy** the grossness of his slanders.

106 **pleases . . . angers . . . laugh . . . beat** He
pleases those libertines who hear his slanders, angers
those who are slandered: the former laugh, the latter
beat him.

107 **fleet** assembly. 'Boarded' continues the nauti-
cal metaphor. The women in their flowing gowns
(like sails) are the ships, grappled with and boarded
by the men. Some suggest that Beatrice makes a
(perhaps unconscious) pun on 'bawd'. Compare *TN*
1.3.56–7: '"Accost" is front her, board her, woo her,
assail her.'

109 **break a comparison** make a disparaging
simile. The metaphor of breaking comes from tilting,
where lances were broken. It is used several times in
this play of combative wit. Compare 2.3.192, or
5.1.131: 'Nay then, give him another staff, this last
was broke cross.'

melancholy, and then there's a partridge wing saved, for the fool will
eat no supper that night. We must follow the leaders.

BENEDICK In every good thing.

BEATRICE Nay, if they lead to any ill, I will leave them at the next turning.

Music for the Dance. [They Dance.] Exeunt [all but Don John,
Borachio and Claudio]

DON JOHN Sure my brother is amorous on Hero, and hath withdrawn her   115
father to break with him about it: the ladies follow her, and but one
visor remains.

BORACHIO And that is Claudio, I know him by his bearing.

DON JOHN Are not you Signor Benedick?

CLAUDIO You know me well, I am he.   120

DON JOHN Signor, you are very near my brother in his love, he is
enamoured on Hero, I pray you dissuade him from her, she is no
equal for his birth: you may do the part of an honest man in it.

CLAUDIO How know you he loves her?

DON JOHN I heard him swear his affection.   125

BORACHIO So did I too, and he swore he would marry her tonight.

DON JOHN Come, let us to the banquet.

Exeunt Don John and Borachio

CLAUDIO Thus answer I in name of Benedick,
But hear these ill news with the ears of Claudio:
'Tis certain so, the prince woos for himself,   130
Friendship is constant in all other things,
Save in the office and affairs of love:
Therefore all hearts in love use their own tongues.
Let every eye negotiate for itself,
And trust no agent: for beauty is a witch,   135

---

114 SD] *Dance. Exeunt* Q; *Exeunt. Musicke for the dance.* F   127 SD] *Exeunt: manet Clau.* Q

111 **partridge wing** Trenery quotes Willughby's *Ornithology*: 'Palate-men and such as have skill in eating, do chiefly commend the Partridge's Wing'; she also suggests a 'thrust' at the 'very valiant trencherman' (1.1.38) since there is little meat on a partridge wing.

112 **leaders** i.e. of the dance.

114 **turning** i.e. in the figure of the dance.

114 *SD The dance continues for a while – perhaps, as Brissenden suggests (p. 50), a cinquepace or galliard, a more lively measure than the pavan that goes with the paired conversations of lines 61–114. Clearly the F SD misplaces a stage-manager's addition in the quarto that served as copy for F.

115–16 Don John should know (from 1.3.36–46)

that Don Pedro is wooing for Claudio. It must be assumed that he recognises Claudio before Borachio identifies him, and at once begins his mischief-making. Garrick's text (1777) makes this explicit by inserting 'Now then for a trick of contrivance' at the beginning of the speech.

115 **amorous on** in love with. For this use of 'on' see Abbott 181. So with 'enamoured on' at 122.

121 **very near ... love** a dear friend of my brother.

126 **tonight** Borachio's invention to increase Claudio's jealousy.

127 **banquet** A light dessert following the dance, not the supper (2.1.1) which was the main meal. Compare *Shr.* 5.2.9–10: 'My banket is to close our stomachs up / After our great good cheer.'

Against whose charms faith melteth into blood:
This is an accident of hourly proof,
Which I mistrusted not: farewell therefore, Hero.

Enter BENEDICK

BENEDICK Count Claudio.
CLAUDIO Yea, the same.   140
BENEDICK Come, will you go with me?
CLAUDIO Whither?
BENEDICK Even to the next willow, about your own business, county:
what fashion will you wear the garland of? About your neck, like an
usurer's chain? Or under your arm, like a lieutenant's scarf? You   145
must wear it one way, for the prince hath got your Hero.
CLAUDIO I wish him joy of her.
BENEDICK Why that's spoken like an honest drovier, so they sell bull-
ocks: but did you think the prince would have served you thus?
CLAUDIO I pray you leave me.   150
BENEDICK Ho now you strike like the blind man, 'twas the boy that stole
your meat, and you'll beat the post.
CLAUDIO If it will not be, I'll leave you.   *Exit*
BENEDICK Alas poor hurt fowl, now will he creep into sedges: but that my
Lady Beatrice should know me, and not know me: the prince's fool!   155
Hah, it may be I go under that title because I am merry: yea but so I
am apt to do myself wrong: I am not so reputed, it is the base (though
bitter) disposition of Beatrice, that puts the world into her person,
and so gives me out: well, I'll be revenged as I may.

143 county] Q; Count F   144 of] Q; off F   156 Hah,] Q; Hah? F

136 **blood** passion.
137 **accident** happening.
137 **proof** demonstration.
143 **willow** The willow garland was the badge of
the unhappy lover. Compare *Oth.* 4.3.51,
Desdemona's 'Willow' song.
143 **county** count. Q uses four spellings, count,
counte, countie and county; see p. 152 below on
Shakespeare's spelling.
145 **usurer's chain** Rich men wore heavy gold
chains, in the style of the chains of office worn by
mayors on official occasions.
145 **lieutenant's scarf** Worn over the left
shoulder and under the right arm. A garland would
normally be worn on the head, and NS suggests that
Benedick is implying Claudio should either get rich
from Don Pedro's bounty, or challenge him to a duel
for the loss of Hero.
148 **drovier** cattle-dealer.
151–2 **blind man ... post** A neat fable of the

effect of anger. It may have a distant source in the
Spanish romance *Lazarillo de Tormes*, where the
rogue-hero in his youth is for a while guide to a blind
man.
154 **hurt ... sedges** Sedges grow in wet or boggy
ground near water, where the injured water-fowl is
imagined taking shelter from hunters.
155 **know ... not know me** 'recognise me, but
pretend not to', or – more likely from what follows –
'be acquainted with me, and yet have such a mistaken view as to call me the prince's fool'.
157–8 **base ... disposition** 'Base' can mean
'counterfeit' and 'disposition' 'placing': so 'by calling
me the prince's fool Beatrice puts me in a false position, and one that is bitter to me.' Such an interpretation (Hulme, p. 284) makes the common emendation to 'the base, the bitter' (Johnson), which is hard
to justify textually, unnecessary.
158 **puts ... person** states her own private
opinion as the general view.

Enter DON PEDRO

DON PEDRO Now, signor, where's the count, did you see him? 160

BENEDICK Troth, my lord, I have played the part of Lady Fame, I found
him here as melancholy as a lodge in a warren; I told him, and I think I
told him true, that your grace had got the good will of this young lady,
and I offered him my company to a willow tree, either to make him a
garland, as being forsaken, or to bind him up a rod, as being worthy to 165
be whipped.

DON PEDRO To be whipped: what's his fault?

BENEDICK The flat transgression of a schoolboy, who being overjoyed
with finding a bird's nest, shows it his companion, and he steals it.

DON PEDRO Wilt thou make a trust a transgression? The transgression is 170
in the stealer.

BENEDICK Yet it had not been amiss the rod had been made, and the
garland too, for the garland he might have worn himself, and the rod
he might have bestowed on you, who (as I take it) have stolen his
bird's nest. 175

DON PEDRO I will but teach them to sing, and restore them to the owner.

BENEDICK If their singing answer your saying, by my faith, you say
honestly.

DON PEDRO The Lady Beatrice hath a quarrel to you, the gentleman that
danced with her told her she is much wronged by you. 180

BENEDICK Oh she misused me past the endurance of a block: an oak but
with one green leaf on it, would have answered her: my very visor
began to assume life, and scold with her: she told me, not thinking I
had been myself, that I was the prince's jester, that I was duller than a

---

159 SD *Enter* DON PEDRO] *Enter the Prince.* F; *Enter the Prince, Hero, Leonato, Iohn and Borachio, and Conrade.* Q
162 think I told] Q; think, told F 163 good will] goodwill Q; will F 165 him up a rod] Q; him a rod F 184 jester,
that] Q; Iester, and that F

---

159 *SD The Q stage direction is clearly excessive;
F may also be defective. Capell and others have given
an entrance here for Leonato and Hero because of
Benedick's reference to '*this* young lady' (163) but in
that case they must stand aloof and not hear the
dialogue between Don Pedro and Benedick.
161 **Lady Fame** The personification of Rumour.
See *2H4*, Induction. The Latin *Fama* could mean
both 'good fame' and 'rumour'; a major source for
the figure is *Aeneid* IV, 173–90. Benedick's trope is
ironic against him, since in spite of his 'I think I told
him true' (162–3), he has given the same false report
that Don John gave maliciously.
162 **melancholy ... warren** The exact meaning
of this has not been explained, but Benedick's essential image, of a shelter for hunters in a large game

reserve, is of isolation which both induces and is a
symptom of melancholy. He found Claudio sulking
by himself.
165 **rod** A bundle of thin twigs, most commonly
birch, used to punish children.
166 **whipped** Still the term, in some old-fashioned
schools, for being beaten on the behind with a cane.
168 **transgression** A lover, as Claudio said,
should 'trust no agent' (135).
176 **sing** The song will be the acceptance of
Claudio's proposal of marriage.
180 **wronged** misrepresented, slandered.
184–5 **duller ... thaw** When roads would be
impassable with mud, skies overcast and fog frequent, and it was necessary to stay at home.

great thaw, huddling jest upon jest, with such impossible conveyance   185
upon me, that I stood like a man at a mark, with a whole army shooting
at me: she speaks poniards, and every word stabs: if her breath were
as terrible as her terminations, there were no living near her, she
would infect to the north star: I would not marry her, though she were
endowed with all that Adam had left him before he transgressed: she   190
would have made Hercules have turned spit, yea, and have cleft his
club to make the fire too: come, talk not of her, you shall find her the
infernal Ate in good apparel. I would to God some scholar would
conjure her, for certainly, while she is here, a man may live as quiet in
hell, as in a sanctuary, and people sin upon purpose, because they   195
would go thither, so indeed all disquiet, horror and perturbation
follows her.

Enter CLAUDIO *and* BEATRICE, LEONATO [*and*] HERO

DON PEDRO Look, here she comes.
BENEDICK Will your grace command me any service to the world's end? I
will go on the slightest errand now to the Antipodes that you can   200

188 as her terminations] Q; as terminations F   197 SD] F; *Enter Claudio and Beatrice* Q

185 **conveyance** dexterity; the 'conveyance' of a
shot could perhaps mean the distance it travelled: see
OED Convey 4b.
186–7 **man . . . me** 'In long distance or "flight"
shooting "it was common to have a marker, whose
business it was to show the shooter where the arrow
had fallen"' (NS). With 'a whole army shooting'
together this would be an impossible and a very
dangerous task.
187 **poniards** daggers.
188 **terminations** terms, epithets.
189 **north star** i.e. the outer limit of the universe.
The unmoving pole star marks the axis upon which
turn all the inner spheres of the Ptolemaic universe.
189 **marry her** Nobody else has suggested that he
should.
190 **Adam . . . transgressed** i.e. dominion over
the rest of creation – with perhaps the implication
that Eve was excluded, having 'transgressed' before
Adam did.
191–2 **Hercules . . . fire** To purge himself of guilt
for the death of Iphitus, Hercules became the slave
of Omphale, Queen of Lydia, for a year. She dressed
him in women's clothes and set him to spin, while
she took his club and lion skin: the classic instance of
the reversal of sex-roles. Benedick says that Beatrice
would have given him even more humiliating tasks.
The turnspit was the lowest of kitchen menials, while
the cleaving of the club is an image of de-sexing.
191 **have turned . . . have cleft** For these past
infinitives, see Abbott 360.

193 **Ate** The goddess of discord appears 'in good
apparel' with Duessa in *FQ*, IV, I, xvii, and there
follows a long account of her dwelling 'Hard by the
gates of hell' (stanza xx).
193–4 **some . . . her** Evil spirits respond to
learned languages. Marlowe's Doctor Faustus 'con-
jures' Mephistophilis in Latin (J. D. Jump (ed.), *Doctor Faustus*, 1962, scene iii, 16–24); Horatio is a fit
person to address the Ghost because he is 'a scholar'
(*Ham.* 1.1.42). Benedick wishes 'Ate' conjured *back*
to Hell, which is quiet as a sanctuary while she is
away (195).
197 *SD If the Folio direction is accepted (rather
than an earlier entry for Leonato and Hero with Don
Pedro at 159 above) it is still appropriate that
Beatrice and Claudio should enter separately from
Hero and Leonato, and preferably from a different
direction.
199–205 Benedick's offers of travel all involve
extreme distances and recall the fantasies in
Mandeville's *Travels*. The Antipodes – the people
whose feet are opposed to ours, not the place they
inhabit, which is the modern sense – were placed in
Ethiopia by John of Trevisa (*OED* Antipodes, first
quotation). It was also the legendary home of Prester
John, who, according to Marco Polo, died in battle
with Ghengis Khan. The Great Cham, Khubla
Khan, ruler of the Mongols, resided in East Asia, as
did, reputedly, the Pygmies. Toothpicks seem to
have been an affectation of travellers: 'your traveller,
/ He and his toothpick at my worship's mess' (*John*
1.1.189–90). Compare also *AWW* 1.1.158.

devise to send me on: I will fetch you a tooth-picker now from the
furthest inch of Asia: bring you the length of Prester John's foot: fetch
you a hair off the Great Cham's beard: do you any embassage to the
Pygmies, rather than hold three words conference with this Harpy:
you have no employment for me?   205

DON PEDRO None, but to desire your good company.

BENEDICK Oh God, sir, here's a dish I love not, I cannot endure my Lady
Tongue.   *Exit*

DON PEDRO Come, lady, come, you have lost the heart of Signor
Benedick.   210

BEATRICE Indeed, my lord, he lent it me a while, and I gave him use for it,
a double heart for his single one: marry once before he won it of me,
with false dice, therefore your grace may well say I have lost it.

DON PEDRO You have put him down, lady, you have put him down.

BEATRICE So I would not he should do me, my lord, lest I should prove   215
the mother of fools: I have brought Count Claudio, whom you sent
me to seek.

DON PEDRO Why how now, count, wherefore are you sad?

CLAUDIO Not sad, my lord.

DON PEDRO How then? Sick?   220

CLAUDIO Neither, my lord.

BEATRICE The count is neither sad, nor sick, nor merry, nor well: but
civil, count, civil as an orange, and something of that jealous
complexion.

DON PEDRO I'faith, lady, I think your blazon to be true, though I'll be   225

207–8 my Lady Tongue] Q; this Lady tongue F   212 his] Q; a F   223 of that] Q; of a F

---

204 Harpy In Greek mythology, a ravenous and
destructive bird with a beautiful woman's face. Dio-
nyza (*Per.* 4.3.46–7) is compared to a harpy with
angel's face and eagle's talons. Benedick's insult
involves a compliment to Beatrice's beauty.

211 use usury; she paid 100 per cent interest, two
hearts for one.

212–13 marry ... dice Beatrice is playing on the
idea of the lovers' exchange of hearts: she gave him
hers, but Benedick only lent his and then took it
back, consequently having two hearts. She lost his
heart because he cheated 'with false dice'. 'Once
before' is confusing, but probably means 'once
before the present occasion' to which Don Pedro
referred, not once before the time when Benedick
'lent' his heart.

215–16 So ... fools 'Put down' (214) as well as
meaning 'get the better of' could have the sense of
the modern slang 'lay'; Beatrice does not want to be
'laid' by Benedick, for if she got pregnant the child,
being his, would certainly be a fool. 'Fool' could,
probably mean 'bastard child': compare Polonius's

pun, 'Tender yourself more dearly, / Or ... you'll
tender me a fool' (*Ham.* 1.3.107–9).

223 civil as an orange Malvolio is 'sad and civil' –
grave and sober (*TN* 3.4.5). 'Civil' was a common
spelling of the time for Seville; the Seville orange is a
bitter orange or (according to Cotgrave under *Aigre-
douce*) 'between sweet and sour'. The pun wittily
sums up Claudio's downcast, angry but still respect-
ful manner, and then offers a diagnosis. NS pointed
out that Nashe had used the phrase in *Strange Newes*
(1592): 'For the order of my life, it is as civil as a civil
orange' (*Works*, I, 329).

223–4 jealous complexion Yellow is traditionally
the colour of jealousy, perhaps because of the association of melancholy with biliousness and jaundice.
Compare *WT* 2.3.104–8.

225 blazon description; perhaps from the techni-
cal sense in heraldry, but fairly frequent at this time
for the detailing of female beauty. Compare Sonnet
106.5–6: 'the blazon of sweet beauty's best, / Of
hand, of foot, of lip, of eye, of brow'.

sworn, if he be so, his conceit is false: here, Claudio, I have wooed in
thy name, and fair Hero is won: I have broke with her father, and his
good will obtained: name the day of marriage, and God give thee joy.

LEONATO Count, take of me my daughter, and with her my fortunes: his
grace hath made the match, and all grace say amen to it.   230

BEATRICE Speak, count, 'tis your cue.

CLAUDIO Silence is the perfectest herald of joy, I were but little happy if I
could say, how much! Lady, as you are mine, I am yours: I give away
myself for you, and dote upon the exchange.

BEATRICE Speak, cousin, or (if you cannot) stop his mouth with a kiss,   235
and let not him speak neither.

DON PEDRO In faith, lady, you have a merry heart.

BEATRICE Yea, my lord, I thank it, poor fool it keeps on the windy side of
care: my cousin tells him in his ear that he is in her heart.

CLAUDIO And so she doth, cousin.   240

BEATRICE Good Lord for alliance: thus goes every one to the world but I,
and I am sunburnt, I may sit in a corner and cry, 'Heigh ho for a
husband.'

DON PEDRO Lady Beatrice, I will get you one.

BEATRICE I would rather have one of your father's getting: hath your   245
grace ne'er a brother like you? Your father got excellent husbands, if a
maid could come by them.

DON PEDRO Will you have me, lady?

BEATRICE No, my lord, unless I might have another for working-days,

239 her] Q; my F   248, 252, 258, 265, 268, 273, 282, 285 SH DON PEDRO] *Prince* Q

226 **conceit** assumption.

230 **grace ... amen** The highest local worldly
power has made the match, and may be the source of all
grace approve it.

238 **poor fool** A deprecatory endearment: 'such
as it is'.

238 **windy side** upwind; thereby either avoiding
bad smells or, if the image is from sailing, having the
advantage, 'taking the wind out of the sails' of care.

241 **alliance** relations. Beatrice responds to
Claudio's pointed claim of relationship in calling her
'cousin' (240).

241 **goes ... world** everyone gets married. The
alternative was to retire from the world, enter the
church, and stay celibate. Compare *AYLI* 5.3.4–5
where Audrey desires 'to be a woman of the world'.

242 **sunburnt** unattractive. It was only with the
development of large-scale factory and office work
that a suntan came to indicate freedom from labour
(and therefore wealth) and became fashionable.
Compare 'The Grecian dames are sunburnt, and not
worth / The splinter of a lance' (*Tro.* 1.3.282–3).

242–3 **Heigh ... husband** Proverbial (Tilley
H833); also the title of a ballad, 'Hey ho for a
husband, or the married wives felicity', entry 1114 (4
April 1657) in H. E. Rollins, *An Analytical Index to the
Ballad-entries ... in the Registers of the Company of
Stationers*, SP 21 (1924), 98. Rollins gives a cross-
reference to a ballad with the same title in the Pepys
Collection, IV, 9.

245 **getting** begetting. Another of Beatrice's
'shrewd' puns; she can't wait until a son 'got' by Don
Pedro is old enough to marry. The joke is a bold one,
unless she has for the moment forgotten the
existence of Don John. It is also an invitation to the
prince to propose. Don Pedro responds (248) with
what is probably a jocular proposal. He reasserts his
willingness to marry Beatrice at 2.3.145, but as this is
in the process of gulling Benedick it is again
equivocal.

249–50 Beatrice sidesteps Don Pedro's question:
he is too good for her, like Sunday clothes on a
working day. But there is embarrassment in
Leonato's excuse (256) to get her out of the way.

your grace is too costly to wear every day: but I beseech your grace   250
pardon me, I was born to speak all mirth, and no matter.

DON PEDRO Your silence most offends me, and to be merry, best
becomes you, for out a question, you were born in a merry hour.

BEATRICE No sure, my lord, my mother cried, but then there was a star
danced, and under that was I born: cousins, God give you joy.   255

LEONATO Niece, will you look to those things I told you of?

BEATRICE I cry you mercy, uncle: by your grace's pardon.   *Exit*

DON PEDRO By my troth a pleasant spirited lady.

LEONATO There's little of the melancholy element in her, my lord, she is
never sad, but when she sleeps, and not ever sad then: for I have   260
heard my daughter say, she hath often dreamed of unhappiness, and
waked herself with laughing.

DON PEDRO She cannot endure to hear tell of a husband.

LEONATO Oh by no means, she mocks all her wooers out of suit.

DON PEDRO She were an excellent wife for Benedick.   265

LEONATO Oh Lord, my lord, if they were but a week married, they would
talk themselves mad.

DON PEDRO County Claudio, when mean you to go to church?

CLAUDIO Tomorrow, my lord: time goes on crutches, till love have all his
rites.   270

LEONATO Not till Monday, my dear son, which is hence a just seven-
night, and a time too brief too, to have all things answer my mind.

DON PEDRO Come, you shake the head at so long a breathing, but I

---

253 out a question] Q; out of question F   261 dreamed] dreampt Q; dreamt F   263 SH DON PEDRO] *Pedro* Q   271,
280 SH LEONATO] Q; *Leonata* F

251 **all ... matter** jokingly and never seriously.

254 **mother cried** i.e. in the pains of child-birth. It is part of Beatrice's essential seriousness and feminism that she insists on this.

254–5 **star danced** A piece of mock astrology: her horoscope (unlike Borachio's, 1.3.9) indicated a cheerful disposition.

257 **I ... pardon** An apology to her uncle, and a request to the prince for permission to leave.

259 **melancholy element** The melancholy humour was cold and dry and corresponded to the element Earth in the physiology of the time. The Dauphin's horse (like Cleopatra on her death-bed (*Ant.* 5.2.289)) is 'air and fire; and the dull elements of earth and water never appear in him' (*H5* 3.7.21–2).

260 **never ... then** only serious when she is asleep, and not always then.

261 **unhappiness** misfortune. Her spirit is so cheerful that she even wakes up laughing after bad dreams.

264 **out of suit** The legal, amatory and dress senses of this word are probably all involved. Beatrice claims (1.1.56) that Benedick changes his hat with every new fashion and we learn at 3.2.25 that he is a fancy dresser, and this may be the association, as well as Benedick's proclaimed misogyny, that prompts Don Pedro's proposal.

267 **themselves** each other.

268 **go to church** get married.

270 **rites** Hearers would not distinguish 'rites' from 'rights'; both would properly include the consummation of the marriage.

271 **son** Leonato anticipates the relationship that will follow the marriage; compare 240 above.

271–2 **a just seven-night** just a week. It is this remark that fixes firmly the time-scheme of the play: see Appendix 1, p. 154 below.

272 **answer my mind** be as I would wish them.

273 **breathing** pause.

warrant thee, Claudio, the time shall not go dully by us. I will in the
interim undertake one of Hercules' labours, which is, to bring Signor   275
Benedick and the Lady Beatrice into a mountain of affection, th'one
with th'other: I would fain have it a match, and I doubt not but to
fashion it, if you three will but minister such assistance as I shall give
you direction.

LEONATO My lord, I am for you, though it cost me ten nights' watchings.   280
CLAUDIO And I, my lord.
DON PEDRO And you too, gentle Hero?
HERO I will do any modest office, my lord, to help my cousin to a good
husband.

DON PEDRO And Benedick is not the unhopefullest husband that I know: 285
thus far can I praise him, he is of a noble strain, of approved valour,
and confirmed honesty. I will teach you how to humour your cousin,
that she shall fall in love with Benedick, and I, with your two helps,
will so practise on Benedick, that in despite of his quick wit, and his
queasy stomach, he shall fall in love with Beatrice: if we can do this,   290
Cupid is no longer an archer, his glory shall be ours, for we are the
only love-gods. Go in with me, and I will tell you my drift.

Exeunt

[2.2] *Enter* [DON] JOHN *and* BORACHIO

DON JOHN It is so, the Count Claudio shall marry the daughter of
Leonato.

---

292 SD *Exeunt*] *Exit.* Q   Act 2, Scene 2

275 **Hercules' labours** i.e. almost impossible
tasks.
276 **mountain of affection** Of the extended
Variorum commentary on this, Newcomer writes, '"a
mountain of affection" is only less familiar, not more
difficult of conception, than a "towering passion"'.
280 **ten ... watchings** ten nights without sleep.
The sense of supervision or spying is not involved.
283–4 Hero's affection for Beatrice is implied in
her reservations – '*modest* office', '*good* husband' –
and this obliges Don Pedro to modify his tone a little.
It is not a practical joke to provoke a mis-match.
285 **unhopefullest** most unpromising.
286 **noble strain** good family. Don Pedro also
means that Benedick has the disposition appropriate
to good breeding.
286 **approved** demonstrated.
287 **honesty** worth, honour.
287 **humour** play upon the idiosyncrasies of.

289 **practise on** persuade, work on; usually with
the sense of guile, and often of downright deceit.
290 **queasy** easily nauseated. 'Stomach' can mean
'courage' or 'disposition', so it is Benedick's rejection
of the idea of love that is in question.
292 **drift** plan; what I am driving at.

Act 2, Scene 2

0 SD The scene is unlocalised, and could be
imagined as being anywhere in Leonato's house or
garden; most editors give 'another room'. NS makes
the scenes continuous, and the SD reads 'they go
within, Hero on the arm of Claudio [2.2] Don John
and Borachio, coming from the banquet, meet them
in the door'. This neatly provides Don John with
evidence for his opening assertion. There is no
internal evidence that time has passed, or that it has
not.

BORACHIO Yea, my lord, but I can cross it.

DON JOHN Any bar, any cross, any impediment, will be medicinable to me, I am sick in displeasure to him, and whatsoever comes athwart his affection, ranges evenly with mine. How canst thou cross this marriage? 5

BORACHIO Not honestly, my lord, but so covertly, that no dishonesty shall appear in me.

DON JOHN Show me briefly how. 10

BORACHIO I think I told your lordship a year since, how much I am in the favour of Margaret, the waiting gentlewoman to Hero.

DON JOHN I remember.

BORACHIO I can at any unseasonable instant of the night, appoint her to look out at her lady's chamber window. 15

DON JOHN What life is in that to be the death of this marriage?

BORACHIO The poison of that lies in you to temper; go you to the prince your brother, spare not to tell him, that he hath wronged his honour in marrying the renowned Claudio, whose estimation do you mightily hold up, to a contaminated stale, such a one as Hero. 20

DON JOHN What proof shall I make of that?

BORACHIO Proof enough, to misuse the prince, to vex Claudio, to undo Hero, and kill Leonato; look you for any other issue?

DON JOHN Only to despite them I will endeavour anything.

BORACHIO Go then, find me a meet hour to draw Don Pedro and the 25 Count Claudio alone, tell them that you know that Hero loves me, intend a kind of zeal both to the prince and Claudio (as in love of your brother's honour who hath made this match, and his friend's reputation, who is thus like to be cozened with the semblance of a maid) that you have discovered thus: they will scarcely believe this without 30 trial: offer them instances which shall bear no less likelihood, than to

---

25 Don Pedro] don Pedro Q; on *Pedro* F   28 match,] match) Q   29 maid)] maid, Q

---

4 **medicinable** like medicine, curative.

5 **I . . . him** my dislike for him makes me sick.

5–6 **comes . . . affection** crosses his desires. The particular inclination is his affection for Hero. Compare 1.1.223.

6 **ranges evenly** runs parallel (opposed to 'athwart', 5).

11 **since** ago.

14 **appoint** make an appointment with. Borachio will not instruct or order Margaret.

17 **temper** mix, prepare.

19 **estimation** reputation.

20 **contaminated stale** corrupted prostitute. The sense of 'contaminated' is probably 'much handled'

rather than 'infected'. Compare Don Pedro's words at 4.1.58–9 below.

22 **misuse** abuse, deceive.

22 **vex** cause great distress to. The modern sense of the word is much weaker.

24 **despite** do malicious injury to.

25 **meet hour** appropriate time.

27 **intend** profess, pretend.

27 **as** to this effect. The long parenthesis beginning with 'as' is the motivation to be offered for Don John's pretended 'zeal'.

29 **cozened** cheated.

30 **discovered thus** made this disclosure.

31 **instances** proofs.

see me at her chamber window, hear me call Margaret Hero, hear
Margaret term me Claudio, and bring them to see this the very night
before the intended wedding, for in the mean time, I will so fashion
the matter, that Hero shall be absent, and there shall appear such   35
seeming truth of Hero's disloyalty, that jealousy shall be called
assurance, and all the preparation overthrown.

DON JOHN Grow this to what adverse issue it can, I will put it in practice:
be cunning in the working this, and thy fee is a thousand ducats.

BORACHIO Be you constant in the accusation, and my cunning shall not   40
shame me.

DON JOHN I will presently go learn their day of marriage.

Exeunt

[2.3] *Enter* BENEDICK *alone*

BENEDICK Boy.

BOY [*within*] Signor.

[*Enter* BOY]

BENEDICK In my chamber window lies a book, bring it hither to me in
the orchard.

BOY I am here already, sir.   5

BENEDICK I know that, but I would have thee hence and here again.

Exit [*Boy*]

---

33 Margaret term] F; Marg.terme Q   36 truth] Q; truths F   40 you] Q; thou F   42 SD *Exeunt*] *Exit.* Q   Act 2, Scene 3

---

33 Claudio This has puzzled editors, for if
Claudio heard Hero call another man 'Claudio, he
might reasonably think her betrayed, but he could
not have the same reason to accuse her of disloyalty'
(Theobald, who proposed to emend 'Claudio' to
'Borachio'). A complex explanation is that Claudio
would assume that he was being mocked as well as
betrayed, 'the baseness of treachery . . . aggravated
by the wantonness of insult' (Mason). In performance there is no time to cogitate subtleties of interpretation, and the problem hardly arises, but the
simplest account is probably that 'Borachio wheedled
Margaret into playing with him at a scene between
the other lovers' (Dyce). (All from Furness.)

36 jealousy suspicion.

37 assurance certainty.

39 the working this Modern usage would be 'the
working of this' or simply 'working this'; see Abbott
93.

42 presently at once.

Act 2, Scene 3

0 SD Editors have taken Benedick's word for it (4)
that the location is Antonio's or Leonato's orchard
(see 1.2.8). The 'arbour' where Benedick hides from
the prince and his companions is required later in
the scene. Perhaps some kind of property hedge was
used, though it is possible that Benedick used the
stage pillars as concealment: see illustrations 1 and 3,
pp. 7 and 9 above.

5 here already The boy's statement means that
he will be back immediately. Benedick (6) takes him
literally, in fun. There is no Q SD for his return and in
some productions he is given a nice business of producing the book from his pocket to cap Benedick's
response.

I do much wonder, that one man seeing how much another man is a
fool, when he dedicates his behaviours to love, will after he hath
laughed at such shallow follies in others, become the argument of
his own scorn, by falling in love: and such a man is Claudio. I have   10
known when there was no music with him but the drum and the fife,
and now had he rather hear the tabor and the pipe: I have known
when he would have walked ten mile afoot, to see a good armour,
and now will he lie ten nights awake carving the fashion of a new
doublet: he was wont to speak plain and to the purpose (like an   15
honest man and a soldier) and now is he turned orthography, his
words are a very fantastical banquet, just so many strange dishes:
may I be so converted and see with these eyes? I cannot tell, I think
not: I will not be sworn but love may transform me to an oyster, but
I'll take my oath on it, till he have made an oyster of me, he shall   20
never make me such a fool: one woman is fair, yet I am well: another
is wise, yet I am well: another virtuous, yet I am well: but till all
graces be in one woman, one woman shall not come in my grace:
rich she shall be, that's certain: wise, or I'll none: virtuous, or I'll
never cheapen her: fair, or I'll never look on her: mild, or come not   25
near me: noble, or not I for an angel: of good discourse, an excellent
musician – and her hair shall be of what colour it please God. Hah!
the prince and Monsieur Love, I will hide me in the arbour.

Enter DON PEDRO, LEONATO, CLAUDIO [*and* BALTHASAR *with*] *music*

27 God.] God, Q   28 SD DON PEDRO] *prince* Q   28 SD *music*] *Musicke* Q; *and Iacke Wilson* F; *after 34* Q *has / Enter Balthaser with musicke.*

8 behaviours The various different ways in which
he shows that he is in love.
9 argument subject.
11 drum ... fife Military music.
12 tabor ... pipe A small hand-drum and a
three-stopped whistle; popular instruments used at
fairs and festivals and particularly associated with
fools, as in *TN* 3.1. For the force of the comparison,
compare *R3*, 1.1.24: 'this weak piping time of peace'.
13 armour suit of armour.
14 carving designing.
15 doublet A close-fitting body-garment.
16 orthography A synecdoche for 'orthographer',
one concerned with refined and elaborate language.
18 may ... converted can I be so transformed?
19 oyster Perhaps the typical lover's moody
silence is what Benedick has in mind. 'Shut me up
like a clam' (Humphreys).

21 well content.
23 graces ... grace Beauty, virtue and wisdom
were the gifts of the three Graces. Benedick puns on
the sense of grace meaning 'good will'.
25 cheapen bargain for.
26 noble ... angel A common pun on the names
of coins: the noble was one-third, and the angel one-
half the value of a pound. 'If she were not noble ...
he would not give 10s. [50p] for her, and if she were
worth only 6s. 8d. [33p] he would not have her though
she were an angel' (Furness).
27 what ... God Her hair must be her own, and
not dyed, and he expresses no preference.
28 *SD* F's rationalisation of Q's two stage directions, and substitution of 'Iacke Wilson' for Balthasar
clearly suggests a theatrical source for the change.
See supplementary note, p. 146 below.

DON PEDRO Come, shall we hear this music?

CLAUDIO Yea, my good lord: how still the evening is,   30
    As hushed on purpose to grace harmony!

DON PEDRO See you where Benedick hath hid himself?

CLAUDIO Oh very well, my lord: the music ended,
    We'll fit the kid-fox with a pennyworth.

DON PEDRO Come, Balthasar, we'll hear that song again.   35

BALTHASAR Oh, good my lord, tax not so bad a voice,
    To slander music any more than once.

DON PEDRO It is the witness still of excellency,
    To put a strange face on his own perfection:
    I pray thee sing, and let me woo no more.   40

BALTHASAR Because you talk of wooing I will sing,
    Since many a wooer doth commence his suit,
    To her he thinks not worthy, yet he woos,
    Yet will he swear he loves.

DON PEDRO   Nay, pray thee come,
    Or if thou wilt hold longer argument,   45
    Do it in notes.

BALTHASAR   Note this before my notes,
    There's not a note of mine that's worth the noting.

DON PEDRO Why these are very crotchets that he speaks,
    Note notes forsooth, and nothing.

                [Music]

BENEDICK Now divine air, now is his soul ravished: is it not strange that   50
    sheep's guts should hale souls out of men's bodies? Well, a horn for
    my money when all's done.

---

29 SH DON PEDRO] *Prince* Q *(and throughout scene)*

34 fit . . . pennyworth give Benedick more than
he bargains for. 'Kid-fox' has not been satisfactorily
explained. Some editors (following Warburton)
emend to 'hid-fox' and make the reference to a children's game as in *Ham.* 4.2.30, 'Hide fox, and all
after.' 'Kid' could be the past participle of the
obsolete 'kithe', to make known, and would contrast
strongly with 'hid' (32). The kid-fox thinks he is hid,
but he is kid (= has been seen).

36 tax task.

38–9 The highly skilled are inclined to denigrate
their own performance.

41 you Balthasar uses the polite 'you' in response
to the prince's familiar 'thee'.

41–4 Balthasar continues to dispraise himself, by
suggesting that the prince only 'woos' out of
courtesy.

46–9 Several senses of 'note' are played on here:

notes of music, brief comments, and the verbal sense
of 'take notice of'. 'Not' and 'nothing' (with the 'th'
pronounced 't' as it commonly was, as various puns
and rhymes make clear) are also involved. Don
Pedro gets a little bored with the game: crotchets are
(1) notes one-quarter of the value of the semi-breve
and (2) quibbles, odd fancies.

50 divine . . . ravished Benedick's language suggests mockery, and the whole passage gives an
impression that Balthasar is conceited and affected –
and not a very good singer.

51 hale haul.

51–2 horn . . . money 'I'd rather follow the hunting horn than listen to fancy singing.' For the
audience this is another cuckold joke, anticipating
'Benedick the married man'. 'The audience certainly
laughed at this line the *second* time they saw the play'
(A. P. Rossiter, *Angel with Horns*, 1961, p. 69).

The Song

[BALTHASAR] Sigh no more, ladies, sigh no more,
          Men were deceivers ever,
          One foot in sea, and one on shore,   55
          To one thing constant never.
          Then sigh not so, but let them go,
          And be you blithe and bonny,
          Converting all your sounds of woe,
          Into hey nonny nonny.   60

          Sing no more ditties, sing no mo,
          Of dumps so dull and heavy,
          The fraud of men was ever so,
          Since summer first was leavy.
          Then sigh not so, but let them go,   65
          And be you blithe and bonny,
          Converting all your sounds of woe,
          Into hey nonny nonny.

DON PEDRO By my troth a good song.

BALTHASAR And an ill singer, my lord.   70

DON PEDRO Ha, no no faith, thou sing'st well enough for a shift.

BENEDICK And he had been a dog that should have howled thus, they
     would have hanged him: and I pray God his bad voice bode no
     mischief, I had as lief have heard the night-raven, come what plague
     could have come after it.   75

DON PEDRO Yea marry, dost thou hear, Balthasar? I pray thee get us

---

65–8] Then sigh not so, & c. Q   72 been] F; bin Q   74 lief] F; live Q

53–68 Peter Warlock (pseudonym of Philip
Heseltine) published a setting of a version of this
song by Thomas Ford (?1580–1648) from a MS. in
Christ Church, Oxford: *Four English Songs of the
Early Seventeenth Century*, 1925. There is an extra
line, following and rhyming with the first, in each
stanza, and of three in Ford's version, only the first
stanza corresponds to the song here (Seng, pp. 58–
60), so it was probably not the tune used originally in
Much Ado. Manifold (p. 163) notes that 'Morley
wrote a wordless air for three voices which fits the
lyrics' and suggests it could be used in productions.
'It is among the sight-reading exercises in the first
part of *A Plain and Easy Introduction to Practical Music*'
(1597).
  58 blithe and bonny cheerful and carefree. The
general sense of 'bonny' is 'having the appearance of

good health' – so, as 'care's an enemy to life' (*TN*
1.3.2), to be bonny is a consequence of being blithe.
  61 mo more in number (*OED* sv *adj.* 2), *pace*
Stanley Wells, who writes 'I think "Sing no more
ditties, sing no mo" looks ridiculous' (*Spelling*, p. 17).
'Mo' is the comparative of 'many'.
  62 dumps (1) sad moods, (2) melancholy tunes,
(3) dismal dances; compare *TGV* 3.2.84: 'Tune a
deploring dump'.
  71 shift makeshift, when there's nothing better.
  74 night-raven Bird with a harsh cry uttered at
night, most probably the nightjar. If the raven is
ominous (*Mac* 1.5.38–9) the night-raven is worse.
  76 Yea marry This and Don Pedro's previous
speech are discontinuous. We must assume some
business in the prince's party while Benedick speaks.

some excellent music: for tomorrow night we would have it at the
Lady Hero's chamber window.

BALTHASAR The best I can, my lord.

DON PEDRO Do so, farewell. 80

Exit Balthasar

Come hither, Leonato, what was it you told me of today, that your
niece Beatrice was in love with Signor Benedick?

CLAUDIO Oh aye, stalk on, stalk on, the fowl sits. I did never think that
lady would have loved any man.

LEONATO No nor I neither, but most wonderful, that she should so dote 85
on Signor Benedick, whom she hath in all outward behaviours
seemed ever to abhor.

BENEDICK Is't possible? Sits the wind in that corner?

LEONATO By my troth, my lord, I cannot tell what to think of it, but that
she loves him with an enraged affection, it is past the infinite of 90
thought.

DON PEDRO May be she doth but counterfeit.

CLAUDIO Faith like enough.

LEONATO Oh God! Counterfeit? There was never counterfeit of passion, came so near the life of passion as she discovers it. 95

DON PEDRO Why what effects of passion shows she?

CLAUDIO Bait the hook well, this fish will bite.

LEONATO What effects, my lord? She will sit you – you heard my
daughter tell you how.

CLAUDIO She did indeed. 100

DON PEDRO How, how, I pray you! You amaze me, I would have
thought her spirit had been invincible against all assaults of
affection.

83 Oh aye] O I Q

---

77 **tomorrow night** We hear no more of this
serenade, and it is assumed sometimes (e.g. by Furness and Trenery) that it is for the night before the
wedding, arranged 'a just seven-night' hence in
2.1.271. Though time indications are vague there is
no necessary conflict: see Appendix 1, p. 154 below.
Long suggests that this music was intended for the
wedding night, and notes the irony of the substitution of the dirge in 5.3, but that is to make all the
events before 3.4 come in the same day as this scene,
which begins at evening (30) even if it ends at 'dinner' time (173).

83 **stalk ... sits** keep on stalking, our quarry is a
sitting duck.

88 **Sits ... corner?** Is that the way the wind

blows? Commonly 'quarter' for 'corner' (Tilley
W419).

90–1 **it ... thought** it's unbelievable (but true).
This phrase can qualify either the assertion that
Beatrice loves Benedick or the degree of her 'enraged affection' (= aroused passion); or it can qualify
both.

95 **life ... it** reality of passion as she displays it.

98 **will sit you** The future-tense form is used for
repeated action in the past; so at 115. 'You' is an
ethical dative; it invites the hearer's attention and
interest. Or possibly 'you' is a repetition, indicating a
pause and the temporary drying-up of Leonato's
invention.

LEONATO I would have sworn it had, my lord, especially against Benedick.

BENEDICK I should think this a gull, but that the white-bearded fellow speaks it: knavery cannot sure hide himself in such reverence.

CLAUDIO He hath ta'en th'infection, hold it up.

DON PEDRO Hath she made her affection known to Benedick?

LEONATO No, and swears she never will, that's her torment.

CLAUDIO 'Tis true indeed, so your daughter says: shall I, says she, that have so oft encountered him with scorn, write to him that I love him?

LEONATO This says she now when she is beginning to write to him, for she'll be up twenty times a night, and there will she sit in her smock, till she have writ a sheet of paper: my daughter tells us all.

CLAUDIO Now you talk of a sheet of paper, I remember a pretty jest your daughter told us of.

LEONATO Oh when she had writ it, and was reading it over, she found Benedick and Beatrice between the sheet.

CLAUDIO That.

LEONATO Oh she tore the letter into a thousand halfpence, railed at herself, that she should be so immodest to write to one that she knew would flout her: I measure him, says she, by my own spirit, for I should flout him, if he writ to me, yea, though I love him I should.

CLAUDIO Then down upon her knees she falls, weeps, sobs, beats her heart, tears her hair, prays, curses, Oh sweet Benedick, God give me patience.

LEONATO She doth indeed, my daughter says so, and the ecstasy hath so much overborn her, that my daughter is sometime afeared she will do a desperate outrage to herself, it is very true.

DON PEDRO It were good that Benedick knew of it by some other, if she will not discover it.

CLAUDIO To what end? He would make but a sport of it, and torment the poor lady worse.

DON PEDRO And he should, it were an alms to hang him: she's an excellent sweet lady, and (out of all suspicion) she is virtuous.

105

110

115

120

125

130

135

118 us of] F; of us Q   134 make but] Q; but make F

106 **gull** trick, deception.

108 **hold it up** keep it going.

115 **smock** slip. The smock was the basic linen undergarment, and Beatrice would probably sleep in hers, or sleep naked and put it on when she got up to write her letter.

120 **between the sheet** in bed. Some editions

following Capell read 'sheet?', so that Leonato asks Claudio 'is that the joke you mean?'

122 **halfpence** tiny pieces. The halfpenny was a small silver coin.

132 **some other** someone else.

136 **And he should** If he did.

136 **alms** good deed; hanging would be too good for him.

CLAUDIO And she is exceeding wise.

DON PEDRO In everything but in loving Benedick.

LEONATO Oh my lord, wisdom and blood combating in so tender a   140
body, we have ten proofs to one, that blood hath the victory: I am
sorry for her, as I have just cause, being her uncle, and her
guardian.

DON PEDRO I would she had bestowed this dotage on me, I would have
daffed all other respects, and made her half myself: I pray you tell   145
Benedick of it, and hear what a will say.

LEONATO Were it good, think you?

CLAUDIO Hero thinks surely she will die, for she says she will die, if he
love her not, and she will die ere she make her love known, and she
will die if he woo her, rather than she will bate one breath of her   150
accustomed crossness.

DON PEDRO She doth well: if she should make tender of her love, 'tis
very possible he'll scorn it, for the man (as you know all) hath a
contemptible spirit.

CLAUDIO He is a very proper man.   155

DON PEDRO He hath indeed a good outward happiness.

CLAUDIO Before God, and in my mind, very wise.

DON PEDRO He doth indeed show some sparks that are like wit.

LEONATO And I take him to be valiant.

DON PEDRO As Hector, I assure you, and in the managing of quarrels   160
you may say he is wise, for either he avoids them with great discre-
tion, or undertakes them with a most christianlike fear.

LEONATO If he do fear God, a must necessarily keep peace: if he break
the peace, he ought to enter into a quarrel with fear and trembling.

145 daffed] daft Q   146 a] Q; he F   157 Before] Q; 'Fore F   159 SH LEONATO] F; *Claudio* Q   161 say] Q; see
F   162 with a most] Q; with a F

140 **blood** passion.

143 **guardian** The clearest indication in the play
that Beatrice is an orphan.

145 **daffed ... respects** put aside other con-
siderations. Compare 2.1.248. There are two major
'respects': the prince's superior rank, and the
absence of any evidence that Beatrice is an heiress.

150 **bate** abate, give up.

151 **crossness** contrariness.

152 **tender** offer. Now usually restricted to commercial contexts.

154 **contemptible** contemptuous.

155 **proper** good-looking, elegant.

156 **good outward happiness** fine external
appearance and behaviour.

157 **Before God** A strong affirmation.

157, 158 **wise, wit** Wit and wisdom are not
synonymous. Wisdom is what the proper exercise of
wit achieves, as in the morality play *The Marriage of
Wit and Wisdom*. The prince's reply is a limiting one
– 'Well, he's quite bright.'

159 SH *LEONATO This question comes more
naturally from Leonato (F) than from Claudio (Q)
who has just returned from a military campaign with
Benedick.

160–5 Don Pedro begins to carry the joke to a
point of mockery of Benedick that endangers the
success of the plot, then realises his error and with
'the man doth fear God' corrects it.

DON PEDRO And so will he do, for the man doth fear God, howsoever it   165
 seems not in him, by some large jests he will make: well, I am sorry
 for your niece: shall we go seek Benedick, and tell him of her love?

CLAUDIO Never tell him, my lord, let her wear it out with good counsel.

LEONATO Nay that's impossible, she may wear her heart out first.

DON PEDRO Well, we will hear further of it by your daughter, let it cool   170
 the while: I love Benedick well, and I could wish he would modestly
 examine himself, to see how much he is unworthy so good a lady.

LEONATO My lord, will you walk? Dinner is ready.

CLAUDIO If he do not dote on her upon this, I will never trust my
 expectation.   175

DON PEDRO Let there be the same net spread for her, and that must
 your daughter and her gentlewomen carry: the sport will be, when
 they hold one an opinion of another's dotage, and no such matter:
 that's the scene that I would see, which will be merely a dumb show:
 let us send her to call him in to dinner.   180

[Exeunt all but Benedick]

BENEDICK This can be no trick, the conference was sadly borne, they
 have the truth of this from Hero, they seem to pity the lady: it seems
 her affections have their full bent: love me? Why, it must be
 requited: I hear how I am censured, they say I will bear myself
 proudly, if I perceive the love come from her: they say too, that she   185
 will rather die than give any sign of affection: I did never think to
 marry, I must not seem proud, happy are they that hear their detrac-
 tions, and can put them to mending: they say the lady is fair, 'tis a
 truth, I can bear them witness: and virtuous, 'tis so, I cannot reprove
 it: and wise, but for loving me: by my troth it is no addition to her   190
 wit, nor no great argument of her folly, for I will be horribly in love

---

167 seek] Q; see F   172 unworthy so] Q; unworthy to have so F   183 have their] Q; have the F

166 **large** gross.

168 **wear ... counsel** endure and overcome it
with wise reflection. 'Counsel' here is probably
reflexive – 'her own thoughts'.

173 **Dinner** The main midday meal for
Elizabethans, but the scene begins in the evening
(30): a minor inconsistency.

174 **upon** (1) after, (2) a consequence of.

174–5 **never ... expectation** never believe that I
can correctly predict anything.

176 **net** An image, like 'stalk' (83), from hunting
birds.

177 **carry** manage, carry out.

178 **they ... dotage** each of them thinks the other
madly in love.

179 **merely a dumb show** A dumb show because
both, in contrast to their usual garrulity, would be
tongue-tied. 'Merely' can have its modern limiting
sense of 'nothing more than', but can also mean
'absolutely, entirely' – 'an absolute pantomime'.

181 **sadly borne** seriously carried on.

183 **have their full bent** are strained to the limit.
A bow has 'full bent' when the string is drawn back
until the head of the arrow touches the bow.

184 **censured** judged; without the usual modern
connotation of 'unfavourably'.

189 **reprove** (1) disprove, (2) deny.

with her: I may chance have some odd quirks and remnants of wit
broken on me, because I have railed so long against marriage: but
doth not the appetite alter? A man loves the meat in his youth, that
he cannot endure in his age. Shall quips and sentences, and these   195
paper bullets of the brain awe a man from the career of his humour?
No, the world must be peopled. When I said I would die a bachelor,
I did not think I should live till I were married – here comes
Beatrice: by this day, she's a fair lady, I do spy some marks of love in
her.   200

Enter BEATRICE

BEATRICE Against my will I am sent to bid you come in to dinner.
BENEDICK Fair Beatrice, I thank you for your pains.
BEATRICE I took no more pains for those thanks, than you took pains to
    thank me, if it had been painful I would not have come.
BENEDICK You take pleasure then in the message.   205
BEATRICE Yea, just so much as you may take upon a knife's point, and
    choke a daw withal: you have no stomach, signor, fare you well. *Exit*
BENEDICK Ha, against my will I am sent to bid you come in to dinner:
    there's a double meaning in that: I took no more pains for those
    thanks than you take pains to thank me: that's as much as to say, any   210
    pains that I take for you is as easy as thanks: if I do not take pity of
    her I am a villain, if I do not love her I am a Jew, I will go get her
    picture.   *Exit*

---

204 been] F; bin Q   206 knife's] knives Q

192 **odd quirks** left-over jokes. 'Odd' has much
the same force as 'remnants'; what is left-over after
the distribution of significant items.

194 **meat** food.

195 **sentences** wise sayings.

196 **paper ... brain** Paper bullets would be
harmless. 'Paper' because borrowed from books;
'bullets of the brain' because a wit-combat is seen as
a duel with guns.

196 **career** course. In horsemanship a 'career' is a
swift short gallop with check and turn. Compare
5.1.129.

202 Benedick's first response to Beatrice makes a
line of verse.

207 **daw** jackdaw.

207 **stomach** appetite.

209 **double meaning** Beatrice appears to have
left no scope for ambiguity – which improves the
comedy of the line in the theatre: perhaps Benedick
wishes to read 'against her will' as meaning that she
does not want him to come in, but rather to stay out
in the garden with her. He proceeds to find a 'double
meaning' in her following words, which are perhaps
what 'that' refers to.

3.[1] *Enter* HERO *and two gentlewomen,* MARGARET *and* URSULA

HERO Good Margaret, run thee to the parlour,
     There shalt thou find my cousin Beatrice,
     Proposing with the prince and Claudio,
     Whisper her ear and tell her I and Ursley
     Walk in the orchard, and our whole discourse   5
     Is all of her, say that thou overheard'st us,
     And bid her steal into the pleachèd bower,
     Where honeysuckles ripened by the sun,
     Forbid the sun to enter: like favourites,
     Made proud by princes, that advance their pride,   10
     Against that power that bred it: there will she hide her,
     To listen our propose: this is thy office,
     Bear thee well in it, and leave us alone.
MARGARET I'll make her come I warrant you, presently.   *Exit*
HERO Now, Ursula, when Beatrice doth come,   15
     As we do trace this alley up and down,
     Our talk must only be of Benedick:
     When I do name him, let it be thy part,
     To praise him more than ever man did merit:
     My talk to thee must be how Benedick   20
     Is sick in love with Beatrice: of this matter

Act 3, Scene 1   3.1] *Actus Tertius* F; *not in* Q   0 SD *gentlewomen*] Q; *Gentlemen* F   0 SD URSULA] F; *Ursley* Q   4
Ursley] Q; *Ursula* F   12 propose:] propose, Q; *purpose* F

Act 3, Scene 1

0 SD The imaginary location is the same as 2.3, and we may assume the same property arbour, if there was one, was used (see 2.3.0 n. above). As there is a clear time-break (dinner at least is over) it is possible that an interval could have been given – in performances on appropriate occasions – at this point. An interval with no change of scene seems to be indicated in *MND* in the Folio stage direction at the end of 3.2, *They sleep all the act* – though Foakes in his edition (1984, pp. 141–3) is sceptical of this interpretation.

1 **parlour** In a great house like Leonato's, a small room used by the family and familiar guests for conversation.

3 **Proposing** Conversing.

4 **Ursley** The familiar pronunciation of Ursula.

7 **pleachèd bower** Compare 1.2.8.

8–11 Hero is a properly educated young lady, and finds a 'sentence' (2.3.195) from her copy-book for the metaphor. It does not seem (to me) likely that Shakespeare intended any specific contemporary reference. Furnivall thought it a reference to the Essex rebellion, and got over the problem of the dates of staying and entry in the Stationers' Register by making it a late two-line addition that could be inserted without any disturbance of the pre-existing lines.

8 **honeysuckles** This name and woodbine (3.1.30) are used both for the same plant, and for a variety of different plants. At *MND* 4.1.42 woodbine and honeysuckle must be distinct plants, but here are the same, and, almost certainly, what we now know as honeysuckle: *Lonicera periclymenum*.

12 *propose Compare 3 above. The word is an unusual one, and the F compositor's substitution of 'purpose' is not unlikely. 'Propose' usually has a more formal or logical sense than here, equivalent to 'proposition'.

14 **presently** at once.

Is little Cupid's crafty arrow made,
That only wounds by hearsay: now begin,

Enter BEATRICE

For look where Beatrice like a lapwing runs
Close by the ground, to hear our conference.   25
URSULA The pleasant'st angling is to see the fish
    Cut with her golden oars the silver stream,
    And greedily devour the treacherous bait:
    So angle we for Beatrice, who even now,
    Is couchèd in the woodbine coverture: 30
    Fear you not my part of the dialogue.
HERO Then go we near her, that her ear lose nothing
    Of the false sweet bait that we lay for it:
    No truly, Ursula, she is too disdainful,
    I know her spirits are as coy and wild,   35
    As haggards of the rock.
URSULA   But are you sure,
    That Benedick loves Beatrice so entirely?
HERO So says the prince, and my new trothèd lord.
URSULA And did they bid you tell her of it, madam?
HERO They did entreat me to acquaint her of it,   40
    But I persuaded them, if they loved Benedick,
    To wish him wrestle with affection,
    And never to let Beatrice know of it.
URSULA Why did you so? Doth not the gentleman
    Deserve as full as fortunate a bed,   45
    As ever Beatrice shall couch upon?
HERO Oh God of love! I know he doth deserve,
    As much as may be yielded to a man:
    But nature never framed a woman's heart
    Of prouder stuff than that of Beatrice: 50
    Disdain and scorn ride sparkling in her eyes,

---

23 SD] *At 25 in* Q

23 only wounds by hearsay wounds by hearsay alone.

24–5 Beatrice perhaps moves with a bobbing motion, sometimes seen, sometimes concealed, and this reminds Hero of the motion of the lapwing attempting to distract predators from its nest.

24 lapwing The peewit, *Vanellus vulgaris*, a common ground-nesting plover.

30 woodbine See 8 n. above.

35 coy disdainful.

36 haggards A haggard is a female hawk that has grown to maturity in the wild, and is consequently much more difficult to train for hawking than one reared by hand. Compare 3.1.112 below.

44–6 Doesn't Benedick deserve a wife at least as good as Beatrice?

Misprising what they look on, and her wit
Values itself so highly, that to her
All matter else seems weak: she cannot love,
Nor take no shape nor project of affection,   55
She is so self-endeared.

URSULA   Sure I think so,
And therefore certainly it were not good,
She knew his love, lest she'll make sport at it.

HERO Why you speak truth, I never yet saw man,
How wise, how noble, young, how rarely featured,   60
But she would spell him backward: if fair-faced,
She would swear the gentleman should be her sister:
If black, why Nature drawing of an antic,
Made a foul blot: if tall, a lance ill-headed:
If low, an agate very vilely cut: 65
If speaking, why a vane blown with all winds:
If silent, why a block moved with none:
So turns she every man the wrong side out,
And never gives to truth and virtue, that
Which simpleness and merit purchaseth.   70

URSULA Sure, sure, such carping is not commendable.

HERO No, not to be so odd, and from all fashions,
As Beatrice is, cannot be commendable:
But who dare tell her so? If I should speak,
She would mock me into air, oh she would laugh me   75
Out of myself, press me to death with wit:

---

56 self-endeared] *Rowe;* selfe indeared Q   60 featured,] *Rowe;* featured. Q   65 vilely] vildly Q

52 Misprising Condemning, despising.

55 'Her mind will not receive the form or even the notion of love.' 'Project' is more vague and distant than 'shape'.

56 self-endeared in love with herself.

60 How However.

61 spell him backward misrepresent him, taking everything the wrong way. It is possibly connected with witchcraft, where the Lord's Prayer spoken backwards could raise the devil.

63 black dark-complexioned.

63 antic grotesque figure.

65 agate Small figures were cut into agate-stones for seal-rings. Compare *Rom.* 1.4.55–6: 'In shape no bigger than an agot-stone / On the forefinger of an alderman'.

66 vane weathercock.

70 purchaseth gains by merit. 'Purchase' was not

restricted to commercial transactions in Shakespeare's day. For the singular verb with conjoined subjects see Abbott 336.

71 commendable Elizabethans would probably have stressed the first syllable.

72–3 No, not ... cannot This accumulation of negatives exercised earlier editors, but the sense is clear and the speech admirably follows the movement of Hero's mind.

75 mock me into air reduce me to nothing.

75–6 laugh ... myself laugh at me so that I am unable to reply.

76 press me to death This was the punishment for persons accused of a felony who refused to plead. Aldis Wright suggests Hero's thought is that she will be first reduced to silence and then blamed for not speaking.

Therefore let Benedick like covered fire,
Consume away in sighs, waste inwardly:
It were a better death, than die with mocks,
Which is as bad as die with tickling.   80

URSULA Yet tell her of it, hear what she will say.

HERO No rather I will go to Benedick,
And counsel him to fight against his passion,
And truly I'll devise some honest slanders,
To stain my cousin with, one doth not know   85
How much an ill word may empoison liking.

URSULA Oh do not do your cousin such a wrong,
She cannot be so much without true judgement,
Having so swift and excellent a wit,
As she is prized to have, as to refuse   90
So rare a gentleman as Signor Benedick.

HERO He is the only man of Italy,
Always excepted my dear Claudio.

URSULA I pray you be not angry with me, madam,
Speaking my fancy: Signor Benedick,   95
For shape, for bearing, argument and valour,
Goes foremost in report through Italy.

HERO Indeed he hath an excellent good name.

URSULA His excellence did earn it, ere he had it:
When are you married, madam?   100

HERO Why every day tomorrow: come go in,
I'll show thee some attires, and have thy counsel,
Which is the best to furnish me tomorrow.

URSULA She's limed I warrant you, we have caught her, madam.

---

79 death, than] Q; death, to F   104 limed] Q; tane F   104] Pope; Q makes a fresh line at we

---

77–8 Therefore ... inwardly Benedick must conceal his passion: his fire must be covered and damped down. It will continue to burn unseen and the interior of the fire will turn to ash and 'waste'. For the consumptive effect of the lover's sighs, see 1.1.185 above.

84 honest slanders There could be no suggestion that Beatrice was not virtuous. When Polonius sends Reynaldo to spy on Laertes in Paris, he advises him to invent 'forgeries' about his misbehaviour, but 'none so rank / As may dishonour him' (*Ham.* 2.1.20–1).

90 prized esteemed.

96 argument power of reason.

101 every day tomorrow After tomorrow I shall be a married woman all the time. 'This reply is a levity, indicating her raised spirits; they are quickly to have a tumble' (Capell).

102 attires head-dresses.

104 *limed Small birds were caught by coating twigs with bird-lime, a sticky substance derived from holly bark. The continuation of the hunting and fowling imagery of this and the previous scene makes it seem probable that F's 'tane' (taken) is a compositor's simplification.

HERO If it prove so, then loving goes by haps,   105
          Some Cupid kills with arrows, some with traps.

                                        Exeunt Hero and Ursula

BEATRICE What fire is in mine ears? Can this be true?
          Stand I condemned for pride and scorn so much?
          Contempt, farewell, and maiden pride, adieu,
          No glory lives behind the back of such.   110
          And Benedick, love on, I will requite thee,
          Taming my wild heart to thy loving hand:
          If thou dost love, my kindness shall incite thee
          To bind our loves up in a holy band,
          For others say thou dost deserve, and I   115
          Believe it better than reportingly.   *Exit*

[3.2] *Enter* DON PEDRO, CLAUDIO, BENEDICK *and* LEONATO

DON PEDRO I do but stay till your marriage be consummate, and then
      go I toward Arragon.
CLAUDIO I'll bring you thither, my lord, if you'll vouchsafe me.
DON PEDRO Nay that would be as great a soil in the new gloss of your
      marriage, as to show a child his new coat and forbid him to wear it: I   5
      will only be bold with Benedick for his company, for from the crown
      of his head, to the sole of his foot, he is all mirth: he hath twice or

---

106 SD] *Exit.* F; *not in* Q   **Act 3, Scene 2**   0 SD DON PEDRO] *Prince* Q   1 SH DON PEDRO] *Prince* Q *(and throughout
scene)*

107–16 'Observe the metre and rhyme. How delicate the dramatic instinct that makes Benedick, in his
first scarce-recognised transport, utter a line of verse
(2.3.202), and here makes Beatrice burst, as it were,
into full song' (Newcomer). Her 'song' makes the
last ten lines of a Shakespearean sonnet.

107 These are rhetorical questions. The proverbial burning of the ears (Tilley E14) seems not appli-
cable here, since that is caused by people talking
about a person in his absence. The fire is started by
what Beatrice has heard from Hero and Ursula, and
her ears burn with shame, though from a different
cause than Adonis's:

Mine ears, that to your wanton talk attended,
Do burn themselves for having so offended.
                              (*Venus and Adonis* 809–10)
Beatrice is ashamed of her 'pride and scorn', and the
fire is also the fire of love.

110 Beatrice thinks that what she has just heard

was spoken 'behind her back': good things are not
said of the contemptuous and proud in their absence.

112 Beatrice develops the idea of herself as a haggard (36). 'The temper of the wild-caught hawk is
. . . far gentler and more amiable when once she is
tamed than is that of a hawk taken from the nest'
(Lascelles, *Falconry*, quoted in Furness).

116 **reportingly** by hearsay. Beatrice has an inner
conviction of Benedick's love.

Act 3, Scene 2
0 SD An unlocalised scene on the main stage, it is
usually specified as in 'Leonato's house' (Theobald)
but could as easily be out of doors.

3 **bring** escort.

7–8 **twice . . . bow-string** Compare 1.1.29–31
and 92–4 for earlier references to Benedick's
immunity to love.

thrice cut Cupid's bow-string, and the little hangman dare not shoot
at him: he hath a heart as sound as a bell, and his tongue is the
clapper, for what his heart thinks, his tongue speaks.   10

BENEDICK Gallants, I am not as I have been.

LEONATO So say I, methinks you are sadder.

CLAUDIO I hope he be in love.

DON PEDRO Hang him, truant, there's no true drop of blood in him to
be truly touched with love: if he be sad, he wants money.   15

BENEDICK I have the tooth-ache.

DON PEDRO Draw it.

BENEDICK Hang it.

CLAUDIO You must hang it first, and draw it afterwards.

DON PEDRO What, sigh for the tooth-ache?   20

LEONATO Where is but a humour or a worm.

BENEDICK Well, everyone cannot master a grief, but he that has it.

CLAUDIO Yet say I, he is in love.

DON PEDRO There is no appearance of fancy in him, unless it be a fancy
that he hath to strange disguises, as to be a Dutchman today, a   25
Frenchman tomorrow, or in the shape of two countries at once, as a

11 been] bin Q   22 cannot] Q; can *Pope*   26–8 or in . . . no doublet] Q; *not in* F

8 **little hangman** Any executioner could be a
hangman at this period, but the phrase is really
jocular – 'rogue'.

9–10 'Sound as a bell' is still current, and Don
Pedro possibly refers to another proverb, 'As the fool
thinks, the bell chinks' (Tilley, F445).

14 **truant** i.e. from love.

17–19 Drawn teeth were hung on display in bar-
bers' shop windows (NS); hanging and drawing (dis-
embowelling) followed by quartering was the punishment for a traitor; and love and toothache were
associated: 'You had best be troubled with the
Tooth-ache too, / For lovers ever are' (*The False One*
2.3, Beaumont and Fletcher, *Works* (1647), Rr1ʳ).
Benedick is a traitor to love, but the associations and
puns are rather weak, unless some refinement is lost
to us. Compare: '*Martino* I pray, what's good, Sir, for
a wicked tooth? *Richardo* Hang'd, drawn, and
quartering; Is't a hollow one?' (Middleton, *The
Widow* (1652), 4.1.108 (G1ʳ); though this is now
taken to be mainly the work of Middleton, Fletcher
and Jonson are also named on the title page of the
early edition).

21 **humour ... worm** Both causes are found in
Stephen Batman, *Upon Bartholome* (1582), in chapter
25, *Of tooth ache*, in Book 7: 'Worms breed in the

cheek teeth of rotted humours that be in the hol-
lownesse thereof.'

22 *****cannot** Pope's emendation – 'can' – is universally accepted, but Benedick's remark makes good
sense: only the person who suffers pain can overcome it. It is probably true, all the same, that the
speech would be normally understood in the
sarcastic sense which Pope's emendation gave it. For
that reason, perhaps, it was so long before the
emendation was provided.

24–9 Don Pedro puns elegantly on 'fancy' meaning (1) love and (2) whim; the order of these senses is
reversed at the end. There is also play with
appearance and disguise.

26–8 *****or ... doublet** It has been conjectured that
the omission of this passage from F had a political
origin, either in King James's known dislike of jokes
about foreigners, or in some more specific occasion,
such as the performance at court during the festivities for the marriage of Princess Elizabeth to the
Elector Palatine in 1613. The English were
frequently mocked for borrowing fashions indis-
criminately from many other countries. Furness
documents this extensively.

German from the waist downward, all slops, and a Spaniard from
the hip upward, no doublet: unless he have a fancy to this foolery, as
it appears he hath, he is no fool for fancy, as you would have it
appear he is.   30

CLAUDIO If he be not in love with some woman, there is no believing
old signs: a brushes his hat a-mornings, what should that bode?

DON PEDRO Hath any man seen him at the barber's?

CLAUDIO No, but the barber's man hath been seen with him, and the
old ornament of his cheek hath already stuffed tennis balls.   35

LEONATO Indeed he looks younger than he did, by the loss of a beard.

DON PEDRO Nay, a rubs himself with civet, can you smell him out by
that?

CLAUDIO That's as much as to say, the sweet youth's in love.

DON PEDRO The greatest note of it is his melancholy.   40

CLAUDIO And when was he wont to wash his face?

DON PEDRO Yea, or to paint himself? For the which I hear what they
say of him.

CLAUDIO Nay but his jesting spirit, which is now crept into a lute-
string, and now governed by stops.   45

DON PEDRO Indeed that tells a heavy tale for him: conclude, conclude,
he is in love.

CLAUDIO Nay but I know who loves him.

DON PEDRO That would I know too, I warrant one that knows him not.

29–30 have it appear] Q; have it to appear F   34 been] F; bin Q   40 SH DON PEDRO] *Prince* F; *Bene.* Q   46 conclude,
conclude] Q; conclude F

27 **slops** loose baggy breeches.

28 **no doublet** Malone explained this as 'no
doublet visible because concealed by a Spanish
cloak'.

35 **old ornament . . . tennis balls** Tennis balls
were stuffed with hair at this time. Compare Nashe,
A Wonderful Strange . . . Prognostication (1591): 'some
. . . may sell their hair by the pound to stuff Tennis
balls' (*Works*, III, 384). Beatrice had indicated
(2.1.23) that she would 'rather lie in the woollen'
than have a bearded husband.

37 **civet** perfume; derived, as Touchstone knew,
'from sacs or glands in the anal pouch' (*OED*) of the
civet cat (*AYLI* 3.2.67–8).

37 **smell him out** discover his secret. The punning on odour is picked up again in 'sweet' (39) and
perhaps 'melancholy' (40) which, while appropriate
for a lover, could also suggest 'bad smelling', since in
those afflicted it produced 'continual sharp and
stinking belchings, as if their meat in their stomachs
were putrefied' (Burton, *The Anatomy of Melancholy*,

Part 1, Sec. 3, Mem. 1, subsect. 1). Compare *1H4*
1.2.77–8: 'the melancholy of Moor-ditch'.

41 **wash** Probably 'use a cosmetic lotion', but it is
possible that Benedick, playing the returned
campaigner, maintained a deliberate unkemptness.

42 **paint himself** use make-up.

42–3 **For . . . him** That's the rumour about him
now.

44–5 **now crept . . . stops** It is often assumed that
the 'stops' are the frets on the fingerboard of the lute,
and as a consequence the second 'now' amended to
'new' (Walker, Dyce). Boas and NS read 'new crept
. . . now governed'. Neither emendation seems justified, since 'stops' can equally (and more commonly
in Shakespeare) apply to wind instruments. Benedick's 'spirit' which used to express itself in jesting
now finds relief in the music of lute or pipe. 'Heavy'
(46) could be a term for melancholy music. The 'now
. . . now' construction suggests rapid shifts of attention. Compare the speed with which Orsino tires of
music in *TN* 1.1.8.

CLAUDIO Yes, and his ill conditions, and in despite of all, dies for him.   50
DON PEDRO She shall be buried with her face upwards.
BENEDICK Yet is this no charm for the tooth-ache: old signor, walk
    aside with me, I have studied eight or nine wise words to speak to
    you, which these hobby-horses must not hear.
                            [Exeunt Benedick and Leonato]
DON PEDRO For my life, to break with him about Beatrice.   55
CLAUDIO 'Tis even so: Hero and Margaret have by this played their
    parts with Beatrice, and then the two bears will not bite one another
    when they meet.

                 Enter DON JOHN *the Bastard*

DON JOHN My lord and brother, God save you.
DON PEDRO Good den, brother.   60
DON JOHN If your leisure served, I would speak with you.
DON PEDRO In private?
DON JOHN If it please you, yet Count Claudio may hear, for what I
    would speak of, concerns him.
DON PEDRO What's the matter?   65
DON JOHN Means your lordship to be married tomorrow?
DON PEDRO You know he does.
DON JOHN I know not that, when he knows what I know.
CLAUDIO If there be any impediment, I pray you discover it.
DON JOHN You may think I love you not, let that appear hereafter, and   70
    aim better at me by that I now will manifest, for my brother (I think
    he holds you well, and in dearness of heart) hath holp to effect your
    ensuing marriage: surely suit ill-spent, and labour ill-bestowed.

---

58 SD DON JOHN] Iohn Q   59 SH DON JOHN] *Bastard* Q *(and subst. throughout scene)*   71–2 brother (I . . . heart)] Q
corr., F; brother, I . . . heart, Q *uncorr.*; brother, I . . . heart *Rowe*   72 holp] Q *corr.*, F; hope Q *uncorr.*

50–1 dies . . . upward 'Dying' was a common
term for sexual orgasm (compare 5.2.77); Beatrice
will be buried under Benedick when she dies for him
in this sense.

52–4 old . . . hear Benedick's intention is
apparently to propose himself as Beatrice's suitor, to
her guardian, Leonato. He does so in fact at 5.4.20–
30, but the duplication is not noticed in
performance.

54 hobby-horses buffoons.

55 break with See 1.1.235 n.

56 Margaret In 3.1 Ursula played the main part
with Hero.

57 Two bears . . . another Compare Thersites in
Tro. (5.7.18–19): 'One bear will not bite another, and
wherefore should one bastard?'; also Tilley w606:
'One wolf (bear) will not . . . bite . . . another.'

60 Good den A contraction of 'God give you good
even', a greeting for any time after noon.

70–3* Don John's syntax is a little involved, but it
seems that the pointing of corrected Q gives as good a
sense as any. It merely clarifies and does not change
the sense of uncorrected Q. Rowe's emendation,
which is followed by many editors (along with
Capell's substitution of a full stop after 'manifest'),
does change the sense, since it relates 'in dearness of
heart' adverbially to the following 'holp', from which
it is firmly separated by the parenthesis of corrected
Q. 'In dearness of heart' is parallel in construction to
'well' and relates to the preceding verb, 'holds'.

72 holp helped.

DON PEDRO Why what's the matter?

DON JOHN I came hither to tell you, and circumstances shortened (for 75
she has been too long a-talking of), the lady is disloyal.

CLAUDIO Who Hero?

DON JOHN Even she, Leonato's Hero, your Hero, every man's Hero.

CLAUDIO Disloyal?

DON JOHN The word is too good to paint out her wickedness, I could 80
say she were worse, think you of a worse title, and I will fit her to it:
wonder not till further warrant: go but with me tonight, you shall see
her chamber window entered, even the night before her wedding
day: if you love her, then tomorrow wed her: but it would better fit
your honour to change your mind. 85

CLAUDIO May this be so?

DON PEDRO I will not think it.

DON JOHN If you dare not trust that you see, confess not that you know:
if you will follow me, I will show you enough: and when you have
seen more, and heard more, proceed accordingly. 90

CLAUDIO If I see anything tonight, why I should not marry her tomorrow in the congregation, where I should wed, there will I shame her.

DON PEDRO And as I wooed for thee to obtain her, I will join with thee,
to disgrace her.

DON JOHN I will disparage her no farther, till you are my witnesses: bear 95
it coldly but till midnight, and let the issue show itself.

DON PEDRO Oh day untowardly turned!

CLAUDIO Oh mischief strangely thwarting!

DON JOHN Oh plague right well prevented! So will you say, when you
have seen the sequel. 100

Exeunt

76 been] F; bin Q   84 her, then] Q; her then, *Hanmer*   91–2 her tomorrow in] Q; her tomorrow, in *Rowe;* her; tomorrow, in *Capell*   96 midnight] Q; night F   100 SD *Exeunt*] *Exit.* F; *not in* Q

75 **circumstances shortened** leaving out the details.

76 **disloyal** unfaithful, unchaste.

80 **paint out** paint in full; 'out' is intensive.

83 **window entered** Borachio did not propose this (2.2.32), nor is it what is later observed (3.3.118–21).

84 ***love her, then** Hanmer's emendation, widely followed, is not necessary. The Q reading adopted here makes perfectly good sense: 'marry her if you love her, but concern for your own honour should make you not love her'.

88 **that . . . that** what . . . what. Don John remains cryptic: 'If you won't trust your own eyes, don't claim

to know anything', or perhaps 'keep quiet about what you have been told'. Compare A. B. Dawson, 'Much ado about signifying', *SEL* 22.2 (1982), 214: 'Like certain pronouncements of Iago, this sentence appears more meaningful, even portentous, than it actually is. It cheats the listener by pretending a meaning that it fails to deliver.'

91–2 ***marry . . . congregation** The punctuation of this passage has regularly been emended to insert a pause after 'tomorrow'; this has the effect of associating 'in the congregation' with the verb 'shame' which follows it. In Q it is attached to 'marry', which provides a perfectly satisfactory reading.

95–6 **bear it coldly** keep cool about it.

[3.3] *Enter* DOGBERRY *and his compartner* [VERGES] *with* [SEACOAL,
WATCHMAN 1, WATCHMAN 2 *and the rest of*] *the Watch*

DOGBERRY Are you good men and true?

VERGES Yea, or else it were pity but they should suffer salvation body
and soul.

DOGBERRY Nay, that were a punishment too good for them, if they
should have any allegiance in them, being chosen for the prince's   5
watch.

VERGES Well, give them their charge, neighbour Dogberry.

DOGBERRY First, who think you the most desartless man to be
constable?

WATCHMAN 1 Hugh Oatcake, sir, or George Seacoal, for they can   10
write and read.

DOGBERRY Come hither, neighbour Seacoal, God hath blessed you
with a good name: to be a well-favoured man, is the gift of Fortune,
but to write and read, comes by nature.

SEACOAL Both which, master constable –   15

DOGBERRY You have: I knew it would be your answer: well, for your
favour, sir, why give God thanks, and make no boast of it, and for
your writing and reading, let that appear when there is no need of
such vanity: you are thought here to be the most senseless and fit
man for the constable of the watch: therefore bear you the lantern: 20

Act 3, Scene 3   10 SH WATCHMAN 1] *Watch 1* Q   10 Oatcake] Ote-cake Q   10 Seacoal] Sea-cole Q *(and throughout
scene)*   15 SH SEACOAL] *Watch 2* Q   15 constable –] *Rowe;* Constable. Q; Constable F

Act 3, Scene 3

0 SD Walter Hodges's drawing (illustration 13, p.
33 above) admirably sets this scene on the
Elizabethan stage. The 'church bench' (74), usually
in the lych-gate of the churchyard, is in the central
discovery area of the tiring-house wall, and the penthouse shelter from the rain (85) is afforded by the
stage canopy. The scene was localised as 'the street'
by Theobald. For an account of the distribution of
the 'WATCH' speeches see Textual Analysis, p. 152
below.

0 SD *compartner* fellow office-bearer; Dogberry
is Master Constable, Verges Headborough (from the
entry for 3.5), a lower office. One reason for the
incompetence of those performing these unpaid civic
offices emerges from the interrogation of Constable
Elbow by Escalus in *MM* 2.1.257–73: 'As they are

chosen, they are glad to choose me for them. I do it
for some piece of money, and go through with all.'
Competent persons could spend their time more
pleasantly or profitably, and so paid a deputy.

0 SD *the Watch* A group of local citizens chosen
for police duties.

2 salvation For 'damnation'. The constables
commonly say the reverse of what they mean. An
opposite word of similar sound is not always so easy
to find as in this case.

7 charge A formal instruction in their duties.

10 George Seacoal He cannot be the Francis
Seacoal referred to at 3.5.45 and who is presumably
the Sexton of 4.2. The name suggests his trade was
supplying 'sea coal', which was brought by sea to
London from the mines in the north of England.

13 well-favoured good-looking.

this is your charge, you shall comprehend all vagrom men, you are
to bid any man stand, in the prince's name.

SEACOAL How if a will not stand?

DOGBERRY Why then take no note of him, but let him go, and presently
call the rest of the watch together, and thank God you are rid of a 25
knave.

VERGES If he will not stand when he is bidden, he is none of the prince's
subjects.

DOGBERRY True, and they are to meddle with none but the prince's
subjects: you shall also make no noise in the streets: for, for the 30
watch to babble and to talk, is most tolerable and not to be endured.

WATCHMAN 2 We will rather sleep than talk, we know what belongs to
a watch.

DOGBERRY Why you speak like an ancient and most quiet watchman,
for I cannot see how sleeping should offend: only have a care that 35
your bills be not stolen: well, you are to call at all the alehouses, and
bid those that are drunk get them to bed.

SEACOAL How if they will not?

DOGBERRY Why then let them alone till they are sober: if they make you
not then the better answer, you may say, they are not the men you 40
took them for.

SEACOAL Well, sir.

DOGBERRY If you meet a thief, you may suspect him, by virtue of your
office, to be no true man: and for such kind of men, the less you
meddle or make with them, why the more is for your honesty. 45

SEACOAL If we know him to be a thief, shall we not lay hands on him?

DOGBERRY Truly by your office you may, but I think they that touch
pitch will be defiled: the most peaceable way for you, if you do take a
thief, is, to let him show himself what he is, and steal out of your
company. 50

VERGES You have been always called a merciful man, partner.

---

23 SH SEACOAL] *Watch 2* Q   31 to talk] Q; talk F   32 SH WATCHMAN 2] *Watch* Q   37 those] Q; them F   38, 42, 46
SH SEACOAL] *Watch* Q; Watch 2 Rowe   51 been] F; bin Q

---

21 **comprehend** For 'apprehend'. Compare
Shakespeare's careful distinction of these terms:
  Such tricks hath strong imagination,
  That if it would but apprehend some joy,
  It comprehends some bringer of that joy . . .
              (*MND* 5.1.18–20)
  21 **vagrom** For 'vagrant' presumably.

24 **presently** at once.
34 **ancient** sober, experienced.
36 **bills** Weapons like the halberd, a spear-point
combined with an axe-head mounted on a long shaft.
  47–8 **touch ... defiled** Ecclus. 13.1 in the
Apocrypha: 'Whoso toucheth pitch, shall be defiled
withal.'

DOGBERRY Truly I would not hang a dog by my will, much more a man
    who hath any honesty in him.
VERGES If you hear a child cry in the night, you must call to the nurse
    and bid her still it.   55
WATCHMAN 2 How if the nurse be asleep and will not hear us?
DOGBERRY Why then depart in peace, and let the child wake her with
    crying, for the ewe that will not hear her lamb when it baas, will
    never answer a calf when he bleats.
VERGES 'Tis very true.   60
DOGBERRY This is the end of the charge: you, constable, are to present
    the prince's own person, if you meet the prince in the night, you may
    stay him.
VERGES Nay by'r Lady that I think a cannot.
DOGBERRY Five shillings to one on't with any man that knows the   65
    statutes, he may stay him: marry, not without the prince be willing,
    for indeed the watch ought to offend no man, and it is an offence to
    stay a man against his will.
VERGES By'r Lady I think it be so.
DOGBERRY Ha, ah ha! Well, masters, good night: and there be any   70
    matter of weight chances, call up me: keep your fellows' counsels,
    and your own, and good night: come, neighbour.
SEACOAL Well masters, we hear our charge, let us go sit here upon the
    church bench till two, and then all to bed.
DOGBERRY One word more, honest neighbours, I pray you watch about   75
    Signor Leonato's door, for the wedding being there tomorrow,
    there is a great coil tonight: adieu, be vigitant I beseech you.
                              Exeunt [*Dogberry and Verges*]

                    Enter BORACHIO *and* CONRADE

BORACHIO What, Conrade?
SEACOAL Peace, stir not.
BORACHIO Conrade, I say.   80
CONRADE Here, man, I am at thy elbow.

---

56 SH WATCHMAN 2] *Rowe; Watch.* Q   64 by'r Lady] birlady Q   69 By'r Lady] Birlady Q   66 statutes] Q; statues
F   73 SH SEACOAL] *Watch.* Q; *Watch.* 2 / *Rowe*   79, 88 SH SEACOAL] *Watch.* Q; *Watch.* 2 / *Capell (subst.)*

52 **hang a dog** Legal penalties were inflicted on
animals. Compare 2.3.72–3, and Launce on his dog:
'I have sat in the stocks for puddings he hath stolen,
otherwise he had been executed' (*TGV* 4.4.30–2).

59 **calf . . . bleats** The bleating calf is the foolish
watchman, so the pronoun 'he' is appropriate. 'Calf'
in the sense of 'fool' is common: see *OED sv sb*¹ 1c,
and compare *LLL* 5.2.247–55.

61 **present** represent. This is not an error of Dogberry's, but contemporary usage.

70 **Ha, ah ha!** A crow of triumph, rather than a
laugh.

77 **coil** bustle, business.

77 **vigitant** For 'vigilant'.

BORACHIO Mass and my elbow itched, I thought there would a scab follow.

CONRADE I will owe thee an answer for that, and now forward with thy tale. 85

BORACHIO Stand thee close then under this penthouse, for it drizzles rain, and I will, like a true drunkard, utter all to thee.

SEACOAL Some treason, masters, yet stand close.

BORACHIO Therefore know, I have earned of Don John a thousand ducats. 90

CONRADE Is it possible that any villainy should be so dear?

BORACHIO Thou shouldst rather ask if it were possible any villainy should be so rich. For when rich villains have need of poor ones, poor ones may make what price they will.

CONRADE I wonder at it. 95

BORACHIO That shows thou art unconfirmed: thou knowest that the fashion of a doublet, or a hat, or a cloak, is nothing to a man.

CONRADE Yes, it is apparel.

BORACHIO I mean the fashion.

CONRADE Yes, the fashion is the fashion. 100

BORACHIO Tush, I may as well say the fool's the fool, but seest thou not what a deformed thief this fashion is?

WATCHMAN 1 I know that Deformed, a has been a vile thief, this seven year, a goes up and down like a gentleman: I remember his name.

BORACHIO Didst thou not hear somebody? 105

CONRADE No, 'twas the vane on the house.

BORACHIO Seest thou not, I say, what a deformed thief this fashion is, how giddily a turns about all the hot-bloods, between fourteen and five and thirty, sometimes fashioning them like Pharaoh's soldiers in

89 Don John] F; Dun Iohn Q   103 SH WATCHMAN 1] *Watch.* Q   103 Deformed] deformed Q   103–4 seven year] Q; VII yeares F

82–3 elbow . . . follow There is a pun on 'scab' as (1) the crust that forms on a wound and (2) a scoundrel. The latter sense seems now restricted to specialised use in industrial disputes. Hilda Hulme quotes from Withals, 'He that is a blab is a scab', which links the pun to 'utter all' (p. 86). Tilley gives 'My elbow itched, I must change my bedfellow' (E98). At *LLL* 5.2.109 itching elbows seem to denote satisfaction.

86 penthouse overhanging roof or porch.

87 true drunkard Alluding to the proverb *in vino veritas*; Borachio derives his name from the Spanish for a drunkard, and he is evidently drunk here.

96 unconfirmed inexperienced.

97 fashion . . . man Borachio means that the fashion of clothes makes no difference to the man inside them. Conrade understands him to say that fashion is of no concern to a man, and demurs. Borachio's point, which he gets to at 118, is that 'the fashion' (Hero's clothes worn by Margaret) has just been mistaken for the woman. Compare 5.1.209.

106 vane weathercock.

109 Pharaoh's soldiers Probably pursuing the Israelites and about to be drowned in the Red Sea (Exod. 14).

the reechy painting, sometime like god Bel's priests in the old   110
church window, sometime like the shaven Hercules in the smirched
worm-eaten tapestry, where his cod-piece seems as massy as his
club?

CONRADE All this I see, and I see that the fashion wears out more
apparel than the man: but art not thou thyself giddy with the fashion   115
too, that thou hast shifted out of thy tale into telling me of the
fashion?

BORACHIO Not so neither, but know that I have tonight wooed
Margaret, the Lady Hero's gentlewoman, by the name of Hero: she
leans me out at her mistress' chamber window, bids me a thousand   120
times good night: I tell this tale vilely, I should first tell thee how the
prince, Claudio and my master planted, and placed, and possessed,
by my master Don John, saw afar off in the orchard this amiable
encounter.

CONRADE And thought they Margaret was Hero?   125

BORACHIO Two of them did, the prince and Claudio, but the devil my
master knew she was Margaret, and partly by his oaths, which first
possessed them, partly by the dark night which did deceive them,
but chiefly, by my villainy, which did confirm any slander that Don
John had made – away went Claudio enraged, swore he would meet   130

---

110 reechy] *Hanmer;* rechie Q   114 and I see] Q; and see F   120 mistress'] mistris Q   121 vilely] vildly Q
122 prince, Claudio] prince Claudio Q   125 they] Q; thy F

---

110 reechy smoky.

110 god Bel's priests Confuted by Daniel in Bel and Dragon in the Apocrypha.

111 shaven Hercules This has puzzled commentators, but Borachio is perhaps thinking of the youthful – and therefore beardless – 'Hercules at the crossroads'. This was a popular motif in the visual arts, and showed the youth choosing the path of virtue and eschewing vice. On each path was a beautiful woman – often Pallas Athene for virtue and Venus (appropriately deshabillée) for vice. It was also well known from emblems (e.g. Geoffrey Whitney's *A Choice of Emblems* (1586), p. 40 – though in Whitney Hercules is bearded). See Erwin Panofsky, *Hercules am Scheidewege*, Studien der Bibliothek Warburg, Leipzig/Berlin, 1930, for many illustrations. By mythographers Samson was sometimes equated with Hercules, and some editors (since the other pictures have Biblical sources) have suggested that this relates to Judges 16, where Delilah shaves off Samson's hair. It is also taken to refer to Hercules' servitude to Omphale (see 2.1.191–2 n. above) – but in that case Hercules should be dressed in women's clothing, which would not include a cod-piece, and he is normally represented heavily bearded in that episode, to emphasise the anomaly. Hercules was a popular subject for tapestries, espe-

cially among kings, from the late Middle Ages until at least the seventeenth century. Henry VIII had no fewer than eight sets of the history of Hercules, including one, of six pieces, in the Removing Guarderobe (BL MS. Harl. 1419).

112 cod-piece On the front of men's breeches, initially serving the function of the modern jockstrap, it later became ornamental and was often large, prominent and elaborately decorated. As Hercules' club symbolised his virtue, its size, relative to the cod-piece, may be part of the joke here. It was old-fashioned by 1580.

116 shifted To shift could also mean to change one's clothes.

120 leans me Another of Borachio's ethical datives. Compare 1.3.43.

122–3 my master ... my master Borachio's syntax is confused. All three were 'planted', but two were 'placed and possessed' by the third.

122 possessed given information; but perhaps coloured by the sense of demonic possession from association with 'the devil my master' at lines 126–7. 'Possessed' has this sense more strongly at 128.

129–30 my ... made Borachio did not, apparently, enter the chamber, as promised by Don John at 3.2.83. It is implied here that there was an interrogation following the 'balcony scene' in which

her as he was appointed next morning at the temple, and there, before the whole congregation shame her, with what he saw o'er night, and send her home again without a husband.

SEACOAL We charge you in the prince's name, stand.

WATCHMAN 2 Call up the right master constable, we have here   135
recovered the most dangerous piece of lechery, that ever was known in the commonwealth.

WATCHMAN 1 And one Deformed is one of them, I know him, a wears a lock.

CONRADE Masters, masters.   140

WATCHMAN 1 You'll be made bring Deformed forth I warrant you.

SEACOAL Masters, never speak, we charge you, let us obey you to go with us.

BORACHIO We are like to prove a goodly commodity, being taken up of these men's bills.   145

CONRADE A commodity in question I warrant you: come, we'll obey you.

Exeunt

[3.4] *Enter* HERO *and* MARGARET *and* URSULA

HERO Good Ursula, wake my cousin Beatrice, and desire her to rise.
URSULA I will, lady.
HERO And bid her come hither.
URSULA Well.   *[Exit]*
MARGARET Troth I think your other rebato were better.   5

---

134 SH SEACOAL] *Watch. 1* Q   142 SH SEACOAL] *Conr.* Q   142 never] Q; *1 Watch.* Never *Theobald*

Borachio 'confessed' to the liaison with Hero, and after this 'away went Claudio enraged'. Such a scenario makes Claudio's later behaviour more tolerable, but it is so lightly sketched that we hardly perceive it.

135 right An honorific, as in 'right honourable'.

136 recovered ... lechery Dogberry's verbal habits influence his inferiors.

139 lock A lovelock, grown by the left ear, vowed to a mistress and often decorated with her favour (compare 'nourish special locks of vowed hair', Sir Philip Sidney, *Astrophel and Stella*, 54.3).

142 *Masters, never speak For the problems of the distribution of speeches here, see supplementary note, p. 146 below.

144–6 An extended commercial pun. A 'commodity' is a parcel of goods bought on credit (or

'taken up with a bill'), sometimes as part of a loan, instead of ready cash. A 'commodity in question' could be one much sought after, or one subject to legal investigation. At the literal level Borachio and Conrade will prove valuable, now they have been captured by the Watchmen armed with bills (36 above).

Act 3, Scene 4

0 SD This scene, 'Hero's apartment in Leonato's house' (Theobald), could perhaps have been played 'above', to suggest its privacy and separation. This was done in Gielgud's notable 1949 production, where Andreu's set allowed an upper acting-area.

5 rebato Probably here the ruff, though it could refer to the wired linen support for the ruff.

HERO No pray thee, good Meg, I'll wear this.

MARGARET By my troth's not so good, and I warrant your cousin will say so.

HERO My cousin's a fool, and thou art another, I'll wear none but this.

MARGARET I like the new tire within excellently, if the hair were a   10
thought browner: and your gown's a most rare fashion i'faith. I saw
the Duchess of Milan's gown that they praise so.

HERO Oh, that exceeds they say.

MARGARET By my troth's but a night-gown in respect of yours, cloth
o'gold and cuts, and laced with silver, set with pearls, down sleeves,   15
side sleeves, and skirts, round underborne with a bluish tinsel – but
for a fine quaint graceful and excellent fashion, yours is worth ten
on't.

HERO God give me joy to wear it, for my heart is exceeding heavy.

MARGARET 'Twill be heavier soon by the weight of a man.   20

HERO Fie upon thee, art not ashamed?

MARGARET Of what, lady? Of speaking honourably? Is not marriage
honourable in a beggar? Is not your lord honourable without marriage? I think you would have me say, saving your reverence, a
husband: and bad thinking do not wrest true speaking, I'll offend   25
nobody: is there any harm in the heavier for a husband? None I
think, and it be the right husband, and the right wife, otherwise 'tis
light and not heavy: ask my Lady Beatrice else, here she comes.

Enter BEATRICE

Act 3, Scene 4   6, 9, 13 SH HERO] Q; *Bero* F   11 i'faith.] yfaith, Q   14 in] F; it Q   15 o'gold] *Capell;* a gold Q

7 **troth's** troth it's. Also at 14. Margaret's speech, particularly in this scene, is nervous and rapid and full of elisions. It is not yet five o'clock (38) and between twelve and one (4.1.78) she was dressed in Hero's clothes and entertaining Borachio.

10 **tire** Elaborate head-dress made up on a frame with ornaments and supplementary hair.

11 **browner** Hero is 'too brown for a fair praise' (1.1.127) and apparently the 'tire' is not a perfect match with her own hair. It is in another room being prepared along with the wedding dress, 'your gown' (11).

13 **that exceeds** that's outstanding.

14 **night-gown** Dressing-gown is the nearest modern equivalent.

14–16 The Duchess of Milan's gown had cloth of gold showing through cuts made in the main fabric of the dress, was embroidered with silver thread and decorated with pearls; it had close-fitting sleeves to the wrist (down sleeves) and in addition long hanging

sleeves from the shoulders (side sleeves) from which the down sleeves emerged. Side sleeves are still to be found on certain academic robes. The 'blueish tin-sel' (a cloth of silk and gold or silver thread) may have decorated the perimeter of the wide skirt, or been displayed at the hem of a rich petticoat revealed beneath it.

17 **quaint** elegant, dainty.

22–3 **marriage honourable** Matrimony . . . is an honourable estate . . . commended of Saint Paul to be honourable among all men' (Book of Common Prayer (authorised by Elizabeth's first parliament), from 'The Form of the Solemnisation of Matrimony'). St Paul's recommendation is in Heb. 13.4.

24 **saving your reverence** A phrase used in advance as an apology when obliged to say something thought necessary but liable to give offence.

28 **light** (1) immoral, (2) not heavy.

HERO Good morrow, coz.

BEATRICE Good morrow, sweet Hero.   30

HERO Why how now? Do you speak in the sick tune?

BEATRICE I am out of all other tune, methinks.

MARGARET Clap's into *Light o'Love*: that goes without a burden: do you
sing it and I'll dance it.

BEATRICE Ye light o'love with your heels, then if your husband have   35
stables enough, you'll see he shall lack no barns.

MARGARET Oh illegitimate construction! I scorn that with my heels.

BEATRICE 'Tis almost five o'clock, cousin, 'tis time you were ready: by
my troth I am exceeding ill, heigh ho.

MARGARET For a hawk, a horse, or a husband?   40

BEATRICE For the letter that begins them all, H.

MARGARET Well, and you be not turned Turk, there's no more sailing
by the star.

BEATRICE What means the fool, trow?

MARGARET Nothing I, but God send everyone their heart's desire.   45

HERO These gloves the count sent me, they are an excellent perfume.

BEATRICE I am stuffed, cousin, I cannot smell.

MARGARET A maid and stuffed! There's goodly catching of cold.

---

33 Clap's] Q; Claps F   33 *Light o'Love*] Rowe; Light a love Q   36 see] Q; looke F

---

33 Clap's into Begin at once; 's (us) is an ethical
dative.

33 *Light o'Love* A popular song and dance, mentioned as early as 1578 in *A Gorgeous Gallery of Gal-
lant Inventions*; there is a reference to it, and a similar
pun, in *TGV* 1.2.80–3. A light o'love is a wanton.

33 burden bass part. Margaret continues her
punning on the various senses of 'light' and 'heavy',
as well as suggesting that they don't need a man to
sing the bass part in this song.

35 ye ... heels Beatrice elaborates the idea of
Margaret dancing 'Light o'Love': she will 'kick up
her heels' or be 'short-heeled', again suggesting
unchastity. Compare Henry Porter, *Two Angry
Women of Abington* (1599), 740: 'Light alove, short
heels, mistress Goursey' (ed. W. W. Greg, 1913).

36 stables ... barns Punning on 'barns' (= farm
buildings) and 'bairns' (= children) (Johnson). If
Margaret is light o'love with her heels – i.e. unchaste
– then her husband will not lack children. For the
spelling 'barns' compare 'Mercy on's, a barne? A
very pretty barne!' (*WT* 3.3.70). Antigonus proposes,
if Hermione is proved unfaithful, to 'keep my stables
where / I lodge my wife' (*WT* 2.1.134–5).

37 illegitimate construction false inference; but
Margaret continues punning with the idea of illegitimate children.

37 scorn ... heels kick it from me. A proverbial
expression, referring to the backward kick of a horse.
It translates the Latin root of 'recalcitrant'.

38 five o'clock Compare *The Puritan, or the
Widow of Watling Street* (1607), by 'W.S.', sometimes
formerly attributed to Shakespeare, 5.1.5–6: 'hie
thee, 'tis past five, bid them open the Church door,
my sister is almost ready'.

39–40 Margaret takes Beatrice's conventionalised
sigh as a reference to the ballad (compare 2.1.242) or
'a cry of encouragement to a horse or hawk' (NS).

41 H i.e. ache – a common pun at the time, since
'ache' was pronounced like the name of the letter.

42 turned Turk radically changed your views (as
if converted to Islam). Proverbial: Tilley T609.

42–3 there's ... star not even the Pole star can
be relied on any more.

45 everyone their This use of the plural form of
the possessive adjective after a non-gendered
singular 'one' is normal in speech.

46 gloves ... perfume Perfumed gloves were a
proper present from a lover; Mopsa was promised 'a
pair of sweet gloves' (*WT* 4.4.250).

47, 48 stuffed Beatrice has a cold in the head;
Margaret suggests that she is pregnant.

BEATRICE Oh God help me, God help me, how long have you professed apprehension?   50

MARGARET Ever since you left it: doth not my wit become me rarely?

BEATRICE It is not seen enough, you should wear it in your cap: by my
troth I am sick.

MARGARET Get you some of this distilled *Carduus benedictus*, and lay it
to your heart, it is the only thing for a qualm.   55

HERO There thou prick'st her with a thistle.

BEATRICE *Benedictus*, why *benedictus*? You have some moral in this
benedictus.

MARGARET Moral? No by my troth, I have no moral meaning, I meant
plain Holy Thistle, you may think perchance that I think you are in   60
love, nay by'r Lady I am not such a fool to think what I list, nor I list
not to think what I can, nor indeed I cannot think, if I would think
my heart out of thinking, that you are in love, or that you will be in
love, or that you can be in love: yet Benedick was such another, and
now is he become a man, he swore he would never marry, and yet   65
now in despite of his heart he eats his meat without grudging, and
how you may be converted I know not, but methinks you look with
your eyes as other women do.

BEATRICE What pace is this that thy tongue keeps?

MARGARET Not a false gallop.   70

---

61 by'r Lady] birlady Q

49–50 professed apprehension set yourself up
for a wit.

51 left it gave it up. Margaret picks up the sense
of 'perceive clearly' in 'apprehension'. Beatrice can
'see a church by daylight' (2.1.59) but has not seen
the trick played on her.

52 It . . . cap It is so insignificant that it won't be
seen unless prominently displayed, 'as the fool does
his coxcomb' (NS).

54 this i.e. the well-known. *Carduus benedictus*,
Holy Thistle (*Carbenia benedicta* in modern tax-
onomy), was a popular and fashionable remedy in the
late sixteenth century, reputed to cure almost anything. It is a downy, yellow-flowered annual, growing
about 2 feet (60 cm.) high; the leaves are dark, with
lighter veins and indented wavy margins ending in
spines. It is 'an Herb of Mars' and 'helps swimmings
and giddiness of the head'. It 'cures the French Pox
by Antipathy to Venus' and by the same antipathy
might be thought a remedy for love, although 'It
strengthens the attractive faculty in man' (Culpeper,
The English Physician (1652), sig. *a3ʳ). Thomas
Brasbridge, in *The Poore Man's Jewell . . . A Treatise of
the Pestilence* (1578), called it 'a preservatiue against

all diseases' (sig. D2ᵛ); his long section on its extraordinary virtues includes a description of how 'it
helpeth the heart'.

55 qualm A sudden feeling of nausea or faintness.

57 moral hidden meaning. Compare 'has left me
here behind to expound the meaning or moral of his
signs and tokens' (*Shr.* 4.4.78–80).

59–68 Margaret's intention is to divert Beatrice –
who has clearly got suspicious with the reference to
Carduus benedictus – and to provoke her further. She
asserts the common humanity of Beatrice and Benedick: they eat their food, use their eyes and fall in
love like other people.

60 Holy Thistle It would be possible to direct a
certain kind of audience to an extended 'moral
meaning' in this passage: 'lay it to your heart' –
embrace passionately; 'qualm' – the sensation of
orgasm; Hero's comment associates thistles and
pricks, and 'wholly thistle' – nothing but pricks.
Margaret's mind, on this marriage morning, is quite
capable of making such associations.

70 false gallop canter. It is false because it is a
trained, not a natural, pace of the horse. Margaret
asserts that what she says is true.

Enter URSULA

URSULA Madam, withdraw, the prince, the count, Signor Benedick,
    Don John, and all the gallants of the town are come to fetch you to
    church.
HERO Help to dress me, good coz, good Meg, good Ursula.

                                                             [*Exeunt*]

[3.5] *Enter* LEONATO *and* [DOGBERRY] *the Constable and* [VERGES] *the
Headborough*

LEONATO What would you with me, honest neighbour?
DOGBERRY Marry, sir, I would have some confidence with you, that
    decerns you nearly.
LEONATO Brief I pray you, for you see it is a busy time with me.
DOGBERRY Marry this it is, sir.   5
VERGES Yes in truth it is, sir.
LEONATO What is it, my good friends?
DOGBERRY Goodman Verges, sir, speaks a little off the matter, an old
    man, sir, and his wits are not so blunt, as God help I would desire
    they were, but in faith honest, as the skin between his brows.   10
VERGES Yes I thank God, I am honest as any man living, that is an old
    man, and no honester than I.
DOGBERRY Comparisons are odorous, palabras, neighbour Verges.
LEONATO Neighbours, you are tedious.
DOGBERRY It pleases your worship to say so, but we are the poor duke's   15
    officers, but truly for mine own part, if I were as tedious as a king, I
    could find in my heart to bestow it all of your worship.

Act 3, Scene 5   6 SH VERGES] *Head.* Q *(and subst. throughout scene)*   8 off] *Steevens², conj. Capell;* of Q

Act 3, Scene 5
  0 SD The scene is unlocalised (though Theobald
provided 'another apartment in Leonato's house').
On Shakespeare's stage it could perhaps be played
close to that side door of the tiring-house associated
from 1.1 with Leonato, while the wedding guests
begin to assemble on the other side of the stage.
  2 confidence For 'conference' – but 'confiden-
tiality' seems to be involved.
  3 decerns For 'concerns'.
  9 blunt For 'sharp'.
  10 honest ... brows Those whose eyebrows
meet are alleged to be untrustworthy, but the origin

of the proverb may be the practice of branding on the
forehead for some felonies. Tilley s506.
  13 odorous For 'odious'; that is, provoking ill-
will. For the confusion, compare Bottom's 'flowers of
odious savours sweet' (*MND* 3.1.82).
  13 palabras The Spanish phrase *pocas palabras*,
'few words', was widely current. Compare Thomas
Kyd, *The Spanish Tragedy*, ed. P. Edwards, 1959,
3.14.118.
  15 poor duke's duke's poor. Compare *MM*
2.1.47.
  16 tedious Dogberry thinks tedious means 'rich'.
  17 bestow ... of A frequent usage, though 'on'
was commoner; see Abbott 175.

LEONATO All thy tediousness on me, ah?

DOGBERRY Yea, and 'twere a thousand pound more than 'tis, for I hear
as good exclamation on your worship as of any man in the city, and   20
though I be but a poor man, I am glad to hear it.

VERGES And so am I.

LEONATO I would fain know what you have to say.

VERGES Marry, sir, our watch tonight, excepting your worship's
presence, ha' ta'en a couple of as arrant knaves as any in Messina.   25

DOGBERRY A good old man, sir, he will be talking as they say, when the
age is in, the wit is out, God help us, it is a world to see: well said
i'faith, neighbour Verges, well, God's a good man, and two men ride
of a horse, one must ride behind, an honest soul i'faith, sir, by my
troth he is, as ever broke bread, but God is to be worshipped, all   30
men are not alike, alas, good neighbour.

LEONATO Indeed, neighbour, he comes too short of you.

DOGBERRY Gifts that God gives.

LEONATO I must leave you.

DOGBERRY One word, sir, our watch, sir, have indeed comprehended   35
two aspitious persons, and we would have them this morning
examined before your worship.

LEONATO Take their examination yourself, and bring it me, I am now in
great haste, as it may appear unto you.

DOGBERRY It shall be suffigance.   40

[Enter MESSENGER]

LEONATO Drink some wine ere you go: fare you well.

MESSENGER My lord, they stay for you, to give your daughter to her
husband.

LEONATO I'll wait upon them, I am ready.

Exit [Leonato with Messenger]

DOGBERRY Go, good partner, go get you to Francis Seacoal, bid him   45

---

19 pound] Q; times F   25 ha'] Q; have F   39 as it may] Q; as may F   40 SD] *Rowe; not in* Q   44 SD *Exit*] *At 40 in* Q
44 SD *Leonato with Messenger*] *Rowe; not in* Q   45 Seacoal] Sea-cole Q

20 **exclamation** For 'acclamation'.
24 **excepting** For 'respecting'. Verges mangles a
polite formula.
26–31 Dogberry strings together platitudes and
proverbs, switching from Leonato to Verges and
back again. The familiar fragments give him the
impression he is talking very wisely.
26–7 **when . . . out** There is a proverb, 'When ale
is in the wit is out' (Tilley W471).

27 **a world to see** a sight worth seeing (Tilley
W878).
28 **God's . . . man** Tilley G195.
28–9 **and . . . behind** Tilley T638.
29–30 **honest . . . bread** Tilley M68.
35 **comprehended** For 'apprehended'.
36 **aspitious** For 'suspicious'.
40 **suffigance** For 'sufficient'.
45 **Francis** See 3.3.10 and n.

bring his pen and ink-horn to the gaol: we are now to examination these men.

VERGES And we must do it wisely.

DOGBERRY We will spare for no wit I warrant you: here's that shall drive some of them to a noncome, only get the learned writer to set down 50 our excommunication, and meet me at the gaol.

Exeunt

4.[1] *Enter* DON PEDRO, DON JOHN, LEONATO, FRIAR [FRANCIS], CLAUDIO, BENEDICK, HERO *and* BEATRICE[; *Wedding Guests*]

LEONATO Come, Friar Francis, be brief, only to the plain form of marriage, and you shall recount their particular duties afterwards.

FRIAR FRANCIS You come hither, my lord, to marry this lady?

CLAUDIO No.

LEONATO To be married to her: friar, you come to marry her. 5

FRIAR FRANCIS Lady, you come hither to be married to this count?

HERO I do.

FRIAR FRANCIS If either of you know any inward impediment why you should not be conjoined, I charge you on your souls to utter it.

CLAUDIO Know you any, Hero? 10

HERO None, my lord.

FRIAR FRANCIS Know you any, count?

LEONATO I dare make his answer, none.

CLAUDIO Oh what men dare do! What men may do! What men daily do, not knowing what they do! 15

---

46 examination] Q; examine F   51 SD] F; *not in* Q   Act 4, Scene 1   4.1] *Actus Quartus* F; *not in* Q   0 SD DON PEDRO, DON JOHN] *Prince, Bastard* Q   3 SH FRIAR FRANCIS] *Fran.* Q   6 SH FRIAR FRANCIS] *Frier* Q *(and throughout scene)*   15 do, not . . . do!] Q; do! F

---

50 **noncome** For 'nonplus', state of bewilderment. 'Noncome' suggests *non compos mentis*, of unsound mind.

51 **excommunication** For 'examination'.

Act 4, Scene 1

0 SD Pope first provided the location 'a church'; on Shakespeare's stage, appropriate properties – candles, vestments – would indicate this. The processional entry would perhaps be in pairs, in the order given in the stage direction. The church set became a major attraction in Irving's production: see illustration 6, p. 16 above.

2 **recount . . . afterwards** A little homily is still expected from the celebrant at the end of a wedding ceremony.

5 **married to her** Leonato misses the threat in Claudio's bald 'no' and assumes a flippant play on the double grammar of 'marry'.

8–9 The words are close to the marriage service in the Book of Common Prayer: 'I require and charge you both, as ye will answer at the dreadful day of judgement . . . that if either of you know any impediment . . . ye do now confess it.'

15* The omission from F of the final clause is an easy compositorial slip.

BENEDICK How now! Interjections? Why then, some be of laughing, as,
    ah, ha, he.

CLAUDIO Stand thee by, friar: father, by your leave,
    Will you with free and unconstrainèd soul
    Give me this maid your daughter?   20

LEONATO As freely, son, as God did give her me.

CLAUDIO And what have I to give you back, whose worth
    May counterpoise this rich and precious gift?

DON PEDRO Nothing, unless you render her again.

CLAUDIO Sweet prince, you learn me noble thankfulness: 25
    There, Leonato, take her back again,
    Give not this rotten orange to your friend,
    She's but the sign and semblance of her honour:
    Behold how like a maid she blushes here!
    Oh what authority and show of truth   30
    Can cunning sin cover itself withal!
    Comes not that blood, as modest evidence,
    To witness simple virtue? Would you not swear
    All you that see her, that she were a maid,
    By these exterior shows? But she is none: 35
    She knows the heat of a luxurious bed:
    Her blush is guiltiness, not modesty.

LEONATO What do you mean, my lord?

CLAUDIO   Not to be married,
    Not to knit my soul to an approvèd wanton.

LEONATO Dear my lord, if you in your own proof,   40
    Have vanquished the resistance of her youth,
    And made defeat of her virginity –

CLAUDIO I know what you would say: if I have known her,
    You will say, she did embrace me as a husband,

---

24 SH DON PEDRO] *Prince* Q *(and subst. throughout scene)*

16 Interjections Benedick puns on the grammar term and quotes William Lyly's *Short Introduction of Grammar* (1538), sig. C.viiiʳ: 'An Interjection . . . betokeneth a sudden passion of mind . . . Some are of laughing: as *Ha, ha, he.*' John Lyly had made the same joke: 'an interjection, whereof some are of mourning: as *eho, vah*' (*Endimion* (1591), 3.3.5). This echo – whether conscious or not – makes Benedick's interjection a little less fatuous.

25 learn teach; not a solecism then.

27 rotten orange Perhaps because an orange may look sound but be bad inside.

30 authority . . . truth show of authority and truth.

36 luxurious lustful.

38 mean Claudio takes Leonato's question not as 'what is your meaning?' but 'what is your intention?'

43 known her had sexual intercourse with her. 'And Adam knew Heva his wife, who conceiving bare Cain, saying: "I have gotten a man of the Lord"' (Gen. 4.1).

> And so extenuate the forehand sin: no, Leonato,   45
> I never tempted her with word too large,
> But as a brother to his sister, showed
> Bashful sincerity, and comely love.

HERO And seemed I ever otherwise to you?

CLAUDIO Out on thee seeming, I will write against it!   50
> You seem to me as Dian in her orb,
> As chaste as is the bud ere it be blown:
> But you are more intemperate in your blood,
> Than Venus, or those pampered animals,
> That rage in savage sensuality.   55

HERO Is my lord well, that he doth speak so wide?

LEONATO Sweet prince, why speak not you?

DON PEDRO   What should I speak?
> I stand dishonoured that have gone about
> To link my dear friend to a common stale.

LEONATO Are these things spoken, or do I but dream?   60

DON JOHN Sir, they are spoken, and these things are true.

BENEDICK This looks not like a nuptial.

HERO   True, oh God!

CLAUDIO Leonato, stand I here?
> Is this the prince? Is this the prince's brother?
> Is this face Hero's? Are our eyes our own?   65

LEONATO All this is so, but what of this, my lord?

CLAUDIO Let me but move one question to your daughter,
> And by that fatherly and kindly power,
> That you have in her, bid her answer truly.

LEONATO I charge thee do so, as thou art my child.   70

HERO Oh God defend me, how am I beset!
> What kind of catechising call you this?

---

50 thee] Q; thy *Pope*; thee! *Seymour*   50 seeming,] Q; seeming! *Collier*   50 it!] it, Q   **61, 104** SH DON JOHN] *Bastard* Q   **70** do so] Q; doe F

45 **forehand sin** sin by anticipation (of the marriage vows).

50 ***Out ... seeming** This passage has been much emended, but there is no need: 'I've had enough of you seeming'.

50 **write ... it** make a public exposure of it.

51 **Dian** Diana, the moon, goddess of chastity. Compare Posthumus's jealous outburst, *Cym.* 2.5, where 'seem', 'write against' and 'Dian' all recur.

52 **blown** fully open.

54 **pampered** overfed and indulged in luxury. Whether a specific species of animal – goats, monkeys – is in Claudio's mind is hard to say. Venus draws the attention of Adonis to the behaviour of his horse, which is certainly a well-fed beast (*Venus and Adonis* 385–408).

59 **common stale** See 2.2.20; a prostitute of the lowest class (*OED* Stale *sb*³ 4).

67 **move** put.

68 **kindly power** natural authority.

CLAUDIO To make you answer truly to your name.

HERO Is it not Hero? Who can blot that name
   With any just reproach?

CLAUDIO   Marry that can Hero,   75
   Hero itself can blot out Hero's virtue.
   What man was he, talked with you yesternight,
   Out at your window betwixt twelve and one?
   Now if you are a maid, answer to this.

HERO I talked with no man at that hour, my lord.   80

DON PEDRO Why then are you no maiden. Leonato,
   I am sorry you must hear: upon mine honour,
   Myself, my brother, and this grievèd count
   Did see her, hear her, at that hour last night,
   Talk with a ruffian at her chamber window,   85
   Who hath indeed most like a liberal villain,
   Confessed the vile encounters they have had
   A thousand times in secret.

DON JOHN   Fie, fie, they are
   Not to be named my lord, not to be spoke of,
   There is not chastity enough in language,   90
   Without offence to utter them: thus, pretty lady,
   I am sorry for thy much misgovernment.

CLAUDIO Oh Hero! What a hero hadst thou been,
   If half thy outward graces had been placed
   About thy thoughts and counsels of thy heart?   95
   But fare thee well, most foul, most fair, farewell
   Thou pure impiety, and impious purity,
   For thee I'll lock up all the gates of love,

---

81 are you] Q; you are F 88 SH DON JOHN] *Iohn* Q 88–9 Fie . . . are / Not . . . spoke of,] Fie . . . lord, / Not . . . spoke of, Q 89 spoke] Q; spoken F 93 been] F; bin Q

73 answer . . . name The first question in the Church of England Catechism is 'What is your name?'

76 Hero itself i.e. the name itself. Borachio had promised that the watchers should hear him 'call Margaret Hero' (2.2.32).

86 liberal coarse or free in speech. Compare *Ham.* 4.7.169–70: 'long purples / That liberal shepherds give a grosser name'. The sense of 'generous' is also involved: he told them freely, without holding anything back.

92 much very great; more freely used as an adjective then than now. See Abbott 51.

92 misgovernment misconduct. Reason and will have not governed her passions as they should.

93–7 The use of elaborate figures – the pun on Hero, the oxymorons of fair foulness, pure impiety – is common for expressing strong emotion. Compare Leonato's extended play on 'mine' (127–31) below, or Juliet's punning on the three senses of 'I' (eye, aye), *Rom.* 3.2.45–50. But compare also the very different style of Beatrice's outburst (291–307) below. Her grief and anger are much more simply expressed – as is Romeo's final resolution.

98 the gates of love the senses, of which sight is predominant; compare *MV* 3.2.63–7: 'fancy . . . is engend'red in the eyes'.

And on my eyelids shall conjecture hang,
To turn all beauty into thoughts of harm,   100
And never shall it more be gracious.

LEONATO Hath no man's dagger here a point for me?

                    [*Hero faints*]

BEATRICE Why how now, cousin, wherefore sink you down?

DON JOHN Come let us go: these things come thus to light,
Smother her spirits up.

                    [*Exeunt Don Pedro, Don John and Claudio*]

BENEDICK   How doth the lady?   105

BEATRICE Dead I think, help, uncle!
Hero, why Hero: uncle: Signor Benedick: friar!

LEONATO Oh Fate! Take not away thy heavy hand,
Death is the fairest cover for her shame
That may be wished for.

BEATRICE   How now, cousin Hero?   110

FRIAR FRANCIS Have comfort, lady.

LEONATO   Dost thou look up?

FRIAR FRANCIS Yea, wherefore should she not?

LEONATO Wherefore? Why doth not every earthly thing
Cry shame upon her? Could she here deny
The story that is printed in her blood?   115
Do not live, Hero, do not ope thine eyes:
For did I think thou wouldst not quickly die,
Thought I thy spirits were stronger than thy shames,
Myself would on the rearward of reproaches
Strike at thy life. Grieved I, I had but one?   120
Chid I for that at frugal nature's frame?
Oh one too much by thee! Why had I one?
Why ever wast thou lovely in my eyes?
Why had I not with charitable hand,
Took up a beggar's issue at my gates,   125

---

102 SD] *Hanmer; not in* Q   105 SD] *Rowe; not in* Q   119 rearward] Q; reward F

---

99 **conjecture** suspicion.

105 **spirits** vital powers; aerial substances supposed to be carried in the bloodstream to control and maintain bodily functions.

111 **look up** i.e. to heaven, as free from blame. Compare *Ham.* 3.3.50–1: 'then I'll look up. / My fault is past.'

115 **printed in her blood** made plain by her blushes; but also 'unchangeably part of her nature'.

119 **rearward of reproaches** following after reproaches. The metaphor is military. If he did not expect the army of her own shame and his reproaches to cause her death, then as a rearguard to that army he would himself literally kill her.

123 **ever** always.

Who smirchèd thus, and mired with infamy,
I might have said, no part of it is mine,
This shame derives itself from unknown loins:
But mine, and mine I loved, and mine I praised,
And mine that I was proud on, mine so much,   130
That I myself, was to myself not mine,
Valuing of her: why she, oh she is fallen
Into a pit of ink, that the wide sea
Hath drops too few to wash her clean again,
And salt too little, which may season give   135
To her foul tainted flesh.

BENEDICK Sir, sir, be patient. For my part I am so attired in wonder, I
   know not what to say.

BEATRICE Oh on my soul my cousin is belied.

BENEDICK Lady, were you her bedfellow last night?   140

BEATRICE No truly not, although until last night,
   I have this twelve month been her bedfellow.

LEONATO Confirmed, confirmed, oh that is stronger made,
   Which was before barred up with ribs of iron.
   Would the two princes lie, and Claudio lie,   145
   Who loved her so, that speaking of her foulness,
   Washed it with tears? Hence from her, let her die.

FRIAR FRANCIS Hear me a little, for I have only been

---

126 smirchèd] Q; smeered F   132 fallen] F; falne, Q   141 No truly not,] No truly, not Q; No truly: not F   142 been]
bin Q   145 two princes] Q; Princes F   148–51 Hear . . . been / Silent . . . unto / This . . . lady. / I have marked] *As
prose* Q

136 foul tainted It does not seem necessary to
follow Dyce's conjecture 'foul-tainted', though many
editors do so.

137–8 Benedick's speech was cut into verse-
lengths by Pope and many later editors have followed
suit, ending the lines at '. . . patient, / . . . wonder /
. . . say./', but the result does not scan easily and in
any case involves a truncated line. The words have a
prose cadence, and it is best to let well alone. No
argument about the overcrowding of this page (G1ʳ in
Q; see 148–51 n. below and p. 42 above) depends
crucially on the assumption that the compositor
made two lines out of three here. 140 also, although
it has ten syllables, has a much less regular stress
pattern than Beatrice's lines at 139 and 141. It is no
discredit to Benedick that he should first express
scepticism, and then ask a sensible question in a
moderately calm manner. The contrast of his
language with Leonato's in rhythm and figure is
notable.

140 bedfellow The sharing of beds by adults of
the same sex was common. Rosalind and Celia did
so, and there seems nothing to arouse suspicion in
Iago's assertion (*Oth.* 3.3.413–26) that he has spent a
night in the same bed as Cassio – unlikely though it
may seem to us that the Adjutant should sleep with
the RSM. For a discussion of the traditional enmity
between the lieutenant and ensign in the company
structure of the Elizabethan army, see T. R. Henn,
The Living Image, 1972, p. 107.

141–2 For Lewis Carroll's proposed emendation
here, in a letter to Ellen Terry, see Appendix 2, p.
157 below.

148–51* This passage is set as prose crowded at
the bottom of the page on G1ʳ. If we assume that the
text was set seriatim and not 'cast off' and set by
formes (see p. 43 above), the most likely explanation
is that the compositor missed a passage out and did
not discover it until this forme of sheet G was made
up and consequently the corresponding forme as
well. The most likely eye-jump (as Newcomer suggested) would be from 'I have' in 148 to 'I have' in

Silent so long, and given way unto
This course of fortune, by noting of the lady.   150
I have marked
A thousand blushing apparitions,
To start into her face, a thousand innocent shames,
In angel whiteness beat away those blushes,
And in her eye there hath appeared a fire,   155
To burn the errors that these princes hold
Against her maiden truth: call me a fool,
Trust not my reading, nor my observations,
Which with experimental seal doth warrant
The tenure of my book: trust not my age,   160
My reverence, calling, nor divinity,
If this sweet lady lie not guiltless here,
Under some biting error.

LEONATO   Friar, it cannot be,
Thou seest that all the grace that she hath left,
Is that she will not add to her damnation   165
A sin of perjury, she not denies it:
Why seek'st thou then to cover with excuse,
That which appears in proper nakedness?

FRIAR FRANCIS Lady, what man is he you are accused of?

HERO They know that do accuse me, I know none: 170
If I know more of any man alive
Than that which maiden modesty doth warrant,
Let all my sins lack mercy. Oh my father,
Prove you that any man with me conversed,
At hours unmeet, or that I yesternight   175
Maintained the change of words with any creature,
Refuse me, hate me, torture me to death.

---

150 lady.] lady, Q   151 marked] markt, Q; markt. F   154 beat] Q; beare F

151, and no incoherence in the text would result. If
the passage is printed as verse a short line is inevit-
able. Most editors have followed Pope, ending the
first line at 'little', but are then tempted to improve
the rhythm of the following line by transposing 'been
silent' into 'silent been'. The order followed here
gives a satisfactory movement to the verse and allows
Friar Francis a significant pause before 'I have
marked . . .'
149 given way unto allowed to proceed.
153 innocent shames feelings of outraged
modesty (Newcomer).
158 observations studies of real events (in contrast to 'reading').

159 experimental seal the seal of experience.
160 tenure of my book tenor of my studies. The
Friar's experience of life confirms what he has
learned from books, and both assure him that Hero
is innocent.
163 biting sharp, corrosive. The Friar probably
also implies 'malicious, slanderous'.
166 not denies Abbott 305.
168 proper appropriate.
174–7 Prove you . . . Refuse me If you can prove
. . . then disown me.
176 change exchange.

FRIAR FRANCIS There is some strange misprision in the princes.
BENEDICK Two of them have the very bent of honour,
        And if their wisdoms be misled in this,   180
        The practice of it lives in John the bastard,
        Whose spirits toil in frame of villainies.
LEONATO I know not: if they speak but truth of her,
        These hands shall tear her, if they wrong her honour,
        The proudest of them shall well hear of it.   185
        Time hath not yet so dried this blood of mine,
        Nor age so eat up my invention,
        Nor fortune made such havoc of my means,
        Nor my bad life reft me so much of friends,
        But they shall find, awaked in such a kind,   190
        Both strength of limb, and policy of mind,
        Ability in means, and choice of friends,
        To quit me of them throughly.
FRIAR FRANCIS   Pause awhile,
        And let my counsel sway you in this case:
        Your daughter here the princes left for dead,   195
        Let her awhile be secretly kept in,
        And publish it, that she is dead indeed:
        Maintain a mourning ostentation,
        And on your family's old monument
        Hang mournful epitaphs, and do all rites,   200
        That appertain unto a burial.
LEONATO What shall become of this? What will this do?

---

195 princes left for dead,] *Theobald;* princesse (left for dead,) Q; Princesse (left for dead) F

---

178 misprision misapprehension.

181 practice cunning trickery. Compare 'This is practice, Gloucester' (*Lear* 5.3.152).

181 bastard This is the first explicit statement of John's bastardy, apart from stage directions and speech headings.

182 in frame of in contriving.

189 reft deprived.

190 in . . . kind in such a manner.

193 quit . . . throughly revenge myself on them thoroughly.

195 *princes See supplementary note, p. 146 below.

198 ostentation ceremony, show; with no adverse connotation. Compare *Ham.* 4.5.216: 'No noble rite nor formal ostentation'.

199 monument family burial vault. Compare

'Her body sleeps in Capel's monument' (*Rom.* 5.1.18).

200 Hang . . . epitaphs Compare: 'Enter . . . the coffin of the virgin, with a garland of flowers, with epitaphs pinned on it' (Middleton, *A Chaste Maid in Cheapside*, ed. A. T. Brissenden, 1968, 5.4.0 SD). See 5.3 below.

202 shall . . . will In the speech which follows the Friar uses 'shall' six times and 'will' thrice. All seem equally to express his confident expectation of the happy consequences of his plan. At the end of the sixteenth century as now these words were in many situations fully interchangeable. But see Abbott 321 on this passage: 'The indefinite unknown consequence is not personified, the definite project is personified.'

FRIAR FRANCIS Marry, this well carried, shall on her behalf,
Change slander to remorse, that is some good,
But not for that dream I on this strange course,   205
But on this travail look for greater birth:
She dying, as it must be so maintained,
Upon the instant that she was accused,
Shall be lamented, pitied, and excused
Of every hearer: for it so falls out,   210
That what we have, we prize not to the worth,
Whiles we enjoy it; but being lacked and lost,
Why then we rack the value, then we find
The virtue that possession would not show us
Whiles it was ours: so will it fare with Claudio: 215
When he shall hear she died upon his words
Th'idea of her life shall sweetly creep
Into his study of imagination,
And every lovely organ of her life,
Shall come apparelled in more precious habit,   220
More moving-delicate, and full of life,
Into the eye and prospect of his soul
Than when she lived indeed: then shall he mourn,
If ever love had interest in his liver,
And wish he had not so accusèd her: 225
No, though he thought his accusation true:
Let this be so, and doubt not but success
Will fashion the event in better shape
Than I can lay it down in likelihood.

---

203 Marry,] Mary Q; Marry F   217 Th'idea] Th Idæa Q; Th'Idea F   221 moving-delicate] *Capell;* moving delicate Q

204 remorse pity. Claudio will 'wish he had not so accusèd her' (225) but the sense of self-blame and the sense of suffering are much stronger in the modern use of the word.

206 travail Picks up the sense of 'travel' (not then distinguished in spelling) from 'this strange course', and shifts to the other sense with 'birth'.

213 rack stretch; a sense preserved in 'rack-renting'.

217 idea image, recollection.

218 study of imagination thoughtful musings.

219 organ of her life There is an apt imprecision about these words. The phrase could mean just her limbs and bodily parts – the organs by which she lives – but since 'her life' carries the sense of her total

behaviour and attitudes, 'organ' is obliged to take on a much more abstract sense. This combination of concrete and abstract-metaphysical is maintained into 'the eye and prospect of his soul' (222), so that she is to be imagined not only as more physically beautiful, but also as more beautiful in her life and relationships.

224 liver The seat of love. Compare 'their love may be call'd appetite, / No motion of the liver, but the palate' (*TN* 2.4.97–8).

227 success what follows; succeeding events.

227–32 Do this, and be confident that things will turn out even better than I am suggesting. But even if everything else fails, the belief that she is dead will put an end to gossip about her disgrace.

But if all aim but this be levelled false,   230
The supposition of the lady's death,
Will quench the wonder of her infamy.
And if it sort not well, you may conceal her,
As best befits her wounded reputation,
In some reclusive and religious life,   235
Out of all eyes, tongues, minds and injuries.

BENEDICK Signor Leonato, let the friar advise you,
And though you know my inwardness and love
Is very much unto the prince and Claudio,
Yet, by mine honour, I will deal in this,   240
As secretly and justly as your soul
Should with your body.

LEONATO   Being that I flow in grief,
The smallest twine may lead me.

FRIAR FRANCIS 'Tis well consented, presently away:
For to strange sores, strangely they strain the cure: 245
Come, lady, die to live, this wedding day
Perhaps is but prolonged: have patience and endure.

Exeunt [Friar Francis, Leonato and Hero]

BENEDICK Lady Beatrice, have you wept all this while?

BEATRICE Yea, and I will weep a while longer.

BENEDICK I will not desire that.   250

BEATRICE You have no reason, I do it freely.

BENEDICK Surely I do believe your fair cousin is wronged.

BEATRICE Ah, how much might the man deserve of me that would right
her!

BENEDICK Is there any way to show such friendship?   255

BEATRICE A very even way, but no such friend.

BENEDICK May a man do it?

---

247 SD *Exeunt . . . Hero] Rowe subst.; Exit* Q

233 **sort** turn out.

238 **inwardness** intimacy. Compare 'Sir, I was an inward of his' (*MM* 3.2.130).

242 **flow in** am carried away by (as in a flood); probably also 'am weeping bitterly'.

244–7 The Friar's quatrain firmly closes the scene of Hero's disgrace, which has been slightly distanced from us by its elaborate rhetoric. What follows – the crucial interview between Beatrice and Benedick – is in the familiar and much less remote medium of prose.

244 **presently** at once.

247 **prolonged** postponed.

250 **I . . . that** I don't want you to do that.

251 **You . . . freely** Beatrice pretends that Benedick meant 'I won't request you to do that', and replies 'There is no need to request me, I do it of my own free will.'

252 **wronged** Benedick does not imply an agent for the wrong – perhaps only 'there's been a terrible mistake'.

253 **right** revenge. Beatrice gives her literal antithesis a much greater force.

256 **even** plain and easy.

BEATRICE It is a man's office, but not yours.

BENEDICK I do love nothing in the world so well as you, is not that
    strange? 260

BEATRICE As strange as the thing I know not: it were as possible for me
    to say, I loved nothing so well as you, but believe me not, and yet I
    lie not, I confess nothing, nor I deny nothing: I am sorry for my
    cousin.

BENEDICK By my sword, Beatrice, thou lovest me. 265

BEATRICE Do not swear and eat it.

BENEDICK I will swear by it that you love me, and I will make him eat it
    that says I love not you.

BEATRICE Will you not eat your word?

BENEDICK With no sauce that can be devised to it: I protest I love thee. 270

BEATRICE Why then God forgive me.

BENEDICK What offence, sweet Beatrice?

BEATRICE You have stayed me in a happy hour, I was about to protest I
    loved you.

BENEDICK And do it with all thy heart. 275

BEATRICE I love you with so much of my heart, that none is left to
    protest.

BENEDICK Come bid me do anything for thee.

BEATRICE Kill Claudio.

BENEDICK Ha, not for the wide world. 280

BEATRICE You kill me to deny it, farewell.

BENEDICK Tarry, sweet Beatrice.

BEATRICE I am gone, though I am here, there is no love in you, nay, I
    pray you let me go.

266 swear] Q; sweare by it F   281 deny it] Q; denie F

258 It . . . yours Beatrice knows that Hero's reputation must be repaired by a successful challenge to
her slanderer, but the man to do this should be a
member of the family, or closely allied to it (compare
5.1.73–85). Benedick is not such a man, and is
besides 'inward' with the prince and Claudio. Her
dismissal allows him to change the subject and
declare his love – so putting himself in a position
where she can call upon him. There may also be the
implication 'you are not man enough to do it'.

260 strange Not to Beatrice, since she has already
been persuaded that Benedick loves her.

261–4 Beatrice can still equivocate, and one sense
of her words is 'I like you as much as I like nothing',
'I care nothing for you', but the equivocation lacks
conviction.

265 By my sword Appropriate for a gentleman as
the means by which in the last resort honour was
defended, and given religious symbolism by the cross
made by the intersection of blade and guard.

266 *eat it eat the oath you have sworn. F would
have him eat the sword, not his words (Tilley w825).

267 eat it eat the sword; i.e. receive it in his body.

271 God forgive me i.e. for the breach of
decorum she was about to make in declaring her love
for Benedick (273–4).

277 protest make objections. A quibble on the
sense 'affirm' in 273.

280 Ha . . . world Benedick has clearly not seen
implications in his declaration of which Beatrice has
been aware – and has almost warned him against.

281 You . . . it That you refuse it kills me.

BENEDICK Beatrice.   285

BEATRICE In faith I will go.

BENEDICK We'll be friends first.

BEATRICE You dare easier be friends with me, than fight with mine
      enemy.

BENEDICK Is Claudio thine enemy?   290

BEATRICE Is a not approved in the height a villain, that hath slandered,
      scorned, dishonoured my kinswoman? Oh that I were a man! What,
      bear her in hand, until they come to take hands, and then with
      public accusation, uncovered slander, unmitigated rancour? Oh
      God that I were a man! I would eat his heart in the market place.   295

BENEDICK Hear me, Beatrice.

BEATRICE Talk with a man out at a window, a proper saying.

BENEDICK Nay, but Beatrice.

BEATRICE Sweet Hero, she is wronged, she is slandered, she is undone.

BENEDICK Beat –   300

BEATRICE Princes and counties! Surely a princely testimony, a goodly
      count, Count Comfect, a sweet gallant surely, oh that I were a man
      for his sake! Or that I had any friend would be a man for my sake!
      But manhood is melted into curtsies, valour into compliment, and
      men are only turned into tongue, and trim ones too: he is now as   305
      valiant as Hercules, that only tells a lie, and swears it: I cannot be a
      man with wishing, therefore I will die a woman with grieving.

BENEDICK Tarry, good Beatrice, by this hand I love thee.

BEATRICE Use it for my love some other way than swearing by it.

BENEDICK Think you in your soul the Count Claudio hath wronged   310
      Hero?

BEATRICE Yea, as sure as I have a thought, or a soul.

BENEDICK Enough, I am engaged, I will challenge him. I will kiss your
      hand, and so I leave you: by this hand, Claudio shall render me a

---

300 Beat –] *Theobald;* Beat? Q   302 count, Count Comfect] Q; Count, Comfect F   304 curtsies] cursies Q   314 so I]
Q; so F

291 approved in the height proved in the
highest degree.

293 bear her in hand delude her with false
hopes.

294 uncovered discovered, suddenly disclosed.

297 a proper saying a likely story.

302 count (1) account, story (following
'testimony'); (2) accusation, legal charge (compare
Oth. 5.2.273: 'when we shall meet at compt'); (3)
'count' as Claudio's title of honour. 'Goodly' is ironic
in all three cases.

302 Count Comfect Count Candy; but also a
'count comfect' could be a made-up story, since
'comfect' = 'confected', 'made up from mixed
ingredients'. 'Confection' was a term in use at this
time for musical or literary compositions.

305 are ... tongue are good for words and
nothing else.

305 trim neat, smooth.

314 this hand hers; not (as at 308) his.

dear account: as you hear of me, so think of me: go comfort your   315
cousin, I must say she is dead, and so farewell.

[Exeunt]

[4.2] *Enter the Constables* [DOGBERRY *and* VERGES] *and the* [SEXTON *as*]
Town Clerk in gowns, [CONRADE *and*] BORACHIO

DOGBERRY Is our whole dissembly appeared?

VERGES Oh a stool and a cushion for the sexton.

SEXTON Which be the malefactors?

DOGBERRY Marry that am I, and my partner.

VERGES Nay that's certain, we have the exhibition to examine.   5

SEXTON But which are the offenders, that are to be examined? Let them
come before master constable.

DOGBERRY Yea marry, let them come before me: what is your name,
friend?

BORACHIO Borachio.   10

DOGBERRY Pray write down Borachio. Yours, sirrah?

CONRADE I am a gentleman, sir, and my name is Conrade.

DOGBERRY Write down Master Gentleman Conrade: masters, do you
serve God?

BORACHIO ⎫
⎬ Yea, sir, we hope.   15
CONRADE ⎭

DOGBERRY Write down, that they hope they serve God: and write God

Act 4, Scene 2   0 SD *Constables . . . the Sexton as Town Clerk in gowns . . .* BORACHIO] *Constables, Borachio, and the Towne clearke in gownes.* Q   1 SH DOGBERRY] *Keeper* Q   2, 5 SH VERGES] *Cowley* Q   4 SH DOGBERRY] *Andrew* Q   8 SH DOGBERRY] *Kemp* Q *(and throughout scene)*   15 SH BORACHIO / CONRADE] *Both* Q   15–17 Yea . . . villains] Q; *not in* F

Act 4, Scene 2

0 SD The location 'a prison' (Theobald) follows
from 3.5.51. Verges' speech (2) indicates that he is
supervising the setting on stage of appropriate
furniture and properties for a court, perhaps by the
Watchmen: there has been time enough since the
departure of the wedding guests for the journeymen
actors to change their costumes.

0 SD SEXTON This is the title in speech headings,
though Town Clerk appears in Q's stage direction.
He is, presumably, the 'learned writer' Francis Seacoal mentioned at 3.5.45.

0 SD gowns A black gown was the official garb of
constable and sexton.

1 SH *DOGBERRY For the rationalisation of the
interesting speech headings all through this scene in
Q see Textual Analysis, p. 153 below.

1 dissembly For 'assembly'. *OED* quotes a passage from Richard Baxter (1684) where it is used
ironically for the play on 'dissemble'.

3 malefactors Dogberry's claim to be one probably comes from his sense of 'factor', an official agent
or steward.

5 exhibition Probably for 'commission',
Leonato's authority for them to 'take their examination yourself' (3.5.38).

11 sirrah A term of contempt. Conrade in
response stands on his dignity.

15–17 *Yea . . . villains This passage was
perhaps removed from F because of the statute of
1606 (3 Jac. 1.c.21) against profanity.

first, for God defend but God should go before such villains: masters, it is proved already that you are little better than false knaves,
and it will go near to be thought so shortly: how answer you for
yourselves?   20
CONRADE Marry, sir, we say we are none.
DOGBERRY A marvellous witty fellow I assure you, but I will go about
    with him: come you hither, sirrah, a word in your ear, sir: I say to
    you, it is thought you are false knaves.
BORACHIO Sir, I say to you, we are none.   25
DOGBERRY Well, stand aside, 'fore God they are both in a tale: have you
    writ down, that they are none?
SEXTON Master constable, you go not the way to examine, you must call
    forth the watch that are their accusers.
DOGBERRY Yea marry, that's the eftest way, let the watch come forth.   30

[*Enter* SEACOAL, WATCHMAN 2 *and the rest of the Watch*]

Masters, I charge you in the prince's name, accuse these men.
SEACOAL This man said, sir, that Don John the prince's brother was a
    villain.
DOGBERRY Write down, Prince John a villain: why this is flat perjury, to
    call a prince's brother villain.   35
BORACHIO Master constable.
DOGBERRY Pray thee, fellow, peace, I do not like thy look I promise
    thee.
SEXTON What heard you him say else?
WATCHMAN 2 Marry that he had received a thousand ducats of Don   40
    John, for accusing the Lady Hero wrongfully.
DOGBERRY Flat burglary as ever was committed.
VERGES Yea by mass that it is.
SEXTON What else, fellow?
SEACOAL And that Count Claudio did mean upon his words, to dis-   45
    grace Hero before the whole assembly, and not marry her.

32, 45 SH SEACOAL] *Watch.I* Q   43 SH VERGES] *Const.* Q   43 mass] Q; th'masse F

17 **defend** forbid. Not a Dogberryan confusion:
compare 2.1.67.
22–3 **go about with** outmanoeuvre; possibly from
sailing.
23 **a word ... ear** a private word. Dogberry is
attempting to catch the accused in a fabrication by
interrogating them separately, as Daniel did the
wicked elders in Susanna 51–9. Since that is a most
famous story of the collusive defamation of an innocent woman, he takes Daniel's behaviour as his
precedent.
26 **are both ... tale** both tell the same story.
30 **eftest** quickest, most convenient; but as 'eft' is
cognate with 'after', Dogberry's nonce-word might
have been understood as 'slowest'.
43 **by mass** by the mass; a mild old-fashioned
oath.

DOGBERRY Oh villain! Thou wilt be condemned into everlasting redemption for this.

SEXTON What else?

SEACOAL This is all.

SEXTON And this is more, masters, than you can deny: Prince John is this morning secretly stolen away: Hero was in this manner accused, in this very manner refused, and upon the grief of this, suddenly died: master constable, let these men be bound, and brought to Leonato's: I will go before and show him their examination. [*Exit*] 55

VERGES Come, let them be opinioned.

CONRADE Let them be in the hands of coxcomb.

DOGBERRY God's my life, where's the sexton? Let him write down the prince's officer coxcomb: come, bind them, thou naughty varlet.

CONRADE Away, you are an ass, you are an ass. 60

DOGBERRY Dost thou not suspect my place? Dost thou not suspect my years? Oh that he were here to write me down an ass! But masters, remember that I am an ass, though it be not written down, yet forget not that I am an ass: no, thou villain, thou art full of piety as shall be proved upon thee by good witness: I am a wise fellow, and which is 65 more, an officer, and which is more, a householder, and which is more, as pretty a piece of flesh as any is in Messina, and one that knows the law, go to, and a rich fellow enough, go to, and a fellow that hath had losses, and one that hath two gowns, and everything handsome about him: bring him away: oh that I had been writ down 70 an ass!

Exeunt

5.[1] *Enter* LEONATO *and his brother* [ANTONIO]

ANTONIO If you go on thus, you will kill yourself,
And 'tis not wisdom thus to second grief,

50 SH SEACOAL] *Watch* Q   55 Leonato's:] Leonatoes, Q; *Leonato,* F   56 SH VERGES] *Constable* Q   57 SH CONRADE] *Theobald; Couley* Q; *Sex.* F   60 SH CONRADE] *Couley* Q   67 is in] Q; in F   71 SD *Exeunt*] *Exit.* Q   Act 5, Scene 1   5.1] *Actus Quintus* F; *not in* Q   1 SH ANTONIO] *Brother* Q (*and throughout scene*)

48 redemption For 'damnation'.
56–60* See supplementary note, p. 147 below, for a discussion of problems of speech attribution here.
58 God's God save.
59 naughty wicked, good for nothing; much stronger than the modern sense.
61–2 my years T. W. Craik points out the pun on my years and my ears associated with 'ass' ('*Much Ado About Nothing*', *Scrutiny* 19 (1952–3), 309).

Act 5, Scene 1
0 SD The location 'before Leonato's house' (Pope) would be indicated by an entry through Leonato's door.

       Against yourself.
LEONATO   I pray thee cease thy counsel,
       Which falls into mine ears as profitless,
       As water in a sieve: give not me counsel,   5
       Nor let no comforter delight mine ear,
       But such a one whose wrongs do suit with mine.
       Bring me a father that so loved his child,
       Whose joy of her is overwhelmed like mine,
       And bid him speak of patience,   10
       Measure his woe the length and breadth of mine,
       And let it answer every strain for strain,
       As thus for thus, and such a grief for such,
       In every lineament, branch, shape and form:
       If such a one will smile and stroke his beard,   15
       And sorrow; wag, cry hem, when he should groan;
       Patch grief with proverbs, make misfortune drunk
       With candle-wasters: bring him yet to me,
       And I of him will gather patience:
       But there is no such man, for, brother, men   20
       Can counsel and speak comfort to that grief,
       Which they themselves not feel, but tasting it,
       Their counsel turns to passion, which before,
       Would give preceptial medicine to rage,
       Fetter strong madness in a silken thread,   25
       Charm ache with air, and agony with words –
       No, no, 'tis all men's office, to speak patience

---

6 comforter] Q; comfort F   7 do] Q; doth F   16 And] Q; Bid *Capell*   16 sorrow] Q; sorry *conj. Steevens*   16 sorrow; ... groan;] *This edn*; sorrow, ... grone, Q   26 words –] words, Q

9 **of** in.

12 **answer ... strain** There is probably a musical metaphor here, as when one instrument answers another in a consort, as well as the sense 'stress of emotion'.

15–18* For a discussion of this passage and the many emendations and comments on it, see supplementary note, p. 147 below.

15 **stroke his beard** A gesture of self-satisfaction. Compare 'Now play me Nestor, hem, and stroke thy beard' (*Tro.* 1.3.165–6).

16 **wag** play the fool.

16 **cry hem** clear the throat.

17–18 These two lines paraphrase and parallel 15 and 16. Smiling and stroking the beard are the recognised prelude to uttering platitudes; clearing the throat and playing the wag go with drinking, not

to drown sorrows, but in foolish revelry. Compare 'when you breathe in your watering, they cry "hem!" and bid you play it off' (*1H4* 2.4.16–17), and 'drinks off candles' ends for flap-dragons, and rides the wild-mare with the boys . . .' (*2H4* 2.4.246–7). Candle-wasting – 'burning the candle at both ends' – has an established association with carousing. Some editors associate it with scholars burning midnight oil.

20–4 Men can give good advice and make comforting speeches about other people's sorrows, but if they felt the same sorrow themselves their good advice would be forgotten in their own suffering, although they had before been trotting out wise precepts as a cure for rage.

26 **air ... words** Words are air, they have no substance; compare 5.2.38–40.

To those that wring under the load of sorrow,
But no man's virtue nor sufficiency
To be so moral, when he shall endure
The like himself: therefore give me no counsel,　　30
My griefs cry louder than advertisement.

ANTONIO Therein do men from children nothing differ.

LEONATO I pray thee peace, I will be flesh and blood,
For there was never yet philosopher,　　　　　35
That could endure the tooth-ache patiently,
However they have writ the style of gods,
And made a push at chance and sufferance.

ANTONIO Yet bend not all the harm upon yourself,
Make those that do offend you suffer too.　　40

LEONATO There thou speak'st reason, nay I will do so,
My soul doth tell me, Hero is belied,
And that shall Claudio know, so shall the prince,
And all of them that thus dishonour her.

Enter DON PEDRO *and* CLAUDIO

ANTONIO Here comes the prince and Claudio hastily.　　45

DON PEDRO Good den, good den.

CLAUDIO　　　　　　　　　　Good day to both of you.

LEONATO Hear you, my lords?

DON PEDRO　　　　　　　We have some haste, Leonato.

LEONATO Some haste, my lord! Well, fare you well, my lord,
Are you so hasty now? Well, all is one.

DON PEDRO Nay do not quarrel with us, good old man.　　50

ANTONIO If he could right himself with quarrelling,
Some of us would lie low.

CLAUDIO　　　　　　　　　Who wrongs him?

---

44 SD DON PEDRO] *Prince* Q　46 SH DON PEDRO] *Prince* Q *(and throughout scene)*　51 right] Q; *rite* F

28 wring are wrung.

30 moral glib with moral precepts.

32 advertisement The general sense was still 'admonition' but the sense of 'public announcement' was already known, and such advertisements would have been cried in the streets.

35–6 Compare 3.2.20–3.

37 However Although.

37 writ . . . gods The Stoic philosophers claimed superiority to suffering and misfortune: this is to claim the attributes of gods. An alternative interpretation is that philosophers have written in an elevated style and (38) got somewhere near a solution of the problems of chance and human suffering.

38 push pish; an expression of 'contempt, impatience or disgust' (*COED*).

38 sufferance suffering; compare *MM* 3.1.79.

45 comes For the singular verb with conjoined subjects see Abbott 335, 336.

46 good den See 3.2.60 n.

49 all is one it doesn't matter. But this is not submission on Leonato's part; it is the prince's haste that does not matter, as the next line indicates.

BENEDICK Sir, I shall meet your wit in the career, and you charge it
    against me: I pray you choose another subject. 130
CLAUDIO Nay then, give him another staff, this last was broke cross.
DON PEDRO By this light, he changes more and more, I think he be
    angry indeed.
CLAUDIO If he be, he knows how to turn his girdle.
BENEDICK Shall I speak a word in your ear? 135
CLAUDIO God bless me from a challenge.
BENEDICK You are a villain, I jest not, I will make it good how you dare,
    with what you dare, and when you dare: do me right, or I will protest
    your cowardice: you have killed a sweet lady, and her death shall fall
    heavy on you: let me hear from you. 140
CLAUDIO Well I will meet you, so I may have good cheer.
DON PEDRO What, a feast, a feast?
CLAUDIO I'faith I thank him, he hath bid me to a calf's head and a
    capon, the which if I do not carve most curiously, say my knife's
    naught: shall I not find a woodcock too? 145
BENEDICK Sir, your wit ambles well, it goes easily.
DON PEDRO I'll tell thee how Beatrice praised thy wit the other day: I
    said thou hadst a fine wit, true said she, a fine little one: no said I, a
    great wit: right says she, a great gross one: nay said I, a good wit: just
    said she, it hurts nobody: nay said I, the gentleman is wise: certain 150
    said she, a wise gentleman: nay said I, he hath the tongues: that I
    believe said she, for he swore a thing to me on Monday night, which
    he forswore on Tuesday morning, there's a double tongue, there's

148 true said] Q; true saies F   153 tongue, there's] F; tongue theirs Q

129 **in the career** at full gallop. Compare 2.3.196; here the image is clearly from tilting.

131 **staff . . . cross** If in a tilting match the lance snapped (broke cross) instead of splintering, it was considered evidence of incompetence or cowardice in the rider. Claudio accuses Benedick of veering aside from the wit-combat 'as a puisne [= young, inexperienced] tilter, that spurs his horse but on one side, breaks his staff like a noble goose' (*AYLI* 3.4.43–5).

134 **turn his girdle** The expression is common (Tilley B698) and seems to mean 'prepare himself to fight', but there is no clear explanation why. Staunton suggested that 'the sword was formerly worn much at the back, and, to bring it within reach, the buckle of the belt or girdle had to be turned behind' (Furness).

137–8 **I will . . . dare** Benedick, as the challenger, offers Claudio the choice of weapons. Compare 1.1.31 n.

138 **protest** publish.

141 **cheer** entertainment. Claudio says he will accept the challenge 'so long as you fight well enough to make it worth my while'.

143–4 **a calf's head and a capon** a fool and a eunuch. For 'calf' compare 3.3.59 n. A capon is a castrated cock, with the consequent implication of 'coward'.

144 **curiously** skilfully.

145 **woodcock** A game-bird famous for its foolishness. Compare 'springes to catch woodcocks' (*Ham.* 1.3.115).

146 **ambles** The amble was the appropriate pace for a lady's horse.

149 **just** exactly.

151 **wise gentleman** fool.

151 **hath the tongues** speaks several languages.

LEONATO Marry thou dost wrong me, thou dissembler, thou:
    Nay, never lay thy hand upon thy sword,
    I fear thee not.
CLAUDIO   Marry beshrew my hand, 55
    If it should give your age such cause of fear,
    In faith my hand meant nothing to my sword.
LEONATO Tush, tush, man, never fleer and jest at me,
    I speak not like a dotard, nor a fool,
    As under privilege of age to brag, 60
    What I have done, being young, or what would do,
    Were I not old: know, Claudio, to thy head,
    Thou hast so wronged mine innocent child and me,
    That I am forced to lay my reverence by,
    And with grey hairs and bruise of many days, 65
    Do challenge thee to trial of a man:
    I say thou hast belied mine innocent child.
    Thy slander hath gone through and through her heart,
    And she lies buried with her ancestors:
    Oh in a tomb where never scandal slept, 70
    Save this of hers, framed by thy villainy.
CLAUDIO My villainy?
LEONATO   Thine, Claudio, thine I say.
DON PEDRO You say not right, old man.
LEONATO   My lord, my lord,
    I'll prove it on his body if he dare,
    Despite his nice fence, and his active practice,
    His May of youth, and bloom of lustihood. 75
CLAUDIO Away, I will not have to do with you.
LEONATO Canst thou so daff me? Thou hast killed my child,
    If thou kill'st me, boy, thou shalt kill a man.

53 Marry thou] Q; Marry y^u F

53 ***thou** Leonato uses the familiar and (in this situation) contemptuous second person singular to address Claudio, and maintains this until his exit. F's 'y^u' is a contraction to avoid an overrun line.

55 **beshrew** ill befall, curse. A weak imprecation.

57 **my hand . . . sword** my hand had no intention to use my sword.

58 **fleer** grin, sneer. Halliwell quotes Palsgrave: 'I fleere, I make an yvell countenaunce with the mouthe by uncoveryng of the tethe' (Furness).

62 **to thy head** to your face.

66 **trial . . . man** single combat.

67–9 **belied . . . lies** In giving Claudio the lie Leonato himself tells one. This scene modulates beautifully between pathos and farce.

75 **nice . . . practice** skill in fencing and excellent training.

78 **daff** brush aside.

79 **boy** We know that Claudio is very young (1.1.11–12), so this denial of his manhood, picked up and repeated by Antonio, will be particularly offensive.

ANTONIO He shall kill two of us, and men indeed,   80
    But that's no matter, let him kill one first:
    Win me and wear me, let him answer me,
    Come follow me, boy, come, Sir Boy, come follow me,
    Sir Boy, I'll whip you from your foining fence,
    Nay, as I am a gentleman, I will.
LEONATO   Brother.   85
ANTONIO Content yourself, God knows, I loved my niece,
    And she is dead, slandered to death by villains,
    That dare as well answer a man indeed,
    As I dare take a serpent by the tongue.
    Boys, apes, braggarts, Jacks, milksops.
LEONATO   Brother Anthony.   90
ANTONIO Hold you content, what, man! I know them, yea
    And what they weigh, even to the utmost scruple:
    Scambling, out-facing, fashion-monging boys,
    That lie, and cog, and flout, deprave and slander,
    Go anticly, and show outward hideousness,   95
    And speak off half a dozen dangerous words,
    How they might hurt their enemies, if they durst,
    And this is all.
LEONATO But brother Anthony –
ANTONIO   Come 'tis no matter,
    Do not you meddle, let me deal in this.   100
DON PEDRO Gentlemen both, we will not wake your patience,
    My heart is sorry for your daughter's death:

---

90 Boys, apes] Q; Boyes' apes F 99 Anthony –] *Theobald*; Anthonie. Q

---

82 **Win . . . wear me** Beat me (in a fight) and *then* you can give me orders (Tilley W408).

82 **answer me** respond to my challenge.

84 **foining** To foin is to thrust with a pointed weapon. Antonio indicates his old-fashioned disapproval of the rapier and the modern style of fighting where only the point and not the edge of the blade was used.

88 **a man indeed** a real man.

90 **Jacks** knaves.

92 **scruple** A very small weight in apothecary's measure.

93 **Scambling** Scrambling, unruly.

93 **fashion-monging** following every new fashion.

94 **cog** cheat.

94 **deprave** denigrate.

95 **Go anticly** Dress and behave like buffoons.

99 ***But . . . Anthony** – Many editors, following Theobald, end Leonato's brief speeches at 85 and 90 above with dashes, as well as this one. They are unsuccessful attempts to attract Antonio's attention rather than interjections which are cut off. In this case, however, the broken line suggests that Antonio has stopped for breath when Leonato speaks. It is evidence of Antonio's extreme agitation that he does not allow Leonato to continue.

101 **wake your patience** disturb you. The passage has been interpreted as ironical (since the two old men are already very impatient) or as corrupt. The prince wishes to end the encounter, and his meaning probably is 'we will not disturb your peace of mind any longer'.

    But on my honour she was charged with nothing
    But what was true, and very full of proof.
LEONATO My lord, my lord –
DON PEDRO   I will not hear you.   105
LEONATO No come, brother, away, I will be heard.
ANTONIO And shall, or some of us will smart for it.
                    Exeunt Leonato and Antonio
DON PEDRO See, see, here comes the man we went to seek.

          Enter BENEDICK

CLAUDIO Now, signor, what news?
BENEDICK   Good day, my lord.
DON PEDRO Welcome, signor, you are almost come to part almost a   110
    fray.
CLAUDIO We had like to have had our two noses snapped off with two
    old men without teeth.
DON PEDRO Leonato and his brother: what think'st thou? Had we
    fought, I doubt we should have been too young for them.   115
BENEDICK In a false quarrel there is no true valour: I came to seek you
    both.
CLAUDIO We have been up and down to seek thee, for we are high
    proof melancholy, and would fain have it beaten away, wilt thou use
    thy wit?   120
BENEDICK It is in my scabbard, shall I draw it?
DON PEDRO Dost thou wear thy wit by thy side?
CLAUDIO Never any did so, though very many have been beside their
    wit: I will bid thee draw, as we do the minstrels, draw to pleasure us.
DON PEDRO As I am an honest man, he looks pale, art thou sick, or   125
    angry?
CLAUDIO What, courage, man: what though care killed a cat, thou hast
    mettle enough in thee to kill care.

---

105 lord –] Lord. Q   107 SD *Leonato and Antonio*] amb. Q *(at 106); ambo* F   108 SD] *At* 107 Q; *at* 105 F   112 like] likt Q

---

109 **my lord** Benedick pointedly ignores Claudio's greeting.

112 **with** by.

115 **doubt** think it probable.

118–9 **high proof** (1) to a very high degree, (2) of tested quality.

121 **in my scabbard** Benedick is in the humour

for fighting not jesting, and Claudio and the prince are slow to recognise this.

124 **draw** i.e. draw (1) a sword from its scabbard, (2) an instrument from its case, or (3) a bow over the strings.

127 **care . . . cat** Proverbial: Tilley C84.

two tongues: thus did she an hour together trans-shape thy particular virtues, yet at last she concluded with a sigh, thou wast the 155
properest man in Italy.

CLAUDIO For the which she wept heartily, and said she cared not.

DON PEDRO Yea that she did, but yet for all that, and if she did not hate him deadly, she would love him dearly, the old man's daughter told us all. 160

CLAUDIO All, all, and moreover, God saw him when he was hid in the garden.

DON PEDRO But when shall we set the savage bull's horns on the sensible Benedick's head?

CLAUDIO Yea and text underneath, 'Here dwells Benedick the married 165
man'?

BENEDICK Fare you well, boy, you know my mind, I will leave you now to your gossip-like humour: you break jests as braggarts do their blades, which God be thanked hurt not: my lord, for your many courtesies I thank you: I must discontinue your company: your 170
brother the bastard is fled from Messina: you have among you killed a sweet and innocent lady: for my Lord Lack-beard there, he and I shall meet, and till then peace be with him.   [*Exit*]

DON PEDRO He is in earnest.

CLAUDIO In most profound earnest, and I'll warrant you, for the love of 175
Beatrice.

DON PEDRO And hath challenged thee?

CLAUDIO Most sincerely.

DON PEDRO What a pretty thing man is, when he goes in his doublet and hose, and leaves off his wit! 180

CLAUDIO He is then a giant to an ape, but then is an ape a doctor to such a man.

177 thee?] *Rowe;* thee. Q

156 properest Compare 2.3.155 n.

159 old man's daughter Hero. This shows remarkable callousness in Don Pedro, since we must assume that he believes Hero to have died the same morning.

161–2 God ... garden An oblique reference to 2.3. After they had eaten the apple of the tree of knowledge Adam and Eve 'hid themselves from the presence of the lord God amongst the trees of the garden' (Gen. 3.8).

163–4 savage ... head Compare 1.1.193–9.

168–9 braggarts ... blades i.e. in private, while pretending it was done in a fight. Compare Peto's answer when the prince asks 'how came Falstaff's

sword so hack'd?' (*1H4* 2.4.303–7): 'Why, he hack'd it with his dagger, and said he would swear truth out of England but he would make you believe it was done in fight.'

179–80 goes ... wit wears clothes (which distinguishes him superficially from the beasts) but forgets the more important faculty of reason (which is the real distinction). 'Doublet and hose' has been taken to imply 'without a cloak', that is, stripped for a fight.

181–2 He ... man A man delivering a challenge seems a hero to a fool, while in fact the fool is the wiser of the two.

DON PEDRO But soft you, let me be, pluck up my heart, and be sad, did
he not say my brother was fled?

Enter DOGBERRY *and* VERGES, CONRADE *and* BORACHIO [*with*
Watchmen]

DOGBERRY Come you, sir, if justice cannot tame you, she shall ne'er   185
weigh more reasons in her balance, nay, and you be a cursing
hypocrite once, you must be looked to.

DON PEDRO How now, two of my brother's men bound? Borachio one.

CLAUDIO Hearken after their offence, my lord.

DON PEDRO Officers, what offence have these men done?   190

DOGBERRY Marry, sir, they have committed false report, moreover they
have spoken untruths, secondarily, they are slanders, sixth and
lastly, they have belied a lady, thirdly they have verified unjust
things, and to conclude, they are lying knaves.

DON PEDRO First I ask thee what they have done, thirdly I ask thee   195
what's their offence, sixth and lastly why they are committed, and to
conclude, what you lay to their charge?

CLAUDIO Rightly reasoned, and in his own division, and by my troth
there's one meaning well suited.

DON PEDRO Who have you offended, masters, that you are thus bound   200
to your answer? This learned constable is too cunning to be understood: what's your offence?

BORACHIO Sweet prince, let me go no farther to mine answer: do you
hear me, and let this count kill me: I have deceived even your very
eyes: what your wisdoms could not discover, these shallow fools   205
have brought to light, who in the night overheard me confessing to
this man, how Don John your brother incensed me to slander the
Lady Hero, how you were brought into the orchard, and saw me

184 SD *Enter . . .* BORACHIO] *Enter Constables, Conrade, and Borachio* Q *(after 177);* Constable F   185 SH DOGBERRY]
Const. Q *(and throughout scene)*

183 **soft you** steady; wait a moment. Compare
Oth. 5.2.338.
183 **pluck . . . sad** The news that Don John has
fled is clearly bad news, and perhaps Don Pedro
immediately suspects that Hero was maligned. Faced
with these misgivings he says: pull yourself together,
my heart, and consider these matters seriously.
186 **reasons** Pronounced much like 'raisins'
(Kökeritz, p. 138), so it has been suggested (initially
by Ritson) that Dogberry's vision of Justice is as a
grocer, weighing dried fruit; but there is nothing

incongruous in Justice weighing reasons (= arguments pro and con), so the joke is not very obvious.
186 **cursing** accursed.
187 **once** in a word. Abbott 57.
189 **Hearken after** Enquire about.
198 **division** In logic or rhetoric, the organisation
of the parts of an argument.
199 **well suited** well dressed up. Dogberry has
said the same thing in six different ways: the idea is
the common one of language as the dress of thought.

court Margaret in Hero's garments, how you disgraced her when
you should marry her: my villainy they have upon record, which I   210
had rather seal with my death, than repeat over to my shame: the
lady is dead upon mine and my master's false accusation: and briefly
I desire nothing but the reward of a villain.

DON PEDRO Runs not this speech like iron through your blood?

CLAUDIO I have drunk poison whiles he uttered it.   215

DON PEDRO But did my brother set thee on to this?

BORACHIO Yea, and paid me richly for the practice of it.

DON PEDRO He is composed and framed of treachery,
    And fled he is upon this villainy.

CLAUDIO Sweet Hero, now thy image doth appear   220
    In the rare semblance that I loved it first.

DOGBERRY Come, bring away the plaintiffs, by this time our sexton hath
reformed Signor Leonato of the matter: and masters, do not forget
to specify when time and place shall serve, that I am an ass.

VERGES Here, here comes Master Signor Leonato, and the sexton too. 225

Enter LEONATO, *his brother* [ANTONIO] *and the Sexton*

LEONATO Which is the villain? Let me see his eyes,
    That when I note another man like him,
    I may avoid him: which of these is he?

BORACHIO If you would know your wronger, look on me.

LEONATO Art thou the slave that with thy breath hast killed   230
    Mine innocent child?

BORACHIO   Yea, even I alone.

LEONATO No, not so, villain, thou beliest thyself,
    Here stand a pair of honourable men,
    A third is fled that had a hand in it:
    I thank you, princes, for my daughter's death,   235
    Record it with your high and worthy deeds,
    'Twas bravely done, if you bethink you of it.

CLAUDIO I know not how to pray your patience,
    Yet I must speak, choose your revenge yourself,
    Impose me to what penance your invention   240

---

225 SH VERGES] *Con.* 2 Q   225 SD LEONATO . . . *Sexton*] Q; *Leonato.* F   230 thou the] Q; thou thou the F   230–1 Art
. . . killed / Mine . . . child?] Q; *as prose* F

209 **Margaret . . . garments** The only time this
circumstantial detail is mentioned.

209 **how . . . her** What happened in the church
was not part of the Watch's discovery.

212 **mine and my** For distinctions in the use of
these see Abbott 237 and 238.

217 **practice** See 4.1.181 n.

240 **Impose me to** Impose on me.

Can lay upon my sin, yet sinned I not,
But in mistaking.
DON PEDRO   By my soul nor I,
          And yet to satisfy this good old man,
          I would bend under any heavy weight,
          That he'll enjoin me to.   245
LEONATO I cannot bid you bid my daughter live,
          That were impossible, but I pray you both,
          Possess the people in Messina here,
          How innocent she died, and if your love
          Can labour aught in sad invention,   250
          Hang her an epitaph upon her tomb,
          And sing it to her bones, sing it tonight:
          Tomorrow morning come you to my house,
          And since you could not be my son-in-law,
          Be yet my nephew: my brother hath a daughter,   255
          Almost the copy of my child that's dead,
          And she alone is heir to both of us,
          Give her the right you should have given her cousin,
          And so dies my revenge.
CLAUDIO   Oh noble sir!
          Your over kindness doth wring tears from me,   260
          I do embrace your offer, and dispose
          For henceforth of poor Claudio.
LEONATO Tomorrow then I will expect your coming,
          Tonight I take my leave: this naughty man
          Shall face-to-face be brought to Margaret,   265
          Who I believe was packed in all this wrong,
          Hired to it by your brother.
BORACHIO   No by my soul she was not,
          Nor knew not what she did when she spoke to me,
          But always hath been just and virtuous
          In anything that I do know by her.   270
DOGBERRY Moreover, sir, which indeed is not under white and black,
          this plaintiff here, the offender, did call me ass, I beseech you let it
          be remembered in his punishment: and also the watch heard them

---

248 **Possess** Make known to.

257 **she . . . us** Compare 1.2.1, where Antonio has
a son.

261 **dispose** The syntax is abrupt – reflecting
perhaps Claudio's relief at getting off so lightly. The
subject of 'dispose' may be understood as 'you' (i.e.

Leonato) or as 'I' – I dispose of poor Claudio (to
your guidance). The sense is much the same.

264 **naughty** See 4.2.59 n.

266 **packed** an accomplice.

271 **under . . . black** in writing.

LEONATO Marry thou dost wrong me, thou dissembler, thou:
          Nay, never lay thy hand upon thy sword,
          I fear thee not.
CLAUDIO   Marry beshrew my hand,   55
          If it should give your age such cause of fear,
          In faith my hand meant nothing to my sword.
LEONATO Tush, tush, man, never fleer and jest at me,
          I speak not like a dotard, nor a fool,
          As under privilege of age to brag,   60
          What I have done, being young, or what would do,
          Were I not old: know, Claudio, to thy head,
          Thou hast so wronged mine innocent child and me,
          That I am forced to lay my reverence by,
          And with grey hairs and bruise of many days,   65
          Do challenge thee to trial of a man:
          I say thou hast belied mine innocent child.
          Thy slander hath gone through and through her heart,
          And she lies buried with her ancestors:
          Oh in a tomb where never scandal slept,   70
          Save this of hers, framed by thy villainy.
CLAUDIO My villainy?
LEONATO   Thine, Claudio, thine I say.
DON PEDRO You say not right, old man.
LEONATO   My lord, my lord,
          I'll prove it on his body if he dare,
          Despite his nice fence, and his active practice,   75
          His May of youth, and bloom of lustihood.
CLAUDIO Away, I will not have to do with you.
LEONATO Canst thou so daff me? Thou hast killed my child,
          If thou kill'st me, boy, thou shalt kill a man.

53 Marry thou] Q; Marry yᵘ F

53 *thou Leonato uses the familiar and (in this situation) contemptuous second person singular to address Claudio, and maintains this until his exit. F's 'yᵘ' is a contraction to avoid an overrun line.
55 beshrew ill befall, curse. A weak imprecation.
57 my hand . . . sword my hand had no intention to use my sword.
58 fleer grin, sneer. Halliwell quotes Palsgrave: 'I fleere, I make an yvell countenaunce with the mouthe by uncoveryng of the tethe' (Furness).
62 to thy head to your face.

66 trial . . . man single combat.
67–9 belied . . . lies In giving Claudio the lie Leonato himself tells one. This scene modulates beautifully between pathos and farce.
75 nice . . . practice skill in fencing and excellent training.
78 daff brush aside.
79 boy We know that Claudio is very young (1.1.11–12), so this denial of his manhood, picked up and repeated by Antonio, will be particularly offensive.

ANTONIO He shall kill two of us, and men indeed,   80
        But that's no matter, let him kill one first:
        Win me and wear me, let him answer me,
        Come follow me, boy, come, Sir Boy, come follow me,
        Sir Boy, I'll whip you from your foining fence,
        Nay, as I am a gentleman, I will.

LEONATO   Brother.   85

ANTONIO Content yourself, God knows, I loved my niece,
        And she is dead, slandered to death by villains,
        That dare as well answer a man indeed,
        As I dare take a serpent by the tongue.
        Boys, apes, braggarts, Jacks, milksops.

LEONATO   Brother Anthony.   90

ANTONIO Hold you content, what, man! I know them, yea
        And what they weigh, even to the utmost scruple:
        Scambling, out-facing, fashion-monging boys,
        That lie, and cog, and flout, deprave and slander,
        Go anticly, and show outward hideousness,   95
        And speak off half a dozen dangerous words,
        How they might hurt their enemies, if they durst,
        And this is all.

LEONATO But brother Anthony –

ANTONIO   Come 'tis no matter,
        Do not you meddle, let me deal in this.   100

DON PEDRO Gentlemen both, we will not wake your patience,
        My heart is sorry for your daughter's death:

---

90 Boys, apes] Q; Boyes' apes F   99 Anthony –] *Theobald;* Anthonie. Q

---

82 Win . . . wear me Beat me (in a fight) and *then* you can give me orders (Tilley w408).

82 answer me respond to my challenge.

84 foining To foin is to thrust with a pointed weapon. Antonio indicates his old-fashioned disapproval of the rapier and the modern style of fighting where only the point and not the edge of the blade was used.

88 a man indeed a real man.

90 Jacks knaves.

92 scruple A very small weight in apothecary's measure.

93 Scambling Scrambling, unruly.

93 fashion-monging following every new fashion.

94 cog cheat.

94 deprave denigrate.

95 Go anticly Dress and behave like buffoons.

99 *But . . . Anthony – Many editors, following Theobald, end Leonato's brief speeches at 85 and 90 above with dashes, as well as this one. They are unsuccessful attempts to attract Antonio's attention rather than interjections which are cut off. In this case, however, the broken line suggests that Antonio has stopped for breath when Leonato speaks. It is evidence of Antonio's extreme agitation that he does not allow Leonato to continue.

101 wake your patience disturb you. The passage has been interpreted as ironical (since the two old men are already very impatient) or as corrupt. The prince wishes to end the encounter, and his meaning probably is 'we will not disturb your peace of mind any longer'.

But on my honour she was charged with nothing
But what was true, and very full of proof.
LEONATO My lord, my lord –
DON PEDRO   I will not hear you.   105
LEONATO No come, brother, away, I will be heard.
ANTONIO And shall, or some of us will smart for it.
          Exeunt Leonato and Antonio
DON PEDRO See, see, here comes the man we went to seek.

     Enter BENEDICK

CLAUDIO Now, signor, what news?
BENEDICK   Good day, my lord.
DON PEDRO Welcome, signor, you are almost come to part almost a 110
  fray.
CLAUDIO We had like to have had our two noses snapped off with two
  old men without teeth.
DON PEDRO Leonato and his brother: what think'st thou? Had we
  fought, I doubt we should have been too young for them. 115
BENEDICK In a false quarrel there is no true valour: I came to seek you
  both.
CLAUDIO We have been up and down to seek thee, for we are high
  proof melancholy, and would fain have it beaten away, wilt thou use
  thy wit?   120
BENEDICK It is in my scabbard, shall I draw it?
DON PEDRO Dost thou wear thy wit by thy side?
CLAUDIO Never any did so, though very many have been beside their
  wit: I will bid thee draw, as we do the minstrels, draw to pleasure us.
DON PEDRO As I am an honest man, he looks pale, art thou sick, or 125
  angry?
CLAUDIO What, courage, man: what though care killed a cat, thou hast
  mettle enough in thee to kill care.

---

105 lord –] Lord. Q 107 SD *Leonato and Antonio*] amb. Q *(at 106)*; ambo F 108 SD] *At 107* Q; *at 105* F 112 like]
likt Q

109 my lord Benedick pointedly ignores
Claudio's greeting.
 112 with by.
 115 doubt think it probable.
 118–9 high proof (1) to a very high degree, (2) of
tested quality.
 121 in my scabbard Benedick is in the humour

for fighting not jesting, and Claudio and the prince
are slow to recognise this.
 124 draw i.e. draw (1) a sword from its scabbard,
(2) an instrument from its case, or (3) a bow over the
strings.
 127 care . . . cat Proverbial: Tilley C84.

BENEDICK Sir, I shall meet your wit in the career, and you charge it
  against me: I pray you choose another subject.   130

CLAUDIO Nay then, give him another staff, this last was broke cross.

DON PEDRO By this light, he changes more and more, I think he be
  angry indeed.

CLAUDIO If he be, he knows how to turn his girdle.

BENEDICK Shall I speak a word in your ear?   135

CLAUDIO God bless me from a challenge.

BENEDICK You are a villain, I jest not, I will make it good how you dare,
  with what you dare, and when you dare: do me right, or I will protest
  your cowardice: you have killed a sweet lady, and her death shall fall
  heavy on you: let me hear from you.   140

CLAUDIO Well I will meet you, so I may have good cheer.

DON PEDRO What, a feast, a feast?

CLAUDIO I'faith I thank him, he hath bid me to a calf's head and a
  capon, the which if I do not carve most curiously, say my knife's
  naught: shall I not find a woodcock too?   145

BENEDICK Sir, your wit ambles well, it goes easily.

DON PEDRO I'll tell thee how Beatrice praised thy wit the other day: I
  said thou hadst a fine wit, true said she, a fine little one: no said I, a
  great wit: right says she, a great gross one: nay said I, a good wit: just
  said she, it hurts nobody: nay said I, the gentleman is wise: certain   150
  said she, a wise gentleman: nay said I, he hath the tongues: that I
  believe said she, for he swore a thing to me on Monday night, which
  he forswore on Tuesday morning, there's a double tongue, there's

---

148 true said] Q; true saies F   153 tongue, there's] F; tongue theirs Q

---

129 **in the career** at full gallop. Compare 2.3.196;
here the image is clearly from tilting.

131 **staff ... cross** If in a tilting match the lance
snapped (broke cross) instead of splintering, it was
considered evidence of incompetence or cowardice
in the rider. Claudio accuses Benedick of veering
aside from the wit-combat 'as a puisne [= young,
inexperienced] tilter, that spurs his horse but on one
side, breaks his staff like a noble goose' (*AYLI*
3.4.43–5).

134 **turn his girdle** The expression is common
(Tilley B698) and seems to mean 'prepare himself to
fight', but there is no clear explanation why. Staunton suggested that 'the sword was formerly worn
much at the back, and, to bring it within reach, the
buckle of the belt or girdle had to be turned behind'
(Furness).

137–8 **I will ... dare** Benedick, as the challenger,
offers Claudio the choice of weapons. Compare
1.1.31 n.

138 **protest** publish.

141 **cheer** entertainment. Claudio says he will
accept the challenge 'so long as you fight well enough
to make it worth my while'.

143–4 **a calf's head and a capon** a fool and a
eunuch. For 'calf' compare 3.3.59 n. A capon is a
castrated cock, with the consequent implication of
'coward'.

144 **curiously** skilfully.

145 **woodcock** A game-bird famous for its
foolishness. Compare 'springes to catch woodcocks'
(*Ham.* 1.3.115).

146 **ambles** The amble was the appropriate pace
for a lady's horse.

149 **just** exactly.

151 **wise gentleman** fool.

151 **hath the tongues** speaks several languages.

two tongues: thus did she an hour together trans-shape thy particu-
lar virtues, yet at last she concluded with a sigh, thou wast the   155
properest man in Italy.

CLAUDIO For the which she wept heartily, and said she cared not.

DON PEDRO Yea that she did, but yet for all that, and if she did not hate
him deadly, she would love him dearly, the old man's daughter told
us all.   160

CLAUDIO All, all, and moreover, God saw him when he was hid in the
garden.

DON PEDRO But when shall we set the savage bull's horns on the
sensible Benedick's head?

CLAUDIO Yea and text underneath, 'Here dwells Benedick the married   165
man'?

BENEDICK Fare you well, boy, you know my mind, I will leave you now
to your gossip-like humour: you break jests as braggarts do their
blades, which God be thanked hurt not: my lord, for your many
courtesies I thank you: I must discontinue your company: your   170
brother the bastard is fled from Messina: you have among you killed
a sweet and innocent lady: for my Lord Lack-beard there, he and I
shall meet, and till then peace be with him.   *[Exit]*

DON PEDRO He is in earnest.

CLAUDIO In most profound earnest, and I'll warrant you, for the love of   175
Beatrice.

DON PEDRO And hath challenged thee?

CLAUDIO Most sincerely.

DON PEDRO What a pretty thing man is, when he goes in his doublet
and hose, and leaves off his wit!   180

CLAUDIO He is then a giant to an ape, but then is an ape a doctor to
such a man.

---

177 thee?] *Rowe;* thee. Q

156 properest Compare 2.3.155 n.

159 old man's daughter Hero. This shows
remarkable callousness in Don Pedro, since we must
assume that he believes Hero to have died the same
morning.

161–2 God ... garden An oblique reference to
2.3. After they had eaten the apple of the tree of
knowledge Adam and Eve 'hid themselves from the
presence of the lord God amongst the trees of the
garden' (Gen. 3.8).

163–4 savage ... head Compare 1.1.193–9.

168–9 braggarts ... blades i.e. in private, while
pretending it was done in a fight. Compare Peto's
answer when the prince asks 'how came Falstaff's
sword so hack'd?' (*1H4* 2.4.303–7): 'Why, he hack'd
it with his dagger, and said he would swear truth out
of England but he would make you believe it was
done in fight.'

179–80 goes ... wit wears clothes (which distinguishes him superficially from the beasts) but
forgets the more important faculty of reason (which
is the real distinction). 'Doublet and hose' has been
taken to imply 'without a cloak', that is, stripped for a
fight.

181–2 He ... man A man delivering a challenge
seems a hero to a fool, while in fact the fool is the
wiser of the two.

DON PEDRO But soft you, let me be, pluck up my heart, and be sad, did
he not say my brother was fled?

Enter DOGBERRY *and* VERGES, CONRADE *and* BORACHIO [*with*
Watchmen]

DOGBERRY Come you, sir, if justice cannot tame you, she shall ne'er   185
weigh more reasons in her balance, nay, and you be a cursing
hypocrite once, you must be looked to.

DON PEDRO How now, two of my brother's men bound? Borachio one.

CLAUDIO Hearken after their offence, my lord.

DON PEDRO Officers, what offence have these men done?   190

DOGBERRY Marry, sir, they have committed false report, moreover they
have spoken untruths, secondarily, they are slanders, sixth and
lastly, they have belied a lady, thirdly they have verified unjust
things, and to conclude, they are lying knaves.

DON PEDRO First I ask thee what they have done, thirdly I ask thee   195
what's their offence, sixth and lastly why they are committed, and to
conclude, what you lay to their charge?

CLAUDIO Rightly reasoned, and in his own division, and by my troth
there's one meaning well suited.

DON PEDRO Who have you offended, masters, that you are thus bound   200
to your answer? This learned constable is too cunning to be understood: what's your offence?

BORACHIO Sweet prince, let me go no farther to mine answer: do you
hear me, and let this count kill me: I have deceived even your very
eyes: what your wisdoms could not discover, these shallow fools   205
have brought to light, who in the night overheard me confessing to
this man, how Don John your brother incensed me to slander the
Lady Hero, how you were brought into the orchard, and saw me

---

184 SD *Enter . . .* BORACHIO] *Enter Constables, Conrade, and Borachio* Q (*after 177*); *Constable* F   185 SH DOGBERRY]
Const. Q (*and throughout scene*)

183 **soft you** steady; wait a moment. Compare
Oth. 5.2.338.

183 **pluck . . . sad** The news that Don John has
fled is clearly bad news, and perhaps Don Pedro
immediately suspects that Hero was maligned. Faced
with these misgivings he says: pull yourself together,
my heart, and consider these matters seriously.

186 **reasons** Pronounced much like 'raisins'
(Kökeritz, p. 138), so it has been suggested (initially
by Ritson) that Dogberry's vision of Justice is as a
grocer, weighing dried fruit; but there is nothing

incongruous in Justice weighing reasons (= arguments pro and con), so the joke is not very obvious.

186 **cursing** accursed.

187 **once** in a word. Abbott 57.

189 **Hearken after** Enquire about.

198 **division** In logic or rhetoric, the organisation
of the parts of an argument.

199 **well suited** well dressed up. Dogberry has
said the same thing in six different ways: the idea is
the common one of language as the dress of thought.

court Margaret in Hero's garments, how you disgraced her when
you should marry her: my villainy they have upon record, which I   210
had rather seal with my death, than repeat over to my shame: the
lady is dead upon mine and my master's false accusation: and briefly
I desire nothing but the reward of a villain.

DON PEDRO Runs not this speech like iron through your blood?
CLAUDIO I have drunk poison whiles he uttered it.   215
DON PEDRO But did my brother set thee on to this?
BORACHIO Yea, and paid me richly for the practice of it.
DON PEDRO He is composed and framed of treachery,
    And fled he is upon this villainy.
CLAUDIO Sweet Hero, now thy image doth appear   220
    In the rare semblance that I loved it first.
DOGBERRY Come, bring away the plaintiffs, by this time our sexton hath
    reformed Signor Leonato of the matter: and masters, do not forget
    to specify when time and place shall serve, that I am an ass.
VERGES Here, here comes Master Signor Leonato, and the sexton too.   225

Enter LEONATO, *his brother* [ANTONIO] *and the Sexton*

LEONATO Which is the villain? Let me see his eyes,
    That when I note another man like him,
    I may avoid him: which of these is he?
BORACHIO If you would know your wronger, look on me.
LEONATO Art thou the slave that with thy breath hast killed   230
    Mine innocent child?
BORACHIO   Yea, even I alone.
LEONATO No, not so, villain, thou beliest thyself,
    Here stand a pair of honourable men,
    A third is fled that had a hand in it:
    I thank you, princes, for my daughter's death,   235
    Record it with your high and worthy deeds,
    'Twas bravely done, if you bethink you of it.
CLAUDIO I know not how to pray your patience,
    Yet I must speak, choose your revenge yourself,
    Impose me to what penance your invention   240

225 SH VERGES] *Con.* 2 Q   225 SD LEONATO . . . *Sexton*] Q; *Leonato.* F   230 thou the] Q; thou thou the F   230–1 Art
. . . killed / Mine . . . child?] Q; *as prose* F

209 **Margaret . . . garments** The only time this
circumstantial detail is mentioned.
209 **how . . . her** What happened in the church
was not part of the Watch's discovery.

212 **mine and my** For distinctions in the use of
these see Abbott 237 and 238.
217 **practice** See 4.1.181 n.
240 **Impose me to** Impose on me.

> Can lay upon my sin, yet sinned I not,
> But in mistaking.
>
> DON PEDRO   By my soul nor I,
> And yet to satisfy this good old man,
> I would bend under any heavy weight,
> That he'll enjoin me to.   245
>
> LEONATO I cannot bid you bid my daughter live,
> That were impossible, but I pray you both,
> Possess the people in Messina here,
> How innocent she died, and if your love
> Can labour aught in sad invention,   250
> Hang her an epitaph upon her tomb,
> And sing it to her bones, sing it tonight:
> Tomorrow morning come you to my house,
> And since you could not be my son-in-law,
> Be yet my nephew: my brother hath a daughter,   255
> Almost the copy of my child that's dead,
> And she alone is heir to both of us,
> Give her the right you should have given her cousin,
> And so dies my revenge.
>
> CLAUDIO   Oh noble sir!
> Your over kindness doth wring tears from me,   260
> I do embrace your offer, and dispose
> For henceforth of poor Claudio.
>
> LEONATO Tomorrow then I will expect your coming,
> Tonight I take my leave: this naughty man
> Shall face-to-face be brought to Margaret,   265
> Who I believe was packed in all this wrong,
> Hired to it by your brother.
>
> BORACHIO   No by my soul she was not,
> Nor knew not what she did when she spoke to me,
> But always hath been just and virtuous
> In anything that I do know by her.   270
>
> DOGBERRY Moreover, sir, which indeed is not under white and black,
> this plaintiff here, the offender, did call me ass, I beseech you let it
> be remembered in his punishment: and also the watch heard them

248 **Possess** Make known to.

257 **she . . . us** Compare 1.2.1, where Antonio has a son.

261 **dispose** The syntax is abrupt – reflecting perhaps Claudio's relief at getting off so lightly. The subject of 'dispose' may be understood as 'you' (i.e.

Leonato) or as 'I' – I dispose of poor Claudio (to your guidance). The sense is much the same.

264 **naughty** See 4.2.59 n.

266 **packed** an accomplice.

271 **under . . . black** in writing.

talk of one Deformed, they say he wears a key in his ear, and a lock
hanging by it, and borrows money in God's name, the which he hath   275
used so long, and never paid, that now men grow hard hearted and
will lend nothing for God's sake: pray you examine him upon that
point.

LEONATO I thank thee for thy care and honest pains.

DOGBERRY Your worship speaks like a most thankful and reverent   280
youth, and I praise God for you.

LEONATO There's for thy pains.

DOGBERRY God save the foundation.

LEONATO Go, I discharge thee of thy prisoner, and I thank thee.

DOGBERRY I leave an arrant knave with your worship, which I beseech   285
your worship to correct yourself, for the example of others: God
keep your worship, I wish your worship well, God restore you to
health, I humbly give you leave to depart, and if a merry meeting
may be wished, God prohibit it: come, neighbour.

Exeunt [Dogberry and Verges]

LEONATO Until tomorrow morning, lords, farewell.   290

ANTONIO Farewell, my lords, we look for you tomorrow.

DON PEDRO We will not fail.

CLAUDIO   Tonight I'll mourn with Hero.

[Exeunt Don Pedro and Claudio]

LEONATO Bring you these fellows on, we'll talk with Margaret, how her
acquaintance grew with this lewd fellow.

Exeunt

280 reverent] Q; reverend F   289 SD *Exeunt*] *After 286* F; *not in* Q   293 SD] *Capell; not in* Q   293–4] Q; *as verse, Pope
and others:* Bring . . . Margaret, / How . . . fellow.

274 **a key** The lovelock of 3.3.139 has now
become a lock and key in Dogberry's imagination.

275 **borrows . . . name** 'He that hath pity upon
the poor, lendeth unto the Lord' (Prov. 19.17). It was
a common text in the mouths of beggars.

283 **God . . . foundation** Dogberry shows himself
an experienced mendicant: 'Such was the customary

phrase employed by those who received alms at the
gates of religious houses' (Steevens in Furness).

289 **prohibit** For 'permit'; perhaps a garbled
reminiscence of 'God preventing us' (meaning 'God
going before us').

294 **lewd** low, common.

[5.2] *Enter* BENEDICK *and* MARGARET

BENEDICK Pray thee, sweet Mistress Margaret, deserve well at my
    hands, by helping me to the speech of Beatrice.

MARGARET Will you then write me a sonnet in praise of my beauty?

BENEDICK In so high a style, Margaret, that no man living shall come
    over it, for in most comely truth thou deservest it.   5

MARGARET To have no man come over me, why, shall I always keep
    below stairs?

BENEDICK Thy wit is as quick as the greyhound's mouth, it catches.

MARGARET And yours, as blunt as the fencers' foils, which hit, but hurt
    not.   10

BENEDICK A most manly wit, Margaret, it will not hurt a woman: and so
    I pray thee call Beatrice, I give thee the bucklers.

MARGARET Give us the swords, we have bucklers of our own.

BENEDICK If you use them, Margaret, you must put in the pikes with a
    vice, and they are dangerous weapons for maids.   15

MARGARET Well, I will call Beatrice to you, who I think hath legs. *Exit*

BENEDICK And therefore will come.

Act 5, Scene 2

0 SD This scene, in terms of the fictional narrative,
must be imagined as following rapidly on the last, or
as being contemporaneous with it, since news of the
disclosures of 5.1 have only just reached Leonato's
house when Ursula enters at 72. We may assume
that Benedick, having delivered his challenge, is on
the way to tell Beatrice so, when he meets Margaret
somewhere in the vicinity of Leonato's house – and
she has not yet been 'talked with' (5.1.293). The
location 'Leonato's house' (Pope) cannot be
accepted in the light of Ursula's 'at home' (74), but
both Margaret and Ursula should come on through
Leonato's door; Benedick through another.
Steevens's 'Leonato's garden' seems still a little too
near, for the same reason, though it is usually followed. Too close a reading of the literal indications
of time and place in this scene and 5.1 produces
anomalies that would never be noticed in
performance.

4 **style** Punning on 'stile'; a high stile would be
difficult to get over.

6–7 **To . . . stairs** Margaret's paradox depends on
two puns, one of them implicit. If no man comes over
her (overcomes her, puts her down – compare
2.1.215–16 n.) then she will remain a servant (below
stairs) since she is nobody's 'mistress', as she might
be if she let herself be 'put down' upstairs in the
bedroom.

9 **blunt . . . foils** i.e. buttoned foils for friendly
practice.

12 **give . . . bucklers** grant you victory (in the
wit-combat).

12–15 In Margaret's reply to Benedick, 'bucklers'
can be understood as 'bellies'; 'swords' then become
phalluses. Benedick extends the punning on bucklers
by referring to their 'pikes' – a short spike screwed
into the centre of the buckler. Humphreys suggests
that 'vice' is 'a bawdy allusion to thighs closed in
intercourse' but perhaps it is nearer in sense to the
modern use of 'screw' for sexual intercourse. The
use of 'vice' for a holding-tool – two jaws brought
together by a screw – is not common before the
seventeenth century. It develops from the earlier
sense of 'screw', 'spiral'.

[*Sings*]   The God of love
                         That sits above,
                         And knows me,   20
                         And knows me:
                         How pitiful I deserve.
I mean in singing, but in loving – Leander the good swimmer,
Troilus, the first employer of panders, and a whole book full of
these quondam carpet-mongers, whose names yet run smoothly in   25
the even road of a blank verse, why they were never so truly turned
over and over as my poor self in love: marry, I cannot show it in
rhyme, I have tried: I can find out no rhyme to lady but baby, an
innocent rhyme: for scorn horn, a hard rhyme: for school fool, a
babbling rhyme: very ominous endings. No, I was not born under a 30
rhyming planet, nor I cannot woo in festival terms.

Enter BEATRICE

Sweet Beatrice, wouldst thou come when I called thee?
BEATRICE Yea, signor, and depart when you bid me.
BENEDICK Oh stay but till then.
BEATRICE Then, is spoken: fare you well now, and yet ere I go, let me 35
     go with that I came, which is, with knowing what hath passed
     between you and Claudio.
BENEDICK Only foul words, and thereupon I will kiss thee.

18–22 The God . . . deserve] *As prose* Q   29, 30 rhyme] rime Q; time F   31 nor] Q; for F   31 SD] F; *after 32* Q

18–22 These lines come from a version of a song
by William Elderton printed in 1562, but lost until
1958. A MS. version was then discovered by James
M. Osborn in his collection, and published in a
modernised version in *The Times*, 17 November
1958, p. 11. It is the song of a sad lover praying for
pity from his hard-hearted mistress. The song was
very well-known and much imitated, so that the
comedy of Benedick in the role of the melancholy
lover would be at once apparent. The text is given in
Appendix 3, p. 159 below. The tune survives in MS.
versions in several libraries, including one in the
Francis Willughby Lute Book in the University of
Nottingham (Seng, p. 63).
23 Leander In Greek myth, the lover of Hero; he
was drowned when swimming the Hellespont to an
assignation with her. Marlowe's poem *Hero and
Leander* was published in 1598, shortly before the
likely date of *Much Ado*'s first production, but

Shakespeare probably knew it in MS., since allusions
to it are found in *Rom.*
24 Troilus The Trojan lover of Cressida –
though no classical source is known for this medieval
romance. Pandarus, Cressida's uncle, was the go-
between for the lovers. Shakespeare's *Troilus and
Cressida* was written in 1601 or 1602.
24 quondam former.
25 carpet-mongers Those who frequented
ladies' chambers, where the floors were carpeted.
28 innocent silly; punning on the innocence of
babies.
29 horn . . . hard These are still names for sexual
erection, and the cuckold joke is also involved, for
horns are hard to bear.
30 ominous endings 'baby', 'horn' and 'fool'
suggest being a cuckold and the nominal father of
bastards; compare 2.1.215–16 and n.
36 came came for.

BEATRICE Foul words is but foul wind, and foul wind is but foul breath, and foul breath is noisome, therefore I will depart unkissed.   40

BENEDICK Thou hast frighted the word out of his right sense, so forcible is thy wit: but I must tell thee plainly, Claudio undergoes my challenge, and either I must shortly hear from him, or I will subscribe him a coward: and I pray thee now tell me, for which of my bad parts didst thou first fall in love with me?   45

BEATRICE For them all together, which maintained so politic a state of evil, that they will not admit any good part to intermingle with them: but for which of my good parts did you first suffer love for me?

BENEDICK Suffer love! A good epithet: I do suffer love indeed, for I love thee against my will.   50

BEATRICE In spite of your heart I think: alas poor heart, if you spite it for my sake, I will spite it for yours, for I will never love that which my friend hates.

BENEDICK Thou and I are too wise to woo peaceably.

BEATRICE It appears not in this confession, there's not one wise man   55
among twenty that will praise himself.

BENEDICK An old, an old instance, Beatrice, that lived in the time of good neighbours: if a man do not erect in this age his own tomb ere he dies, he shall live no longer in monument than the bell rings and the widow weeps.   60

BEATRICE And how long is that think you?

BENEDICK Question: why an hour in clamour and a quarter in rheum, therefore is it most expedient for the wise, if Don Worm (his conscience) find no impediment to the contrary, to be the trumpet of his own virtues, as I am to myself; so much for praising myself, who I   65
myself will bear witness is praiseworthy: and now tell me, how doth your cousin?

BEATRICE Very ill.

---

59 monument] Q; monuments F   59 bell rings] Q; Bels ring F   65 myself; so] *Rowe;* myself so Q

39–40 Proverbial: Tilley w833.

42 **undergoes** has received and must accept the consequences of.

43–4 **subscribe** write him down, publicly proclaim him.

57–60 Compare Tilley N117: 'He has ill neighbours that is fain to praise himself.'

59 **live . . . than** have no memorial longer than.

62 **Question** An interesting question.

62 **hour in clamour** The period of the tolling of the funeral bell. There are many tales of the rapidity with which widows changed their state.

62 **rheum** weeping.

63–4 **Don Worm (his conscience)** Compare *R3* 1.3.221: 'The worm of conscience still begnaw thy soul.' The image is traditional and derives from Mark 9.44, as that in turn from 'for their worm shall not die, neither shall their fire be quenched' (Isa. 66.24).

65 ***myself; so much** Rowe's semi-colon, or a full point, has been accepted by most editors, but the reading of Q can be defended: Benedick is a trumpet to his own virtues so much *in order to* praise himself, who is, as he is prepared to assert, worthy of praise.

BENEDICK And how do you?

BEATRICE Very ill too.   70

BENEDICK Serve God, love me, and mend: there will I leave you too, for
here comes one in haste.

Enter URSULA

URSULA Madam, you must come to your uncle, yonder's old coil at
home, it is proved my Lady Hero hath been falsely accused, the
prince and Claudio mightily abused, and Don John is the author of   75
all, who is fled and gone: will you come presently?

BEATRICE Will you go hear this news, signor?

BENEDICK I will live in thy heart, die in thy lap, and be buried in thy
eyes: and moreover, I will go with thee to thy uncle's.

Exeunt

[5.3] *Enter* CLAUDIO, DON PEDRO *and three or four [Attendants] with
tapers [and music]*

CLAUDIO Is this the monument of Leonato?

LORD It is, my lord.

[He reads the] epitaph
Done to death by slanderous tongues,
Was the Hero that here lies:
Death in guerdon of her wrongs,   5
Gives her fame which never dies:
So the life that died with shame,

---

79 uncle's] *Malone;* vncles Q   **Act 5, Scene 3**   0 SD DON PEDRO] *Prince* Q   2 SD *He reads the*] *This edn*   3 Done] Q;
CLAUDIO Done *Capell and others*

73 **old coil** a great to-do. 'Old' in this intensive
sense is still quite common in colloquial use.

78–9 **die ... eyes** Dying as a euphemism for
orgasm was common; he will be buried in her eyes
because he will see his own image there as he gazes
into them. Compare Donne in 'The Ecstasy':

And pictures in our eyes to get
Was all our propagation.

Act 5, Scene 3

0 SD *tapers* wax candles; they indicate night and
suggest religious ceremony.

1 **monument** This provides the location for the
scene. Evidently from 25–8 it is in the open air,
though Pope indicated 'a church'. The central discovery space would probably have been used on

Shakespeare's stage. Walter Hodges makes the
attractive suggestion that the resurrected Hero
should emerge from the same space with the other
disguised ladies in 5.4; see illustration 14, p. 40
above.

2 SD *He reads* Nearly all editors follow Capell in
inserting a speech heading for Claudio at this point
in spite of the fact that he is given one in Q at 11.
Similarly the couplet after the song (22–3) which has
the heading *Lo.* in Q and F is given (following Rowe)
to Claudio. This is hard to justify textually: it does
not seem out of character for Claudio to do his griev-
ing by proxy, as he did his wooing.

5 **guerdon** recompense.

7 **with** as a consequence of; Abbott 193.

Lives in death with glorious fame.
Hang thou there upon the tomb,
Praising her when I am dumb.   10

CLAUDIO Now music sound and sing your solemn hymn.

Song

Pardon, goddess of the night,
Those that slew thy virgin knight,
For the which with songs of woe,
Round about her tomb they go: 15
Midnight assist our moan,
Help us to sigh and groan.
Heavily, heavily.
Graves yawn and yield your dead,
Till death be utterèd,   20
Heavily, heavily.

LORD   Now unto thy bones good night,
Yearly will I do this rite.

DON PEDRO Good morrow, masters, put your torches out,
The wolves have preyed, and look, the gentle day   25
Before the wheels of Phoebus, round about
Dapples the drowsy east with spots of grey:
Thanks to you all, and leave us, fare you well.

CLAUDIO Good morrow, masters, each his several way.

[*Exeunt Attendants*]

---

10 dumb] F; dead Q   11 SH CLAUDIO] Q; *Capell and others delete*   16–17] F3; *one line* Q   21 Heavily, heavily] Q; *Heauenly, heauenly* F   22–3] *Rowe; one line* Q   23 rite] right Q   24, 30 SH DON PEDRO] *Prince* Q

12–21 If Jack Wilson sang 'Sigh no more' (2.3.53) he very likely sang this song too, but not necessarily in the person of Balthasar as NS proposes. However the song suggests a plurality of singers – those, they, our, us. Perhaps the first four lines were sung solo, the rest by the 'three or four' of the opening SD, and possibly in parts. There is no contemporary setting known for the song, but Collier cites a reference in *Laugh and Lie Down* (1605) to a ballad sung to the tune of 'Heavily, heavily'. It provides an ironic fulfilment of Don Pedro's request for a serenade at 2.3.77–8, as Long noted (p. 130).

13 knight devoted servant. Compare 'Diana no queen of virgins, that would suffer her poor knight surpris'd' (*AWW* 1.3.114–15). It is true that the first two words depend on Theobald's conjecture, but nevertheless Helena describes herself as the poor knight of the queen of virgins. See also *TNK* 5.1.140.

19–21* These three lines are difficult to make sense of, and the problem is in the meaning of 'uttered'. There are two main views. (1) uttered

means 'fully expressed'. In that case the graves are called upon to open so that the dead may assist in the lamentation. (2) uttered means 'outered', driven out. In that case the end of the song looks towards the resurrection, and F's 'Heavenly, heavenly' becomes a much more attractive reading. The objection to (1) is that the invocation to the dead to take part comes just as the ceremonial is ending; the objection to (2) is that it is a very strained use of 'uttered'. The ease of misreading 'heavily' as 'heavenly' or vice-versa has about equal force for either case. We may agree with Manifold that the song 'is among Shakespeare's worst' (p. 181). Perhaps Don Pedro and Claudio were mediocre poets.

22 SH LORD See 2 SD n. above.

24–33 The alternating rhymes of the last ten lines maintain the ceremonial quality of the scene, but – as with the coming of the dawn – there is a considerable lightening of tone.

26 Phoebus Apollo, the sun god.

DON PEDRO Come let us hence, and put on other weeds,   30
    And then to Leonato's we will go.
CLAUDIO And Hymen now with luckier issue speeds,
    Than this for whom we rendered up this woe.

                                              Exeunt

[5.4] *Enter* LEONATO, BENEDICK, MARGARET, URSULA, ANTONIO,
FRIAR [FRANCIS *and*] HERO

FRIAR FRANCIS Did I not tell you she was innocent?
LEONATO So are the prince and Claudio who accused her,
    Upon the error that you heard debated:
    But Margaret was in some fault for this,
    Although against her will as it appears,   5
    In the true course of all the question.
ANTONIO Well, I am glad that all things sorts so well.
BENEDICK And so am I, being else by faith enforced
    To call young Claudio to a reckoning for it.
LEONATO Well, daughter, and you gentlewomen all,   10
    Withdraw into a chamber by yourselves,
    And when I send for you come hither masked:
    The prince and Claudio promised by this hour
    To visit me: you know your office, brother,
    You must be father to your brother's daughter,   15
    And give her to young Claudio.

                                       Exeunt Ladies

Act 5, Scene 4   0 SD BENEDICK] Q; BENEDICK, BEATRICE *Capell*   0 SD ANTONIO] *Rowe;* old man Q   7, 17 SH
ANTONIO] *Old* Q   7 sorts] Q; sort F

30 weeds garments. They are dressed for mourning and must change for the wedding.

32 Hymen Roman god of marriage.

32–3 'And Hymen is now rapidly approaching
with the promise of a happier outcome than this of
Hero's.' An alternative possibility is that 'speeds' is a
contraction of 'speed us' – 'may Hymen bless us'
(Thirlby).

Act 5, Scene 4

0 SD There is no need to delete Margaret from
this entrance as some have done: Leonato's reproof
is gentle, and suggests her rehabilitation. Most
editors since Capell have provided an entrance for
Beatrice at this point, but it seems unlikely that the

discussion of Hero's innocence and Benedick's challenge to Claudio would pass without some comment
from her, were she present. Benedick's failure to
distinguish her at 72 might also be harder to accept –
though some deliberate confusion engineered by the
ladies may be assumed as well. The order of names
for this entry suggests that Friar Francis escorts
Hero. The location is 'Leonato's house' (Pope).

3 Upon As a consequence of. Abbott 191.

5 against her will unintentionally. She would
never, of deliberate intent, have acted in a way to
cause Hero harm.

7 sorts turns out; 'all things' is probably thought
of as 'everything' and so gets the singular verb. See
Abbott 333.

ANTONIO Which I will do with confirmed countenance.

BENEDICK Friar, I must intreat your pains, I think.

FRIAR FRANCIS To do what, signor?

BENEDICK To bind me, or undo me, one of them: 20
    Signor Leonato, truth it is, good signor,
    Your niece regards me with an eye of favour.

LEONATO That eye my daughter lent her, 'tis most true.

BENEDICK And I do with an eye of love requite her.

LEONATO The sight whereof I think you had from me,   25
    From Claudio and the prince, but what's your will?

BENEDICK Your answer, sir, is enigmatical,
    But for my will, my will is, your good will
    May stand with ours, this day to be conjoined,
    In the state of honourable marriage,   30
    In which (good friar) I shall desire your help.

LEONATO My heart is with your liking.

FRIAR FRANCIS   And my help.
    Here comes the prince and Claudio.

Enter DON PEDRO *and* CLAUDIO, *with Attendants*

DON PEDRO Good morrow to this fair assembly.

LEONATO Good morrow, prince, good morrow, Claudio: 35
    We here attend you, are you yet determined,
    Today to marry with my brother's daughter?

CLAUDIO I'll hold my mind were she an Ethiop.

LEONATO Call her forth, brother, here's the friar ready.

                                    [*Exit Antonio*]

DON PEDRO Good morrow, Benedick, why what's the matter,   40
    That you have such a February face,
    So full of frost, of storm, and cloudiness?

CLAUDIO I think he thinks upon the savage bull:

---

33 Here ... Claudio] Q; *not in* F   33 SD DON PEDRO] *Prince* Q   33 SD *with Attendants*] F; *and two or three other.* Q
34 SH DON PEDRO] *Prince* Q (*and subst. throughout scene*)   39 SD] *Theobald; not in* Q

---

17 **confirmed countenance** straight face.

20 **undo** Punning on the senses of 'unbind' and 'ruin'.

38 **Ethiop** Negress.

41 **February face** Some reserve on Benedick's part towards the prince and Claudio might be expected, but his pun on 'undo' (20) suggests he may have other misgivings – at least about being ridiculed for his change of attitude.

43 **savage bull** Compare 1.1.193 and 5.1.163. Claudio's quip suggests that he is aware that Benedick is to be married at the same time as himself, though this is hardly possible. In performance this slight inconsistency is a virtue, since it chimes with the audience's knowledge of the lines preceding Claudio's entrance.

Tush fear not, man, we'll tip thy horns with gold,
And all Europa shall rejoice at thee,   45
As once Europa did at lusty Jove,
When he would play the noble beast in love.

BENEDICK Bull Jove, sir, had an amiable low,
And some such strange bull leaped your father's cow,
And got a calf in that same noble feat,   50
Much like to you, for you have just his bleat.

Enter ANTONIO, HERO, BEATRICE, MARGARET *[and]*
URSULA *[masked]*

CLAUDIO For this I owe you: here comes other reckonings.
Which is the lady I must seize upon?

LEONATO This same is she, and I do give you her.

CLAUDIO Why then she's mine, sweet, let me see your face.   55

LEONATO No that you shall not, till you take her hand,
Before this friar, and swear to marry her.

CLAUDIO Give me your hand before this holy friar,
I am your husband if you like of me.

HERO And when I lived I was your other wife,   60
And when you loved, you were my other husband.

CLAUDIO Another Hero?

HERO   Nothing certainer.
One Hero died defiled, but I do live,
And surely as I live, I am a maid.

DON PEDRO The former Hero, Hero that is dead.   65

LEONATO She died, my lord, but whiles her slander lived.

FRIAR FRANCIS All this amazement can I qualify,
When after that the holy rites are ended,

---

46 Europa] Q; *Europa* F   50 And] Q; A F   51 SD ANTONIO . . . *and* URSULA *masked*] Theobald; brother . . . , Ursula
Q   63 defiled] defilde Q; *not in* F

45, 46 *Europa F italicises the second Europa, distinguishing the name of the continent from the figure in classical mythology. Italics are not used in the text of Q, but proper names are normally italicised in F, while geographical names rarely are. Europa was the daughter of Agenor, king of Phoenicia. Jove admired her, transformed himself into a bull and carried her off on his back across the sea to Crete.

44–5 Claudio implies that Benedick will be 'a glorious cuckold' (Foakes) and the laughing-stock of Europe.

48–51 Benedick's reply – sweetened perhaps by being in rhyme – is: you are a fool and a bastard.

52 I owe you I'll pay you back.

54 SH *LEONATO Many editors follow Theobald's attribution of this line to Antonio, and some give him 56–7 as well, because he is supposed to be the father of the veiled Hero at this point. It seems unnecessary: some business could be made with Leonato jumping in just as Antonio is about to speak; or perhaps Antonio cannot carry off the role with 'a confirmed countenance', and Leonato has to take it over.

59 like of See Abbott 177.

63 defiled slandered.

67 qualify moderate.

I'll tell you largely of fair Hero's death:
Meantime let wonder seem familiar,   70
And to the chapel let us presently.

BENEDICK Soft and fair friar, which is Beatrice?

BEATRICE I answer to that name, what is your will?

BENEDICK Do not you love me?

BEATRICE   Why no, no more than reason.

BENEDICK Why then your uncle, and the prince, and Claudio,   75
Have been deceived, they swore you did.

BEATRICE Do not you love me?

BENEDICK   Troth no, no more than reason.

BEATRICE Why then my cousin, Margaret and Ursula
Are much deceived, for they did swear you did.

BENEDICK They swore that you were almost sick for me.   80

BEATRICE They swore that you were wellnigh dead for me.

BENEDICK 'Tis no such matter, then you do not love me?

BEATRICE No truly, but in friendly recompense.

LEONATO Come, cousin, I am sure you love the gentleman.

CLAUDIO And I'll be sworn upon't, that he loves her,   85
For here's a paper written in his hand,
A halting sonnet of his own pure brain,
Fashioned to Beatrice.

HERO   And here's another,
Writ in my cousin's hand, stol'n from her pocket,
Containing her affection unto Benedick.   90

BENEDICK A miracle, here's our own hands against our hearts: come, I
will have thee, but by this light I take thee for pity.

BEATRICE I would not deny you, but by this good day, I yield upon great
persuasion, and partly to save your life, for I was told, you were in a
consumption.   95

BENEDICK Peace I will stop your mouth.

DON PEDRO How dost thou, Benedick the married man?

75–6] Q; *as prose* F   80, 81 swore that] Q; swore F   82 such matter] Q; matter F   96 SH BENEDICK] *Theobald; Leon.* Q

---

69 **largely** in detail.

70 **let ... familiar** treat these extraordinary events as commonplace.

71 **presently** at once.

72 **Soft and fair** Don't go too fast.

83 **friendly recompense** Compare 4.1.255–6. Beatrice obliquely acknowledges that Benedick has proved himself a friend.

84 **cousin** See 1.2.1 n.

87 **halting ... brain** sonnet that scans badly and

is all his own work. Compare 5.2.27–31. 'Sonnet' at this time was not restricted to the fourteen-line poem, but could apply to any short lyric.

95 **consumption** Compare 1.1.185 n.

96 SH *BENEDICK It is necessary to accept Theobald's emendation here: it is hard to think of any argument that could justify this speech in Leonato's mouth, while there are many parallels for Benedick. Compare Beatrice's advice to Hero at 2.1.235.

BENEDICK I'll tell thee what, prince: a college of witcrackers cannot
flout me out of my humour: dost thou think I care for a satire or an
epigram? No, if a man will be beaten with brains, a shall wear   100
nothing handsome about him: in brief, since I do purpose to marry,
I will think nothing to any purpose that the world can say against it,
and therefore never flout at me, for what I have said against it: for
man is a giddy thing, and this is my conclusion: for thy part,
Claudio, I did think to have beaten thee, but in that thou art like to   105
be my kinsman, live unbruised, and love my cousin.

CLAUDIO I had well hoped thou wouldst have denied Beatrice, that I
might have cudgelled thee out of thy single life, to make thee a
double dealer, which out of question thou wilt be, if my cousin do
not look exceeding narrowly to thee.   110

BENEDICK Come, come, we are friends, let's have a dance ere we are
married, that we may lighten our own hearts, and our wives' heels.

LEONATO We'll have dancing afterward.

BENEDICK First, of my word, therefore play music. Prince, thou art sad,
get thee a wife, get thee a wife, there is no staff more reverend than   115
one tipped with horn.

Enter MESSENGER

MESSENGER My lord, your brother John is ta'en in flight,
And brought with armed men back to Messina.

BENEDICK Think not on him till tomorrow, I'll devise thee brave
punishments for him: strike up, pipers.   120
Dance [and exeunt]

103 for what I] Q; for I F   115 reverend] F; reverent Q

100–1 if . . . him a man who was afraid of mockery by clever people wouldn't even dress fashionably.
Compare 3.2.24–9.

104 my conclusion the end of my argument. Also
perhaps 'my firm intention'.

105 in that since, because.

108–9 single . . . dealer Claudio would have obliged Benedick to marry Beatrice, giving up his
'single life', but as a husband he would certainly be
unfaithful.

112 hearts . . . heels Brissenden (p. 52) draws
attention to the parallel with 3.4.33–5.

113 dancing afterward Leonato perhaps means
'lovemaking'; compare the opening lines of Heywood's *A Woman Killed With Kindness*, ed. R. W. Van
Fossen, 1961:

Sir Fra. None lead the bride a dance?
Sir Cha. Yes, she would dance 'The Shaking of the
Sheets':
But that's the dance her husband means to lead her.

115–16 staff . . . horn The reverend staff is a
badge of rank, a support for the aged and, possibly,
also the wife herself, who is a support for her
husband. The horn carries the usual innuendo of
cuckoldry, reinforced when it is a tip. Tip and top are
variants of 'tup', a sheep breeder's term for the male
animal and its act; compare *Oth.* 1.1.89, 3.3.396.

120 pipers A generic term for instrumentalists at
this time.

120 SD Dance This would clearly have been a
lively dance. Long (p. 136) suggests the 'cushion'
dance to a galliard tune, in which 'the men and
women kissed as they entered and left the centre of
the dancing area'; a round country dance is another
possibility. No other play of Shakespeare's concludes
with a general dance of the company. It is a familiar
symbol of restored social order, as J. R. Mulryne
pointed out (*Shakespeare: 'Much Ado About Nothing'*,
1965, p. 24).

SUPPLEMENTARY NOTES

2.3.28 SD BALTHASAR There has been much conjecture about the identity of the singer Jack Wilson in F – records of four musical Wilsons have been discovered – but there is no clear evidence. The most popular candidate is Dr John Wilson (1595–1674) who became Professor of Music in Oxford in 1656. He was first claimed as the singer by E. F. Rimbault (*Who was Jack Wilson?*, 1846) following suggestions from Collier. Wilson became 'a gentleman of the King's chapel' in 1626. Of his earlier years nothing is known, but he was clearly too young to have been the singer in the original production. 'Mr Wilson the singer' dined with Edward Alleyn on his 28th wedding anniversary, 22 October 1620 (W. Young, *The History of Dulwich College*, 1889, II, 192), and it is sometimes assumed (by Furness and NS, for example) that he was the same person. John Wilson provides in his *Cheerful Ayres* (1660) a setting of Autolycus's song, 'Lawn as white . . . ' (*WT* 4.4.218–30), and names the composers of other Shakespearean songs. There is also a setting by Wilson of 'Take, O take those lips away' (*MM* 4.1.1–6), probably for the use of the song in Fletcher's *The Bloody Brother*: see J. W. Lever's note in his edition of *MM* (1965). A musical objection, perhaps, is 'that Wilson's style is that of the Lawes brothers, not Shakespearian so much as Davenantian' (Manifold, p. 140). W. W. Greg preferred 'John, the son of Nicholas Wilson, christened at St Bartholomew the Less in April 1585, and still residing in the parish in 1624' (*FF*, p. 280). He was first proposed by Halliwell.

3.3.142–3 Masters . . . us There is an apparent error here in Q, which attributes to *Conr.* a speech, most of which, at least, must belong to a member of the Watch.

Masters, never speak, we charge you, let us obey you to go with us.

Most editors follow Theobald in inserting a new speech heading for one of the Watch before 'never'. This division is not necessary: there is no anomaly in one of the Watch addressing Conrade and Borachio as 'masters', and in my text I have attributed the whole speech to Seacoal. However, I have a more elaborate theory about this crux. I advance it here because I have a conservative resistance to loading the text with conjectural emendations when much simpler ones produce satisfactory sense. The line is on F1ʳ and involves some of the most puzzling corrections that are found in the variant formes of Q. On this page alone – and not, for example, on E4ᵛ facing it – the speech heading *Con.* was corrected to *Conr* or *Conr.* These variants are in the corrected forme (see Hinman, Q, p. viii) and there must have been some motive for the correction. Is it possible that 'the right master constable' (135) – Dogberry – was called up? 'And there be any matter of weight chances, call up me' was his injunction at 71, and at 135 WATCHMAN 2 proposes doing so. On this hypothesis there should be an entry for Dogberry before 140, and the speeches at 140 and 142 could be his, under the appellation *Con.* or *Const.* It is to be noted that the speech headings for 140 and 142 read simply *Conr* (with no point following). This omission is very unusual for Q, and it distinguishes these headings from the other two corrected on F1ʳ at 125 and 146 which read *Conr.* and are correctly attributed to Conrade. Dogberry is *Const.* exclusively in 5.1, where Verges is *Con.2*, and in 3.5 is variously *Const. Dog.*, *Con. Do.*, *Constable*, as well as *Dogbery* and *Dogb.* Out of 22 occurrences of 'master' in various forms in the play, seven come from Dogberry, and 'let us obey you to go with us' is a fine Dogberryism. Conrade uses 'master' three times only, and all in the speeches, 140 and 142, here in question. It is true that a misreading of *Const.* as *Conr.* is not very likely in Secretary hand, but we are making conjectures about 'foul papers', it is usually assumed, and the copy may have had *Con.* in all four places. The corrector, advised that something was wrong with the speech headings on F1ʳ, and unable to decipher what, at least preserved a distinction between them, expanding two instances of *Con.* to *Conr.* and the other two to *Conr*, instead of changing them to *Const.* These two contracted speech headings, without a terminal full stop, are most abnormal for Sims's Compositor A, so perhaps a different hand was at work. J. C. Meagher advanced very much the same argument in 'Conrade conned: or, the career of Hugh Oatcake', *SQ* 24 (1972), 90–2, though I was not aware of this when I developed my own theory.

4.1.195 princes Theobald's emendation is universally accepted, although Q makes perfectly good sense. The problem arises from Hero being called 'the princesse' in the Q reading. Leonato is Governor of Messina, but (like Benedick) he is plain 'Signor', not even a count as Claudio is. On the other hand a certain laxness in the use of titles is apparent in Friar Francis, and others: he includes Claudio as one of the 'princes' at 178 and Benedick's response 'Two of them . . .' links Claudio and Don Pedro as princes by excepting John. The old explanation of compositorial error from mis-hearing copy read aloud carries little conviction, and the punctuation of Q, if it does not derive from copy (and therefore in substance represent the author's intention), must be the compositor's attempt to impose sense on what he found obscure. But the reading proposed by Theobald is not obscure, and if it were in the copy would not have required elucidation by the compositor. Nor does Q's 'princesse' suggest that copy had 'princes' as at 178. The balance of probability seems to be that the compositor followed his copy and that the reading of Q is in substance authorial. Either Shakespeare thought it appropriate for Friar Francis to call Hero 'princess' or he forgot that she was not entitled to it, as he forgot (for example) that he had given her a mother in stage directions for 1.1 and 2.1, and a male cousin in 1.2.1. There is a similar problem in *The Tempest* (1.2.173), and Stephen Orgel argues in his edition (1987) that 'princesse' is a possible Shakespearean spelling of 'princes'.

4.2.56–60 Come . . . ass Here the confusion in speech headings seems to have come from the similarity of *Const.*, *Conr.* and *Couley* (or *Cowley*), perhaps in a contracted form, in the manuscript copy for Q. An editor is obliged to decide who is intended by *Const.* at 43, by *Constable* at 56 – the common choice is Verges in both cases – and to sort out the confusion caused by the heading *Couley* at 57 and 60 for speeches that cannot – at least in their entirety – be given to Verges, the part played by Richard Cowley originally. I have followed Theobald in giving the whole of 57 to Conrade. This is the simplest emendation. The Folio gives the line to the Sexton, but this is not an acceptable reading either. Most editors since Warburton divide the line, giving the last two – or sometimes three – words to Conrade, and the first six – or sometimes five – variously to the Sexton, Dogberry or Verges. Various minor alterations are proposed to the wording of the line as well. The proposal to give Conrade the interjection 'Off coxcomb!' is certainly attractive. The difficulty is the number of alternative proposals for the left-over beginning of the line, and the impossibility of deciding between them on any objective grounds. If the line is taken as an aside by Conrade to Borachio, which is overheard by Dogberry, it makes good sense and requires no tinkering. The speech heading can be explained as a misreading of *Con.* as *Cou.*, which was then expanded as *Couley*. It was clear from the immediately preceding heading that it couldn't be intended for *Constable*, and Conrade had not spoken since line 21. Though he had identified himself at 12 his name had been left out of the entry at the beginning of the scene. It was easy then for the same thing to happen at 60 – and no later editor has disagreed with Rowe's attribution of this line to Conrade.

5.1.15–18 Two solid pages of small type annotate this passage in the Furness *Variorum*, and there is no consensus among more recent editors as to what the reading should be. In the face of this I offer my own conjecture – which requires only minimal modification of the text of Q – with some misgiving. Q reads:

> If such a one will smile and stroke his beard,
> And sorrow, wagge, crie hem, when he should grone,
> Patch griefe with proverbes, make misfortune drunke,
> With candle-wasters: bring him yet to me,
> And I of him will gather patience.   (15–19)

The most favoured emendations to 16 are 'Bid sorrow wag' (essentially Capell's reading, and followed by Humphreys), and 'And, sorry wag,' (originally proposed by Steevens and found, for example, in Foakes). Lewalski retains, in substance, the reading of Q and glosses 'wag' as 'go away'. Riverside reads 'And, sorrow wag' and glosses 'letting sorrow go hang'. It is my contention that if a heavier pause is indicated after 'sorrow' and 'grone', then the passage makes perfectly good sense.

> If such a one will smile and stroke his beard
> And sorrow; wag, cry hem, when he should groan;

It may be paraphrased, 'If such a one will smile and stroke his beard when he is sorrowful; play the fool and clear his throat when he ought to be groaning . . .' Two activities indicating well-being are in each case linked to one of grief, and these are then paralleled in the following lines with single oppositions. Smiling and stroking the beard are appropriate preliminaries to the enunciation of platitudes – 'Patch grief with proverbs' (compare *Tro.* 1.3.165–6). To wag is to play the fool or talk foolishly, and crying 'hem' may be a prelude either to tedious speech or drinking; so 'candle-wasters' may be either scholars at their midnight oil or revellers burning their candles at both ends. Both interpretations have been proposed: my preference is for the second, and supporting parallels are given in the note to 5.1.17–18.

TEXTUAL ANALYSIS

The nature of the copy for Q and the problems of the text for editor and producer

The copy for the quarto of *Much Ado* was a manuscript in Shakespeare's own hand, or something derived very closely from it. It was not a finished transcript, a carefully revised final version, which had been worked over with the stage-manager: Q shows all the symptoms which have been deduced by scholars of Shakespeare's text as evidence of 'foul papers'. There are inconsistencies within the text both on a large scale (characters who are introduced to no purpose, statements made at one point which are contradicted at another) and in smaller detail (variant spellings, inconsistency in the naming of characters, missing or inadequate stage directions). What the text offers, in short, is a becoming, a process, not a finished product.

The first stage direction of the play presents a problem: Hero's mother, Leonato's wife, is given an entry and a name, Innogen. She is listed again (unnamed) in the entry for 2.1, but thereafter disappears. As she never speaks a word, editors since Theobald have assumed that Shakespeare found no use for her as the play developed with his writing. A mother might have mitigated the pathos of the rejected Hero in 4.1, and must surely have had something to say in her daughter's defence. Innogen is not the only ghost in the play: 2.1 introduces, as well as Leonato's brother, 'a kinsman' who has no part in the action, unless he is the 'good cousin' of 1.2.20, one of the 'several persons' who 'cross the stage' in the SD Theobald proposed, and who is addressed although he does not speak. But here further confusions arise, for Leonato's brother is not named 'brother Anthony' until 5.1.99. Earlier he is referred to as 'brother' or 'old man'. The Signor Antonio whom Ursula identifies by the waggling of his head at 2.1.84 has always the speech heading *Antho.* in Q, but previously in that scene the title for Leonato's brother has been *Brother* exclusively. The brother of 1.2 has a son, but at 5.1.257, where Hero is to be resurrected as Antonio's daughter, Leonato says 'she alone is heir to both of us'. Again it seems simplest to assume that the relationships between the characters became clarified as the writing of the play proceeded. If Hero had a young male cousin, as is implied at 1.2.1, there would be a clear onus upon him to challenge Claudio to maintain her honour, but though there is 'a very even way' to right Hero, Beatrice says there is 'no such friend' (4.1.256). The climactic moment of the discovery of their mutual love by Beatrice and Benedick depends on this fact. The comic pathos of Antonio's challenge to Claudio (5.1.80–100) similarly depends on there being no person of suitable age in the family to do this office. Rowe's conflation, in his edition of 1709, of 'old man', 'brother', 'Signor Antonio', and 'brother Anthony' has been generally followed, though Furness demurred.[1]

---

[1] More recently Guy Lambrechts has argued that there is nothing to support the identification: 'Proposed new readings in Shakespeare: the Comedies', *Bulletin de la Faculté des Lettres de Strasbourg* (May–June 1965), 945–58. Furness's comment is in his note to the entry for 1.2.

The first report of 'noting' (compare 2.3.46–9) in the play clearly gives Antonio a separate establishment:

The prince and Count Claudio walking in a thick-pleached alley in *mine* orchard, were thus much overheard by a man of *mine*.   (1.2.7–9, my italics)

While this is never contradicted, it loses significance, and we easily assume that the 'orchard' of 2.3 and 3.1 is the same place although it is clearly associated with Leonato's establishment; and Antonio himself seems increasingly a member of the household of the Governor of Messina. It is a nice point to consider why he is not included in Q stage directions for the wedding, and whether the Antonio who challenges Claudio in 5.1 believes Hero dead or knows that she is alive.[1] But while Antonio's status may be left vague, as a matter of little consequence to the dramatist, it would be rash to assume the same of the variations in the reports about who intends to woo and marry Hero. The audience hears Don Pedro's plan in the last lines of 1.1. In the next scene, only nine lines later, we are given the false report of the 'good sharp fellow' that the prince himself will marry Hero. In 1.3 Borachio gives a further account of overhearing: a true report of the plan made in 1.1 but in a different location. Before the mask in 2.1 it appears that all of Leonato's household including Hero expect the prince to propose for himself, and this supposition is asserted by Don John and Borachio to Claudio later in the scene and believed by Benedick later still. It has often been noted that Claudio's lines "'Tis certain so . . .' at 2.1.130–8 and the ease with which he accepts the false report prepare us for the rapidity with which he becomes jealous later on. It is less commonly pointed out that Hero, too, must make a rapid switch of attachment. At 2.1.48 it appears that she is, without protest, expecting a proposal of marriage from the prince. At 226–8 she is handed over to Claudio, equally without comment or protest.

Here, Claudio, I have wooed in thy name, and fair Hero is won: I have broke with her father, and his good will obtained: name the day of marriage, and God give thee joy.   (2.1.226–8)

Hero's silence is open to interpretation in either case, and must be interpreted on the stage. What it suggests most strongly perhaps is subservience to the parental will. She is not prepared to act on Beatrice's advice, and 'make another curtsy, and say, father, as it please me' (2.1.41). But all these are instances of the relation between report and event that is central to the play's concern, both in the plot to bring Beatrice and Benedick 'into a mountain of affection, th'one with th'other' (2.1.276) and in the calumniation of Hero. In this case it is by design rather than by inattention that we get such a variety of reports about the same plans and relationships.

The staging of the mask in Act 2 raises a number of problems, not only because of the clearly corrupt stage direction in Q, *Enter . . . Balthaser or dumb Iohn* (2.1.60). Masking was a common amusement in the great Elizabethan households, and was given greater formality in the masques of the Stuart court. Commonly a group of masked male dancers would enter the chamber and take partners from among the assembled guests. An

---

[1] J. C. Maxwell argued strongly – and against the practice of 'the current' National Theatre production – that Antonio should not be present in the church scene (*N&Q* n.s. 14 (1967), 135). It appears to be the 1966 revival of Zeffirelli's production that he refers to.

entertainment of this kind does not go as planned in *Love's Labour's Lost*, and another, planned but not performed, is the means of Jessica's escape from her father's house in *The Merchant of Venice*; it is the occasion of Romeo's meeting with Juliet and of King Henry VIII's with Anne Boleyn. The quarto of *Much Ado* does not indicate a mask, though it is clear from the dialogue that this is what takes place. F's addition at 2.1.60 of *Maskers with a drum* may be understood as in apposition to the list of names which it follows, as well as indicating other attendants. The specific mention of the drum suggests that the musicians necessary for the dancing did not come on to the main stage but entered above and played in the gallery in Shakespeare's theatre. They could be present from the opening of the scene, or come on when required for the dance. They belong to Leonato's household, whereas Balthasar is clearly in Don Pedro's entourage.

Balthaser or dumb Iohn has been variously explained. *Dumb Iohn* is clearly Don John – Dun Iohn is found in Q at 3.3.89. I am not persuaded by Dover Wilson's proposal (NS, p. 95) that *Balthaser* emerges from an incorrect expansion of a 'scribbled' insertion 'B or Don John', where 'B or' was intended to indicate Borachio. It is true that Borachio requires an entrance, and that none is provided in Q or F; it is also true that he is on some grounds an appropriate partner in the dance for Margaret. However, the dialogue of 71–81 does not suggest that Margaret's partner is much in her favour, as Borachio claims to be at 2.2.11–12. The switch in the speech headings from *Bene.* to *Balth.* half way through that exchange adds to the confusion, but while a 'Bo' (Borachio) 'Be' (Benedick) confusion is more likely in Secretary hand than a 'Bo' 'Ba' (Balthasar), the Dover Wilson proposal involves both, as well as the expansion by the compositor to the forms found in Q, which is difficult to accept. It seems most probable that *Balthaser* was in the copy for the stage direction (why should B be so expanded otherwise? – if he loses his dialogue with Margaret he does not speak until 2.3) but the initial drafting of the dialogue may have partnered Benedick with Margaret. If this was followed by the realisation that he was a more appropriate partner for Beatrice, there might have been a failure to correct the earlier speech headings. There are sound arguments for the propriety of Balthasar's participation.[1] It is hardly probable that the mask would have been managed like an 'excuse me' foxtrot, though this was proposed by Capell, by J. P. Collier, and more recently by C. T. Prouty.[2] The maskers were not normally members of the household but guests – or even gate-crashers as in *Romeo and Juliet*. This makes the presence of Antonio – if he is Leonato's brother – a little anomalous, the more so as he is present with the family before the masking guests arrive. His exit and re-entry are awkward. Leonato's 'The revellers are entering, brother, make good room' (60) may be a warning for him to leave, as he should be with that party, or perhaps a request for him to clear the room for the dancing while Leonato formally welcomes his guests.

But this raises another problem. Neither Q nor F marks an entry for Margaret and Ursula, and Rowe, whose procedures must be taken seriously, as the editor nearest in time to Shakespeare's own theatre, added entries for them at the beginning of this scene,

---

[1] A. T. Brissenden, 'The case for Balthasar', *N&Q* n.s. 26 (1979), 116–17.
[2] 'A lost piece of stage business in *Much Ado About Nothing*', *MLN* 65 (1950), 207–8. It has also been effectively presented on the stage in this way, as in the 1982 RSC production.

though they do not speak before the dance.[1] But if they have been present all along, Ursula's recognition of Antonio loses much of its point, since there is no time for him to change his costume. Further evidence that the play was taking shape as Shakespeare wrote it is provided by the ghostly 'wife' and 'kinsman' of the opening direction of the scene. It is possible that 'old man', 'brother' and 'Antonio' had not at this stage come together firmly as they do in the 'brother Anthony' of 5.1. Nevertheless the touchy pride of the old man in that little exchange with Ursula chimes very nicely with the outburst of the challenge to Claudio later.

Directors will work out a solution to these problems in the light of their own situation in terms of casting, stage design, and overall understanding of the play's concerns. What I would favour myself as a way of resolving the confusions of the text would be an exit for Antonio when the maskers are announced followed by a rapid return, masked and perhaps with a long cloak thrown over his costume, to tag on to the tail of the group – Don Pedro, Claudio, Benedick and Balthasar, with attendants and musicians. A roll on the drum and formal greetings between Leonato and the maskers would allow time for others to assemble, to watch and participate, Don John and Borachio, Margaret and Ursula among them. If Balthasar chose Margaret, interrupting an amorous interlude with Borachio, it would give some point to his opening remark.

There is also the problem of what Claudio does in this scene. He enters as a masker, and so should dance, but remains on stage alone at the end of the dance. If he dances, it is silently, and with a partner not otherwise distinguished in the play. Whether he is a wallflower or a dancer, his attention should be clearly on Don Pedro and Hero. Perhaps some business could be made of his less than courteous attention to, and rapid desertion of, a hopeful partner.[2] The dance that accompanied the four paired dialogues was most probably a pavan,[3] and would have been followed by a livelier measure.

It is difficult to assess how far the disguises, in a celebration of this kind, were a matter of convention or a matter of fact. In *Henry VIII* 1.4 Wolsey recognises the king with no difficulty, but this was not the case according to Shakespeare's source, Holinshed.[4] In performances of *Much Ado* it is very common for members of Leonato's household to put on masks when the disguised visitors enter, but this was not the original practice. It is clear anyway that Don Pedro makes an immediate approach to Hero (though she, 'too low for a high praise . . . too little for a great praise' (1.1.126–7), may be assumed to be the smallest in the company and recognisable even if she were masked).[5] The dialogue of 2.1.92–7 implies that Beatrice is not disguised. The men have a wish not to be

---

[1] Rowe is followed in the present by Foakes. Wells, *Foul-Papers*, p. 6, notes the problem, and writes that while it is not 'appropriate' for them to come on with the maskers, 'in production it would be better for the girls to slip on with the revellers' rather than be present with nothing to say for the opening of the scene.

[2] Stage practice has varied: in Gielgud's 1949 production (see above, p. 22) Claudio danced with a spare gentlewoman; in some, at least, of Bridges-Adams's productions he was a wallflower.

[3] See Brissenden, *The Dance*, pp. 49–51.

[4] R. A. Foakes (ed.), *King Henry the Eighth*, 1957, 1.4.85–6 n.

[5] At a late stage I read the synopsis of the paper 'My visor is Philemon's roof' by Margaret Twycross, to be delivered at the Conference of the Société Internationale pour l'Étude du Théâtre Mediéval at Perpignan, 7–12 July 1986. The concluding words of her outline are pertinent. When the king puts on a mask it provides 'an illusory freedom . . . more dangerous for the other players than the King himself'.

recognised – as with Antonio, or Benedick's assertion of Beatrice, 'she told me, not thinking I had been myself' (2.1.183–4) – though it seems the most likely assumption in this play that they are identified. This question must be distinguished from the operation of the stage convention of disguise. The audience generally knows who is who, and does not take Sebastian for Cesario/Viola, and would miss half the fun of the mask of Muscovites in *Love's Labour's Lost* if they did not remember all the time that the gentlemen are paying court to the wrong ladies. In that play the ladies *are* masked, but the princess's statement 'ladies, we will every one be mask'd' (5.2.127) suggests that this is exceptional. If the men are masked in 2.1 and the ladies not, as seems most likely, this makes a pointed contrast with the final scene, 5.4. There the 'gentlewomen all' (5.4.10) return to the stage masked. Even after Hero is revealed, Benedick still has to enquire which is Beatrice. The final dance of the play follows.

The distribution of speech headings presents particular problems in the two scenes involving the Watch, 3.3 and 4.2. In 3.3 the speeches of members of the Watch are ascribed in speech headings to *Watch 1*, *Watch 2* and, in most cases, just to *Watch*. We can only guess at the number of 'bill carriers' that might have walked on for this scene in Shakespeare's theatre: it could well have varied with the exigencies of different occasions. If we may judge from Burleigh's letter to Walsingham (reprinted from Collier by Furness for his note on this scene) a watch might number ten or a dozen men. The text implies a minimum of three: Seacoal, Oatcake and the first Watchman to speak, who nominates them. In the edition of the play 'as arranged for the stage by Henry Irving' (1882) most of the speeches go to Seacoal, a few to Oatcake, and a few remain simply *Watch*. Directors will make their own divisions in the light of the resources available. I have not identified Oatcake, but have assumed that Seacoal (*Watch 2* in Q at 15, where he responds to Dogberry's address) is the anxious enquirer about the scope of his functions as constable, and the voice of authority at 134 (*Watch 1* in Q – but Irving made the same attribution at this point, as have many editors). Watchman 2 is the humorist who will rather sleep than talk, and Watchman 1, who nominates Seacoal, is the character concerned about that 'vile thief' Deformed. In 4.2 the lines of *Watch 1* are given to Seacoal. I make no greater claim than that this is a not inconsistent distribution of the speeches. There are further problems in the attribution of speeches, particularly in scenes involving the Watch. These, which do not bear seriously on the larger understanding of the play, are discussed, with other textual cruxes, in the notes to the particular passages.

The variety of spellings in Q also suggests an authorial manuscript as the copy for that text. I was led to an examination of the use of 'master' by the frequency of the alternative spelling 'maister'. It seemed possible that it was intended as a dialect variant for the speech of the Watch – to the modern ear 'maister' has a mummerset ring. But such a view is not tenable: Dogberry has three 'masters' and four 'maisters'. The prince says 'maisters' (twice) and Claudio 'masters'. This indicates, perhaps, the vagaries of Shakespeare's spelling. There are five different spellings of 'sheriff' in five lines of Hand D in *Sir Thomas More*. The three spellings of 'country' in that text can be set beside the spellings 'count', 'counte', 'countie' and 'county' for Claudio's title, and the alternation of 'master' and 'maister' is also found in *More*. On the assumption that Hand D is

Shakespeare's,[1] this supports the view that his manuscript is close behind Q 1600.

The speech headings that are found in the quarto in 4.2 can be accounted for by the same assumption. Here, in place of the names of the characters Dogberry and Verges, or an indication of their official functions – Constable, Headborough or some variation – as is found elsewhere in the play, we find the names of two actors in the Lord Chamberlain's company, Kemp and Cowley.[2] Will Kemp was the great clown and the part of Dogberry was clearly written with him in mind. Of Richard Cowley less is known, but as Verges, though a smaller role, is equally clearly a character part, he must have had special talents and may have been Kemp's regular partner. The other parts in the scene are less specialised and so may not have been thought of as the province of particular individuals. It seems preferable to think that it was the author's hand that wrote 'Kemp' and 'Cowley' in the speech headings, rather than a stage-manager. A stage-manager would not need to indicate a player's name more than once, and, if the play had been cast for production, would have the names of all the actors, not just two of them. Nor is it likely that he would start distributing parts half way through the play. This last objection does not apply so strongly to the author, though it might seem to. The name Dogberry is found in Q in the initial direction for 3.3 and is used in the dialogue of that scene at line 7. Verges' name is never found in a stage direction and occurs in the dialogue only at 3.5.8, 13 and 28. Honigmann, in discussing the many anomalies in Shakespeare's use of names and other matters, points out that the simple assumption that a play would be written straight through from beginning to end is not necessarily correct, and that in collaborative plays there is clear evidence of non-consecutive composition. He suggests (p. 41) that 3.3 may have been written after later Dogberry scenes. It is only in that scene, in any case, that the names Dogberry and Verges are used for speech headings.

---

[1] The assumption is challenged by Carol Chillington in 'Playwrights at work: Henslowe's, not Shakespeare's, *Book of Sir Thomas More*', *ELR* 10 (1980), 439–79.

[2] This is already a simplification: the first speech heading is *Keeper*, and this is usually interpreted as an expansion by the compositor of *Ke.* (for Kemp) in his copy. The heading for line 4 is *Andrew*, a title for the comedian – the 'Merry Andrew' – of the company. *Kemp* is found in the rest of the scene, though the speeches usually given to Verges are sometimes *Cowley*, sometimes *Constable*; see collation for full details.

APPENDIX 1: THE TIME-SCHEME OF
MUCH ADO ABOUT NOTHING

The time-scheme of the play is quite straightforward: there are two major ceremonial scenes which can be clearly dated in relation to each other – Leonato's entertainment for Don Pedro and his court, 2.1, and the scene in church of Hero's repudiation, 4.1. All other scenes can be fixed reasonably precisely before or after these two: the major time-lapse comes between the end of Act 2 and the beginning of Act 3. This makes it likely that if the play was performed with an interval in Shakespeare's theatre it would have come at this point. The scenes of the gulling of Benedick and Beatrice are similar and contrasted, and the arbour property was used in both. There is an interval with a lapse of time but no change of location indicated in the Folio stage direction in *A Midsummer Night's Dream* at the end of 3.2, *They sleep all the act*.[1]

The play begins with the announcement of Don Pedro's arrival in Messina after the successful completion of his war against his bastard brother John. There had been an earlier visit to Messina on the way to the war (1.1.223–4). Leonato is making 'great preparation' for a royal entertainment, and there will be 'revelling tonight' (246). The prince initially intends to stay 'at least a month' (110) and the date 'the sixth of July' is mentioned (211), though this may be no more than a joke. In 1.2 the preparations continue, and at the end of 1.3 Don John and his henchmen leave to attend 'the great supper' (52). Apparently they are too late for the feast but arrive in time for the dancing afterwards. It is in this scene, 2.1, that the marriage of Claudio and Hero is arranged and the date of the ceremony fixed for Monday 'which is hence a just seven-night' (271–2). When the scene ends it is probably early on Tuesday morning, the party is ending, and the company disperse to go to bed. NS provided a stage direction that made 2.2 directly continuous with 2.1, but it need not be so. The earliest possible – and perhaps the most natural – time for 2.3, the scene of the gulling of Benedick, is the day after the entertainment, Tuesday. It may be a little later, though, for Benedick has already had time to get bored with Claudio in the role of lover. It is in this scene that Don Pedro asks Balthasar for some music 'tomorrow night . . . at the Lady Hero's chamber window' (77). Some editors have felt that this conflicts with Don John's plot (Furness, Trenery, Humphreys, for example), but it does not. Borachio's window scene is planned for the night before the wedding, that is, if the wedding is to be on a Monday, Sunday night. But as we have seen, 2.3 may be no later than Tuesday: there is plenty of time for the serenade. The scene does contain an anomaly, though, for it begins in the evening (30) and ends at dinner time, which, by normal Elizabethan practice, would have been in the middle of the day.

The first scene of Act 3 is clearly fixed as the day before the wedding – therefore presumably the following Sunday.

[1] But see the discussion of this stage direction by R. A. Foakes in his edition of *MND*, 1984, pp. 141–3.

URSULA When are you married, madam?
HERO Why every day tomorrow.   (100–1)

The next scene is on the same day: 'Means your lordship to be married tomorrow?' Don John asks (3.2.66). He invites Claudio and Don Pedro to see Hero's 'chamber window entered' that night (83). At the opening of this scene Don Pedro is proposing to depart for Arragon as soon as Claudio's marriage is 'consummate' (thus cutting down the month's stay he originally proposed) and to take only Benedick with him as a travelling companion. In the chaffing of Benedick that follows, it is apparent that the gulling in the arbour of 2.3 has had the desired effect, and probable that two or three days have passed. Benedick has had time to visit the barber and shave off his beard, to wear several fancy changes of clothes (24–8) and to demonstrate other lover-like behaviour. The first scene with the Watch (3.3) is that night. Borachio has played his window scene, and at 4.1.78 we are told that it took place between 'twelve and one'. The Watch are due to go off duty at two (3.3.74). The scene that follows is early in the morning of the wedding day, Monday: ''Tis almost five o'clock' (3.4.38). The next scene, 3.5, where Dogberry successfully fails to convey the information that could prevent Hero's disgrace, immediately precedes the church scene, 4.1. The trial of Borachio takes place later the same day: the Sexton has already had time to hear of Hero's repudiation and presumed death, and also that Don John 'is this morning secretly stolen away'(4.2.52). The long scene that follows, beginning with Leonato's grief (the Sexton has not yet reported to him on Borachio's trial), proceeding to Benedick's challenge of Claudio, and ending with the confession of Borachio's guilt and the proposal for the marriage to Antonio's 'daughter', belongs to the afternoon of the same day, if we may rely on the prince's greeting – 'Good den, good den' (5.1.46). In it the public rehabilitation of Hero and the ceremony of remorse are proposed for 'tonight', and the new marriage for 'tomorrow' (252, 253). In 5.2 Benedick seeks out Beatrice to tell her of his challenge, and while they are talking Ursula brings the happy news that Hero's name is cleared. The night scene at Leonato's family monument follows, and the dawn of the second Tuesday is breaking as it ends. The final scene of joyful reconciliation and union – though it does not proceed to actual marriage – follows, and the play ends with the dance at the end of 5.4.

Although this structure is quite firm, and the linked time-references make it clear that the duration of the action is from one Monday to the Tuesday of the following week, the impression of reading or performance will probably be of a longer span. Certain tiresome questions may be asked. When has Hero had opportunities to meet Borachio at 'vile encounters . . . A thousand times in secret' (4.1.87–8)? It must be before the engagement to Claudio, and Borachio may be assumed a native of Messina since he has been 'in the favour of Margaret' (2.2.12) for more than a year – and this would give a certain circumstantial credibility to his story. He need not have been one of those with Don John when he 'stood out' (1.3.15) against his brother, and he is sufficiently well known in Leonato's household to be 'entertained for a perfumer' (1.3.42). Don John's accusations are, on the whole, rather less incredible than Iago's insinuations, but only if we invent an elaborate story for which the play offers no evidence. There is very little time, either, for Beatrice's attempts at sonnet writing – or for the evidence to be picked from her pocket. She was persuaded that Benedick loved her sometime on Sunday; on Monday morning she had a bad cold, and she would have hardly been in the mood for writing sonnets before the news came of Hero's rehabilitation – she is still feeling 'very ill' at 5.2.70.

We could also enquire what everybody is doing between Tuesday and the following Sunday, and why no start is made in the plot to persuade Beatrice to love Benedick until just before the wedding. But questions like this only bring out more clearly the general irrelevance of the earlier ones. Stage time is not real time, and when characters are not in front of us they are not doing anything – although we may be told later that they have done things, and may believe it, for the purposes of our enjoyment of the play. All that we require is an outline and a sequence of events within it that are not too obviously at odds with the possibilities of time as we understand it. Within that framework the events of the play will arrange themselves and expand to occupy it, as events do in subjective experience, where, as Locke pointed out, measured duration and our experience of the passage of time are very different matters.

We see that one who fixes his thoughts very intently on one thing . . . lets slip out of his account a good part of that duration, and thinks that time shorter than it is.[1]

This time-scheme was worked out long ago – by P. A. Daniel in 1887 – and Furness, with his usual good sense, argues that Shakespeare uses 'two clocks' (p. 371).

[1] *An Essay Concerning Human Understanding*, Book 2, chap. 14, section 4.

APPENDIX 2: LEWIS CARROLL'S LETTER TO ELLEN TERRY ON PROBLEMS IN THE PLOT OF *MUCH ADO ABOUT NOTHING*

This letter, in its whimsical way, is a neat example of the absurdity produced by asking 'real' questions of fictitious situations. It is evident from the second paragraph quoted here that Carroll was well aware of this.

Christ Church, Oxford
March 20, 1883

Dear Mrs Wardell,

This letter needs no answer. Now that I have learned the fact (I think it was Polly who revealed it) that you find letter-writing a tiring occupation, I am loth to do anything to add to your fatigues – for I am sure you are *very* hard-worked. But *reading* a letter takes very little time or trouble: besides, you are not *obliged* to read it, you know! . . .

Now I'm going to put before you a 'Hero-ic' puzzle of mine: but please remember, I do *not* ask for your solution of it, as you *will* persist in believing, if I ask your help in a Shakespeare difficulty, that I am only jesting! However, if you won't attack it yourself, perhaps you would ask Mr Irving some day how *he* explains it?

My difficulty is this: Why in the world did not Hero (or at any rate Beatrice when speaking on her behalf) prove an 'alibi,' in answer to the charge? It seems certain she did *not* sleep in her own room that night: for how could Margaret venture to open the window and talk from it, with her mistress asleep in the room? It would be sure to wake her. Besides, Borachio says, after promising that Margaret shall speak with him out of Hero's chamber-window,'I will so fashion the matter that Hero shall be absent.' (How *he* could possibly manage any such thing is another difficulty: but I pass over that.)

Well, then, granting that Hero slept in some other room that night, why didn't she say so? When Claudio asks her, 'What man was he talked with you yesternight Out at your window betwixt twelve and one?' why doesn't she reply, 'I talked with no man at that hour, my lord: Nor was I in my chamber yesternight, But in another, far from it remote.' And this she could of course prove by the evidence of the housemaid, who *must* have known that she had occupied another room that night.

But even if *Hero* might be supposed to be so distracted as not to remember where she had slept the night before, or even whether she had slept *anywhere*, surely *Beatrice* has her wits about her? And when an arrangement was made, by which she was to lose, for that one night, her twelve-months' bedfellow, is it conceivable that she didn't know *where* Hero passed the night? Why didn't she reply

> But, good my lord, sweet Hero slept not there:
> She had another chamber for the nonce.
> 'Twas sure some counterfeit that did present
> Her person at the window, aped her voice,
> Her mien, her manners, and hath thus deceived
> My good lord Pedro and this company?

With all these excellent materials for proving an 'alibi,' it is incomprehensible that no one should think of it. If only there had been a barrister present, to cross-examine Beatrice! 'Now, ma'am, attend to me, if you please: and speak up, so that the jury may hear you. Where did you sleep last night? Where did Hero sleep? Will you swear that she slept in her own room? Will you swear you do not know where she slept? Etc., etc.' I quite feel inclined to quote old Mr Weller, and to say to Beatrice at the end of the play (only I'm afraid it isn't quite etiquette to speak across the footlights), 'Oh Samivel, Samivel, vy vorn't there a halibi?'

But I shall bore you if I go on chattering . . .

By the way, I must not forget to say that I thought the change in the fainting business a *great* improvement. I presume the change was made owing to some one else having suggested it, before *I* did (as you do not say it was owing to me), but even so I am glad to have my opinion thus confirmed.

Love to the children.

Yours ever,
C. L. Dodgson

At this time Ellen Terry was married to Charles Wardell, her second husband (see p. 15 above). The reference to the 'fainting business' at the end of the letter is explained by an entry in Lewis Carroll's Diary, five days before this letter. He

went up to town to fulfil my promise to Lucy Arnold – to take her for her *first* visit to the theatre . . . We got to the Lyceum in good time, and the play [Henry Irving and Ellen Terry in *Much Ado about Nothing*] was capitally acted. I had hinted to 'Beatrice' how much she could add to Lucy's pleasure by sending round a 'carte' of herself: she sent a 'cabinet'– besides one for Ethel; she is certainly an adept in giving gifts that gratify! We concocted a note of thanks, and sent it round to her. In my [earlier] note . . . I had suggested that Hero fainting *twice* is awkward, and that she had better fall, once for all, where she means to be: this was done tonight, but whether owing to me or not, Miss Terry did not say.

The full text of this letter is to be found in Morton N. Cohen (ed.), *The Letters of Lewis Carroll*, 2 vols., 1979, I, 488–90. Extracts, slightly shorter than those given here, are included in *Ellen Terry's Memoirs*, ed. Edith Craig and Christopher St John, 1933, pp. 142–3. She introduces the letter with these words:

He was a splendid theatre-goer, and took the keenest interest in all the Lyceum productions, frequently writing to me to point out slips in the dramatist's logic which only he would ever have noticed! He did not even spare Shakespeare. I think he wrote these letters for fun, as some people make puzzles, anagrams, or Limericks!

APPENDIX 3: BENEDICK'S SONG, 5.2.18–22

The song that Benedick attempts is the opening of a well-known piece by William
Elderton, a ballad-writer and actor who probably died in 1592. The song appeared in
1562, and its popularity is demonstrated by the number of imitations, parodies and
references to it which have survived. The original was unknown until discovered in the
collection of James M. Osborn in 1958, when a modernised version was published in *The
Times* on 17 November. It was set to a tune well known as a dance in its own right,
'Turkeyloney', but with several other manifestations in English. It relates to melodies
printed in Italy before the middle of the sixteenth century (Seng, pp. 62–3). Benedick's
version varies a little from Osborn's manuscript in 'The Braye Lute Book'.

> The gods of love that sits above
>   and know me, and know me,
>   how sorrowful I do serve,
> grant my request that at the least
>   she show me, she show me,
>   some pity when I deserve;
> that every brawl may turn to bliss
> to joy with all that joyful is.
>   Do this my dear and bind me
> for ever and ever your own;
>   And as you here do find me
>   so let your love be shown,
> for till I hear this unity
>   I languish in extremity.

> As yet I have a soul to save
>   uprightly, uprightly;
>   though troubled with despair,
> I cannot find to set my mind
>   so lightly, so slightly,
>   as die before you be there.
> But since I must needs you provoke,
>   come slake the thirst, stand by the stroke,
> that when my heart is tainted
>   the sorrowful sighs may tell
> you might have been acquainted
>   with one that loved you well.
> None have I told the jeopardy
>   that none but you can remedy.

Those cursed eyes that were the spies
　　to find ye, to find ye,
　　　　are blubbered now with tears;
and eke the head that fancy led
　　to mind ye, to mind ye,
　　　　is fraught with deadly fears;
and every part from top to toe
　　compelleth the heart to bleed for woe.
　　　　Alas, let pity move you
some remedy soon to send me,
　　and knowing how well to love you
　　　　yourself vouchsafe to lend me.
I will not boast the victory
　　but yield me to your courtesy.

I read of old what hath been told
　　full truly, full truly,
　　　　of ladies long ago
whose pitiful hearts have played their parts
　　as duely, as duely,
　　　　as ever good will could show;
and you therefore that know my case
　　refuse me not but grant me grace
　　　　that I may say and hold me
to one triumph and truth –
　　even as it hath been told me
　　　　so my good lady doth;
so shall you win the victory
　　with honour for your courtesy.

With courtesy now so bend, so bow,
　　to speed me, to speed me,
　　　　as answereth my desire;
as I will be if ever I see
　　you need me, ye need me,[1]
　　　　as ready when you require.
Unworthy though to come so nigh
　　that passing show that feeds mine eye,
　　　　yet shall I die without it
if pity be not in you.
　　　　But sure I do not doubt it
nor anything you can do –
to whom I do commit, and shall,
　　my self to work your will with all.
　　　　　　finis

---

[1] This line in Seng reads:
　　yow nede me ye nede me.
　　The 'ye' could alternatively be understood as 'yea' (= yes) in modern English.

I have modernised the spelling and inserted punctuation in the type facsimile of the original given in Seng (pp. 63–5), where a fuller account may be found of the music and related songs. This lyric seems to have little distinction to account for its popularity, but the same could be said of many lyrics of the present – or indeed any time – when divorced from their music. The syntax is loose and the diction commonplace. The surface meaning of the song presents a languishing lover in the courtly tradition praying for 'pity' from his lady, and concluding with a little hope for her 'courtesy' towards his service. At the same time there are several opportunities for double entendre within the song that may have been sharper to the Elizabethans than they can be to us.

READING LIST

This list provides details of the more important books and articles referred to in the Introduction and Commentary, together with a few additional items, and may serve as a guide to those who wish to undertake further study of the play.

Barish, Jonas A. 'Pattern and purpose in the prose of *Much Ado About Nothing*', *Rice University Studies* 60.2 (1974), 19–30
Charlton, H. B. *Shakespearian Comedy*, 1938
Craik, T. W. '*Much Ado About Nothing*', *Scrutiny* 19.4 (1953), 297–316
Dawson, A. B. 'Much ado about signifying', *SEL* 22.2 (1982), 211–21
Dusinberre, Juliet. *Shakespeare and the Nature of Women*, 1975
Evans, Bertrand. *Shakespeare's Comedies*, 1960
Everett, Barbara. '*Much Ado About Nothing*', *CQ* 3.4 (1961), 319–35
French, Marilyn. *Shakespeare's Division of Experience*, 1981
Hunter, G. K. *Shakespeare: The Late Comedies*, 1962
Kermode, Frank. 'The mature comedies', in B. Harris and J. R. Brown (eds.), *The Early Comedies*, 1961
Kirsch, Arthur. *Shakespeare and the Experience of Love*, 1981
Leggatt, Alexander. *Shakespeare's Comedy of Love*, 1974
Lewalski, Barbara. 'Love, appearance and reality: much ado about something', *SEL* 8 (1968), 235–51
Mueschke, Paul and Miriam. 'Illusion and metamorphosis in *Much Ado About Nothing*', *SQ* 18 (1966), 53–65
Mulryne, J. R. *Shakespeare: 'Much Ado About Nothing'*, 1965
Palmer, John. *Comic Characters in Shakespeare*, 1946
Prouty, C. T. *The Sources of 'Much Ado About Nothing'*, 1950
Rossiter, A. P. *Angel with Horns*, 1961
Smith, J. *Shakespearian and Other Essays*, 1974
Storey, Graham. 'The success of *Much Ado About Nothing*', in John Garrett (ed.), *More Talking About Shakespeare*, 1959
White, R. S. *Shakespeare and the Romance Ending*, 1981

The following anthologies of criticism may be useful: they include a number of the more important essays listed above, but not always in their complete form.

Brown, J. Russell (ed.). *'Much Ado About Nothing' and 'As You Like It': A Casebook*, 1979
Davis, Walter R. (ed.). *Twentieth Century Interpretations of 'Much Ado About Nothing'*, 1969
Lerner, Laurence (ed.). *Shakespeare's Comedies: An Anthology of Modern Criticism*, 1967
Muir, K. (ed.). *Shakespeare: The Comedies; A Collection of Critical Essays*, 1965